THE SOVIET SEA CHALLENGE

THE SOVIET SEA CHALLENGE

REAR ADMIRAL **ERNEST McNEILL ELLER** , USN (Ret.)

Foreword by Admiral **ARLEIGH BURKE** , USN (Ret.)
Past Chief of Naval Operations

COWLES BOOK COMPANY, INC.

A Subsidiary of Henry Regnery Company

To Those Who Serve

Contents

Preface and Acknowledgments

"They that go down to the sea in ships, that do business in great waters; these see the works of the Lord, and his wonders in the deep," sang the Psalmist. He could have added that in the deep they would also see the slow growth of freedom and dignity of man. From ancient history we can trace the decisive effect of power at sea in promoting and preserving freedom—when the superior maritime power was exercised by a nation whose leaders were dedicated to liberty.

The sudden surge of the Soviet Union toward maritime predominance has grave significance. One cannot help but be perturbed as the world's strongest land power—a tyrannical government—reaches toward supremacy at sea. Therefore, when Charles N. Heckelmann, editor of Cowles Book Company, proposed a study comparing the relative sea strengths of the United States and the Soviet Union, I accepted. In the year and a half I have spent working on the book I have become even more concerned about the subject. The world approaches what may well be one of the major turning points in civilization, and the outlook is not one to encourage an observant American. Serious consequences will face the United States if she does not reverse her slide toward second place at sea.

In order to explain the problem facing the free world at the outset, Chapter 1 of this volume capsulizes the present maritime capabilities of the two nations. This summary serves as a point of departure. As navigators know, one can best steer the present course and plan for the next if he has sailing directions founded on experience—the accumulated knowledge of the past. Accordingly, it is appropriate to recount highlights of the influence of the world's oceans on the growth of America and Russia from their individual beginnings to their present world stature.

For that reason, Chapters 2 and 3 relate something of the rich maritime heritage of the United States through World War II— although the limited space here forced omission of all but a fraction of the heroism, dedicated service, and significant achievements of those millions of Americans who have contributed to much to our nation's advancement.

Long ago John Adams said of those citizens who fought for independence ashore and afloat, "Posterity! You will never know how much it cost the present generation to preserve your freedom! I hope you will make use of it."

The same words apply to each succeeding generation through the present one; which has sacrificed for freedom in World War II, Korea, and Southeast Asia. Following a chapter that deals with Russia's maritime heritage, Chapters 5 through 8 treat events of the last quarter of a century. The next five chapters expand on the comparisons of maritime power summarized in Chapter 1. As the narratives moves on, the sheer weight of events on the international scene will stir within the reader a deep sense of concern—a concern that mounts as the final pages survey the sweeping geopolitical gains that expanding power at sea has already brought the U.S.S.R.—from Southeast Asia to the Middle East to Cuba.

Leaders such as President Nixon, Secretary of Defense Laird, Secretary of the Navy Chaffee, the late Mendel Rivers, Senator Harry Jackson, Senator John Stennis, Admiral Arleigh Burke, Admiral Thomas Moorer, Admiral George Anderson, Vice Admiral Hyman Rickover, James Hannan, President of the Navy League, and Hanson Baldwin— to name but a few—have pointed out the peril facing America at sea. The purpose of this book will have been served if it induces more Americans to heed the warnings of these men, who understand the full extent of the dangers our nation may be facing.

No man accomplishes anything that does not include the assistance, direct and indirect, of countless others. To the authors of many books, magazine articles, news items, speeches, reports, summary accounts, and releases of various government and private activities I extend my gratitude. I regret that I can mention only a few of them.

Scores of dedicated men in military service and out have assisted me by furnishing information, and many of them, by reviewing secNATO nations of Europe.

tions of the manuscript. While they have been very helpful, they are not responsible for the text as it appears. The conclusions, projections, and opinions are my own.

I especially wish to thank the following: Vice Admiral Thomas F. Connolly and his associates, Rear Admiral Malcolm W. Cagle, Captain J. B. Hansen, and Captain T. P. McGinnis; Vice Admiral Turner F. Caldwell, Jr., Rear Admiral F. J. Harlfinger II; Rear Admiral George H. Miller; Rear Admiral O. D. Waters; Rear Admiral Frank W. Vannoy; Captain L. C. McCarty; Captain O. L. Norman; Commander J. R. Davey; Commander J. C. Mackercher; Commander E. P. Stafford; Commander T. J. Glancy.

In a special group are Vice Admiral E. B. Hooper, Director of Naval History, and these able members of his staff: Dr. Dean C. Allard, Jr.; B. F. Calvlcante, Oscar P. Fitzgerald, Mrs. Agnes F. Hoover, F. S. Meigs, John C. Reilly, Jr., Mrs. Phyllis D. Sherrill, and Mr. Robert L. Scheina, who, while carrying a heavy work load himself, has found time to render great assistance to this book from beginning to end.

Another special group includes Professor Robert W. Daly, a leading expert on Russian naval history; Colonel Robert D. Heinl, USMC (Ret.), noted historian of the Corps; and Captain Robert H. Mereness, USN (Ret.) of the Shipbuilders Council of America, whose publication *Shipyard Weekly* proved invaluable with its timely and accurate information.

On two occasions Mr. Thomas J. Maloney generously made "Casa Maloney" available to us. It is located on the secluded Arrabida coast of Portugal. This proved to be an ideal place to draft much of the historical part of the manuscript. The casa's southern exposure opens like a ship's bridge to the encircling arc of the sea. And what significant history has been shaped on the waters beyond! Over the horizon toward the noonday sun lie famed Cape Vincent and Sagres. On this southwest point of Europe one can still visit relics of Prince Henry the Navigator's school for mariners, which opened the world to Portuguese seamen—and the phenomenal age of sea discovery that produced Columbus and brought about European colonization of a new world.

From Sagres to Gibraltar—an arc of only a few degrees in one's mental line of sight—there are also memories of world struggle between Britain and Napoleon. It is easy to fix in the direction of the decisive naval battle of Trafalgar. Nelson's victory there was as momentous as Salamis two millennia earlier and as Midway—scarcely yesterday on history's record—in shaping civilization's course toward freedom. Thus seapower will basically decide today's struggle between Communist oppression and liberty as represented by America and the

Most of all I must express gratitude to my beloved wife Agnes

Pfohl Eller, who has helped in every way possible. No one else could have been as thoughtful, understanding, and considerate.

This work was undertaken because it deals with one of the most critical problems facing the United States in the future. A storm rushes toward us like a typhoon that destroys the unprepared, the uncertain, and the weak—regardless of their ideals or their purposes. Like life, the great waters respect only the ready, the resolute, and the brave. They respect those who understand that it is not wealth, comfort, ease, leisure, pleasure, or even scientific knowledge and industrial achievement that make a nation great—but rather the virtues of wisdom, preparation, and willingness to sacrifice for the common good.

This truth was best expressed more than two thousand years ago by Pericles. He exhorted his fellow Athenians:

> I would have you day by day fix your eyes upon the greatness of Athens until you become filled with the love of her; and when you are impressed by the spectacle of her glory, reflect that this empire has been acquired by men who knew their duty and had the courage to do it.

E. M. ELLER

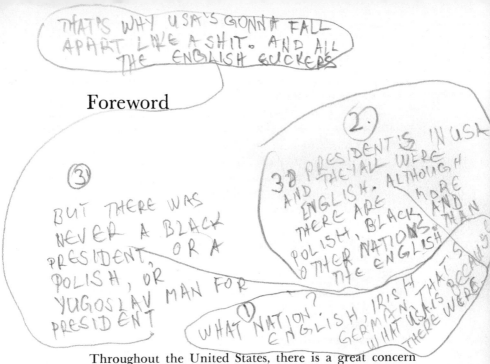

[handwritten annotations:]

THAT'S WHY USA'S GONNA FALL APART LIKE A SHIT. AND ALL THE ENGLISH SUCKERS

②. 32 PRESIDENT'S IN USA AND THEY ALL WERE ENGLISH. ALTHOUGH THERE ARE MORE POLISH, BLACK AND OTHER NATIONS THAN THE ENGLISH

③ BUT THERE WAS NEVER A BLACK PRESIDENT, OR A POLISH, OR YUGOSLAV MAN FOR PRESIDENT

① WHAT NATION? ENGLISH, IRISH, GERMAN. WHAT USA'S BECAUSE THERE WERE

Foreword

Throughout the United States, there is a great concern for the future of our beloved country. Our nation's leaders and our people are confronted with many serious problems, but no one of these problems is more urgent than the growing might of the Soviets at sea.

In the last fifty years the Soviets have repeatedly stated their goals and objectives to dominate the world. Few have believed them. In recent years their plan of action has become evident. It is time we all recognize the shifting balance of power and the ominous consequences to the United States should the Soviet Union continue her aggressive development of her national power at sea and we permit ours to decline.

Admiral Eller appreciates that one of the best guides to the future is cold knowledge of what has happened in the past. His expert historical summaries of United States and Russian history give a clear insight to the heritages of the two nations.

In the early days of World War II the Soviets took a terrific beating from the Germans. The Soviet Navy was practically immobilized. The manufacturing areas of Russia were overrun. The Allies came to the rescue of the Soviets by delivering essential equipment through Murmansk and Iran but took terrific losses at sea from German submarines and raiders.

After the war the Soviets coldly analyzed the operations of the last war and realized what many nations have realized before them —that control of the sea is essential to success in war between powerful nations. Stalin built a navy stressing submarines, but also build-

xiii

ing many cruisers, destroyers, and smaller surface ships. Russian ships were good but not as good as those of her old allies. Her navy personnel were inexperienced, especially in sustained operations on the high seas. They had not assimilated properly the strategy and tactics necessary to gain and maintain control of the seas.

The Soviets realized the shortcomings of their naval posture. In the 1950s they again evaluated their seagoing capability and came to understand that their foundation for sea power was not broad enough and that it would be necessary to spend years to develop real capability in her naval personnel.

Regardless of the shortage of consumer goods, of low living standards of the people, of dissent in the Soviet Union, the Soviet hierarchy methodically developed solid foundations for sea power. Many high-capacity shipyards were built. Fishing fleets were radically expanded. Great efforts were made in oceanography. Russia increased its merchant fleet about seven times. Research on weapons systems and ship design was emphasized. Now, fifteen years later, the Soviets have a tremendous, well-equipped base in each of the fundamental elements of sea power, all capable of being quickly expanded. As the author points out, the Soviets also have large numbers of modern submarines, new weapons systems, and new surface ships.

The greatest achievement of the Soviets in the last decade is the obvious increase in the effectiveness of their naval personnel. No longer is the Soviet Navy tied to the apron strings of the army. It takes years and resolute, concentrated effort to develop naval people with a high degree of skill in operations at sea and in the mutual support so necessary to naval operations. The Soviet Navy people are now experienced. They have learned to operate in the tropics as well as the arctic. They have gained much logistic knowledge. All of their people are well disciplined, apparently enthusiastic, and proud of their achievements.

The trends in relative national power over the past ten years are clear and definite.

It is time to do something about this problem, too.

Admiral ARLEIGH BURKE, USN (Ret.)

THE SOVIET SEA CHALLENGE

1

Soviet Menace from The Sea

THE sea has shaped our land's destiny profoundly since that fateful day in 1492 when the cry of "Land ho!" opened a new era for man. It has strengthened and swelled the tides of freedom that have surged through the world since 1776. It has been both a power and a weakness for the United States: a barrier and a highway for invasion, an unbreachable moat, and an avenue of destruction. What is it today?

The sea brought strength with untold benefits when superior sea power (her own or that of others) shielded the United States. It brought sorrow and disaster when she was weak at sea.

Honest and concerned Americans must, therefore, have grave concern over the current decline of America's maritime power and the swift rise of the power of the Soviets. The Cuban missile confrontation could only be a preview of an ominous future.

Maritime power depends upon several fundamentals ashore and afloat, some of which are outside the average person's understanding of what makes up strength at sea.

Key *shore-going* elements in our atomic space age include: ample territory with a large population that is resolute and courageous; extensive production of food and raw materials to provide fuel for the national economy; a broad industrial and a secure financial foundation; modern shipyards and ship-repair facilities; and naval bases at home and overseas.

Afloat elements of sea power are composed primarily of: a competitive, thriving merchant marine with reserves of ships and men capable of meeting the demand for shipping that swells with explosive speed whenever war breaks out; active fishing, survey, hydrographic, and other craft that extend knowledge of the sea and widen experience in the control and use of it; a balanced navy, well equipped, well led, well maintained, and widely experienced in distant operations.

Soviet Sea Power Builds Up at Full Speed

A nation can still become a major sea power without possessing all of these fundamentals, but it can become especially powerful if it has all of them. Where do the Soviets stand?

Their great capabilities in the shore elements of sea power are obvious in territory, population, agriculture, raw materials, and industry. These give the U.S.S.R. a foundation for world power at sea of the first order. What about shipyards and naval bases?

Shipyards

In the two decades of NATO's existence the U.S.S.R. has made phenomenal maritime advances. These have sobering implications for the Western alliance of freedom, which would deteriorate without control of the sea. To achieve these amazing advances the U.S.S.R. and its satellite countries have vigorously expanded older shipyards and built new ones. The principal yards (which will be covered later in more detail) lie on the Baltic and Black Seas, but valuable ones exist elsewhere, such as the major submarine yards on the White Sea and in eastern Siberia.

Initially, to sustain the concurrent swift expansion of their naval, merchant, and fishing fleets, the Soviets relied heavily on Western shipbuilders. This dependence gradually decreased as iron curtain yards began to develop. Thus today, although heavily absorbed in turning out warships, Soviets also launched up to about 40 percent of their merchant ships. Other nations in the bloc (principally Poland and East Germany) provide about 30 percent. Yugoslavia and Finland launch much of the remainder, and allies of United States—such as Great Britain, West Germany, Holland, Italy, and Japan—build the rest.

Naval Bases

Since World War II the Soviets have rebuilt and expanded bases in the Far East, the Baltic, and the White and Black Sea areas. Most of the bases suffer somewhat from lack of constant free access to the great oceans, although in recent years these handicaps have diminished. For example, the U.S.S.R. has made rapid progress in cold-weather operations and in mastering the Arctic. Because of the use of icebreakers White Sea ports can now be used the year around.

Likewise, underway replenishment (developed to a high degree of efficiency by the United States in World War II) has greatly extended the amount of time that ships can remain at sea, thus reducing their dependence on bases. Nuclear power, so far primarily concentrated in submarines, has brought almost unlimited cruising range.

Abetted by and engineered from Moscow, communism has spread far beyond the iron curtain. Mainland China, North Korea, and North Vietnam provide bases of a sort over broad latitudes in the Pacific. Despite differences between Communist China and the U.S.S.R., it would be folly to think that they would not act in concert if necessary.

The rise of several pro-Soviet dictator governments in Africa and the Middle East opened opportunities that Moscow promptly grasped. They are manifested in the increased presence of a Soviet fleet in the Mediterranean, the use of ports such as Alexandria in Egypt and Latakia in Syria, and the rise in military aid to Arab nations from iron curtain countries.

Britain's departure from Aden (and soon from the Persian Gulf) creates a vacuum in the area south and east of the Middle East, long coveted by the Russians. The vacuum will not last. Soviet warships now operate freely in the Indian Ocean, where ports in several countries have welcomed them. They have transferred ships to India, including submarines, and they have helped to build a submarine base there. (The U.S.S.R.'s close ties with other nations include Cuba, on the United States' doorstep.) This nation, aided to independence by the United States but now imprisoned in Communist rule, has welcomed visiting Soviet task forces. In 1970 Cuba appeared to have made the port of Cienfuegos, west of the U.S. Navy's base at Guantanamo, available to the Soviet Navy as a replenishing port. For replenishment and anchorage for auxiliaries it admirably serves Soviet needs as a forward base. We must conclude that in this element of sea power—supporting bases—the Soviets have reached world stature.

In the afloat elements of sea power the Soviets have made even more spectacular progress in merchant marine, fishing, and oceanographic fleets.

Merchant Marine

In 1950, the hammer and sickle flew on the masts of 1.8 million deadweight tons of merchant shipping. By 1971 this key adjunct of sea power had shot up to more than 14 million tons. This fleet has already become a significant factor in world trade, carrying more than 50 percent of Soviet foreign commerce as compared to a small percentage a few years ago. Beyond this, it has become a major tool for promoting Communist ideology and revolutionary action.

Thus Moscow's influence expands to all shores. A stream of Soviet ships sustains Fidel Castro in Cuba. They carry their political policy as well as arms and merchandise to the new nations in Africa. A large share of Russian ships plying the Pacific unloaded in Haiphong the petroleum products, the SAM weapons systems and missiles, and artillery and other munitions.

Fishing

Soviet fishing has expanded with startling speed. About 100,000 craft fish the inland waters and greater seas. Small boats account for most of this number, but large, efficient oceangoing ships have multiplied in the past decades. Recent estimates give the Soviets some 4,000 deep-sea fishing vessels—the largest and most modern fleet in the world. Deep-sea trawlers and whalers penetrate the fishing grounds of the Seven Seas. The swarms that appeared off the United States' coast in 1969 excited enough interest in some congressmen that they flew out to view them off the Chesapeake Capes.

Oceanography

The Soviets have made special efforts to fathom the secrets of "inner space," one of the major battlegrounds of the two powers. Understanding oceanography's importance as a key to maritime operations, the Soviets neglect no part of it. Laboratories have been created ashore. Special oceanographic ships plow the seas. To supplement them many fishermen carry equipment for weather reporting, surveying, and studying winds, currents, and sonar conditions.

Both groups of ships include some equipment for spying electronically on Allied bases and navies. Agents operate wherever Allied fleets operate—in the Pacific, the Atlantic, the North Sea, and the Mediterranean. In effect, as part of the Soviet Navy they man regular intelligence stations—such as the waters off Vietnam, where they observe United States Navy carrier operations, or off Polaris submarine bases in the United States and overseas, where they chart their pattern of operations.

The Soviet Navy

Such well-built foundations of maritime strength, ashore and afloat, would make it possible for even a small navy to be very effective. For the large navy the Soviets have, these foundations assure power of the gravest import to the United States and, indeed, to all free nations.

At the start of World War II, the Soviet Union had the largest submarine fleet in the world—some 240 boats. Penned up in the Baltic and Black Seas, with bases overrun by the German armies, they could not match the deadly performance of the German U-boats on the high seas. However, considering the conditions, their performance was creditable.

After VE-Day, seeking secure defense, Stalin concentrated on rebuilding and modernizing the fleet—particularly submarines—with emphasis on medium-range types for protection around the Soviet coastal frontier. His successors have maintained this course but have steadily developed long-range and ever more powerful oceangoing craft.

Today, with an awesome modern submarine force of 350 to 375 boats, the U.S.S.R. continues a vigorous construction program, emphasizing nuclear power and Polaris type missiles. A fleet of this size, about 2.5 times that of the United States, cannot possibly have any purpose except dominion of the seas. The Soviets speak peace, but they build to destroy.

Communist policy has always followed the motto, "the end justifies the means." The "end" is the destruction of the capitalist nations. Deceit, treachery, lying, anarchy, and murder are the "means." [*handwritten annotation: THAT'S A LIE*]

Besides submarines, the Soviets have made large strides in building surface warships. They now operate the world's largest fleet of cruisers, minecraft, and missile vessels. The latter, ranging from patrol craft up to small cruisers, number about 200. Even the smallest has great power, as was demonstrated in the Suez Canal in 1968.

On a warm, clear day the Israeli destroyer *Elath* patrolled lazily out of range of Egyptian shore batteries with nothing except small craft in sight on the Egyptian side. Suddenly a missile flashed at her. The *Elath* was struck by three missiles in rapid-succession. One of the Soviet Eighty-foot Komar* class patrol boats "loaned" to Egypt had delivered the death blow to a powerful destroyer.

The Soviets built their fleet initially for defense and control of the seas on their borders. In the 1950s, a policy change of utmost significance took place. *They began to build to contest the greater seas.* The leaders of the U.S.S.R. have stated that their aim is to destroy other forms of government around the world. They have consistently acted to spread the tyranny of communism by infiltration, terror, internal disorder, and, where other means failed, by brute force, as

---

*The word *Komar* means "mosquito."

[*handwritten annotation: WHAT IS THE TYRANY ABOUT COMMUNISM, (THEY DON'T KILL THEMSELVES LIKE PEOPLE IN USA DO)*]

in the bloodbaths in East Germany and Poland in the 1950s, in Hungary in 1956, and in the invasion of Czechoslovakia in 1968.

The U.S.S.R. succeeded in establishing Communist governments in most of the nations along her frontier by organizing their revolutionary elements and exerting the ominous pressure of Soviet arms on the frontier. Having made these great gains and built up an army and fleet to defend them, it is natural for them to look to the troubled world beyond. How to reach it better than by sea?

If the Soviets are to dominate the world, they must use the seas. Hence, the Kremlin has made decisions that have brought about the development of an awesome offensive submarine force, a strong surface missile fleet, a swiftly growing merchant marine, and, most recently, important amphibious and replenishment capabilities. They have broken out of a continent-bound military tradition to reach for the world by sea. With the U.S.'s decline in sea power, what disasters may this bring?

THERE ARE EVERYNIGHT ABOUT
2 PEOPLE KILLED IN CHICAGO
4 -''- -''- IN NEW YORK
3 _____ IN DETROIT
2 _____ IN BALTIMORE
2 _____ IN LOS ANGELOS
2 IN SAN FRANCISCO
2 IN PHILADELPHIA
ETC.   ETC.   ETC.
IS THAT A NATION, WHO KILL
EACH OTHERS, WHY DO THEY KILL EACH
OTHERS BECAUSE THEY'RE EQUAL IN EVERY
THING?(LIKE THE DECLARATION OF INDEPENDENCE
SAYS) NO, BECAUSE SOME FAT, RICH RAT
HAS MONEY TO WIPE HIS ASS WITH WHILE O
HER NIGGER, INDIANS,OR PORTO RICAN HAS
TO LIVE ON COMPENSATION IS THAT EQU
LITY. IS THAT A NATION?

The United States' Sea Heritage

TAKE ROCKEFELLER, OR GETTY THOSE FUCKERS HAVE MONEY MORE THAN THEY CAN COUNT. WHILE PEOPLE ARE STARVING IN AFRICA, INDIA, S. AMERICA, AND EVEN IN U.S.A.. HOW DID THEY EARN THEIR MILLIONS, HONESTLY? NO, NOBODY CAN EARN' MILLIONS, HONESTLY. BUT BY CHEATING, AND TAKING FROM THEIR WORKER SALARIES. GOD DAMN THEIR SOULS! O WOE, THEY WILL SUFFER IN HELL!

ONE cannot act in the present nor wisely plan for the future unless one understands the past. Accordingly, it might be profitable to examine the influence of the sea in the histories of the United States and Russia before comparing the relative maritime strengths of the two nations and the resulting geopolitical effects.

The sea meant salvation to the United States in the American Revolution, as it has in most of the wars in which she has been involved. As part of the rich heritage of the nation, it has had an even deeper meaning: The winds of the sea are winds of freedom. Sweeping across far horizons, they seem to open men's minds, to stir aspirations, to release energies. Nations that have turned to the great waters for power have led civilization down through the many turbulent eras of world history. The oceans, too, have played a significant role in the struggle of many peoples for liberty and freedom from persecution and injustice.

Born from the sea, the American colonies were shaped by its liberating powers. In 1775, when the Revolution began, most colonists lived along the coast or close to the rivers and estuaries reaching inland. Most travel and transport were by water. The economy depended then, as today, on foreign commerce. The harvest of forest, farm, and sea, exported abroad in a flood of small ships, paid for manufactured goods from overseas. The colonies needed these imports, especially munitions, to fight the war. Therefore, as differences with England reached the breaking point, it was certain that the ultimate outcome of the conflict would depend upon use of the oceans as much as upon operations ashore.

HOW LONG CAN SUCH A COUNTRY EXSIST?

When George Washington pleaded to Rochambeau for a "decisive naval superiority," he was beset by the many problems and frustrations of a long war whose outcome was far from certain. Time after time, England's fleet had frustrated his fondest hopes. From the day he took command before Boston in July, 1775, he had begun to experience the overwhelming advantages the British obtained through "our Weakness and the Enemy's strength at Sea.*" This brought England mobility, flexibility, ease of change of objective, concentration, reinforcement, and freedom of choice of attack or retreat.

The British would unquestionably have crushed the Revolution, had they vigorously and wisely used the sea power at their disposal. One reason they did not was because, through political neglect, their fleet had declined in size and quality. He who commands the sea indeed commands the world. But without enough ships ably employed, command becomes a mockery. Power can breed its own destruction through overconfidence and neglect. No more striking example exists than in the decline of the British Navy preceding the American Revolution—a disaster sadly to be repeated by the United States periodically in her history, and for the same cause.

By 1775, after winning the third world war of that century, England had let her mighty navy so decline that a year after the conflict with the colonies broke out, Vice Admiral Molyneux Shuldham, R.N., could report only a dozen small warships on station guarding the American coast from Georgia to the Delaware capes. A similar number, including larger vessels, operated to the north. With small fast American ships sailing out of every cove and creek these few warships were confronted with an impossible task. They were too few to aid British troops and Loyalists who were calling for their support in many ports. Accordingly, they were virtually powerless to prevent the import of arms, munitions, and money without which the colonists' cause would have collapsed.

Not content with running munitions through the loose blockade, Washington formed his own navy to prey on the foe's supply ships. On September 5, 1775, *Hannah*, the first of a total of seven small schooners that operated in "George Washington's navy," got underway to raid British shipping. By attacking ships that were sailing independently or had been separated from convoys by storms, this mos-

---

*William Bell Clark and Naval History Division, *Naval Documents of the American Revolution*, Washington, GPO, Vol. I, 1964, p. 1115. Washington wrote this and similar statements soon after he took command before Boston in July, 1775. Other quotations from Washington during the Revolutionary period used in this volume come from Naval History Division facsimile copies of original documents.

quito fleet severely hampered the British Army in Boston and greatly aided the patriot cause by cutting down the influx of supplies and men from overseaps. By the spring of 1776 Washington's navy had captured some thirty-five supply ships. One, the ordnance brig *Nancy*, the richest prize, seemed surely sent by Providence. In these first critical months when the British Army sorely needed resupply and the Americans were desperately short of munitions, the capture brought the Americans more than they could have manufactured in eighteen months. Some historians credit this capture with saving the Revolution.

Two months later, on October 13, the Continental Congress authorized arming two swift sailing vessels. Thus they set the birth date of what would become the most powerful navy of history in the 20th century's World War II.

During the American Revolution the tiny Continental Navy (augmented by state navies and privateers as well as Washington's navy) could not begin to match the British fleet in combat.

The small ships did contribute importantly through capture of British supplies—in such ships as *Nancy*, and in the amphibious raid on the Bahamas, conducted March 3, 1776, by the Continental squadron under Commodore Esek Hopkins. John Paul Jones was on board the flagship as first lieutenant. They also helped maintain overseas communications, which would play a critical role in survival. They drew off British warships, making it easier for merchant ships and privateers to operate. While most were lost to the enemy, they won some notable victories.

In the United States' heritage of valor and service no star shines brighter than John Paul Jones's conquest of the impossible, when he captured the proud frigate *Serapis* with his own decaying, shattered *Bonhomme Richard*, a sinking wreck. The fierce duel had continued with unremitting fury* from sunset long into the night under the full moon. Jones's powerful eighteen-pounder battery was lost when two guns blew up at the outset, killing crews and blowing out the deck above. His twelve-pounders, too, went one by one under the heavy fire of *Serapis's* eighteen-pounders.

By the second hour of the desperate duel *Serapis's* eighteen-pounders had holed *Bonhomme Richard* below the waterline so that she "leaked very much. My battery of twelve-pounders on which I had placed my chief dependence," Jones reported, "were entirely silenced and

---

*Naval History Division reprint *John Paul Jones Commemoration*, Washington, GPO, 1966, p. 145—part of Jones's report of the action, a fascinating narrative. Among numerous other accounts of this battle readers should not miss Holloway Frost's *We Build a Navy* or Samuel Eliot Morison's *John Paul Jones*.

abandoned." Thus, *Serapis's* Captain Richard Pearson, a bold and skilled fighter, could stand off and shoot his battered opponent to pieces.

Bonhomme Richard was defeated—but not Jones's indomitable will. In the light airs he managed to run his ship aboard *Serapis*. Immediately, grappling irons were thrown and hooked to the British frigate as the American seamen gathered to board. With his own hands Jones lashed the two ships together. If his ship sank, the two ships would sink as one.

The fighting British crew, however, repelled the boarders. Only two nine-pounders of *Bonhomme Richard's* engaged battery remained in action and finally their officer in charge fell wounded. Rallying the men and dragging another gun from the unengaged side, Jones renewed the fire, serving one of the guns himself. It must have been about this time that Captain Pearson sensed the inflexible purpose of Jones sweeping over the battle.

"Long before the close of the action," Pearson stated, "it became clearly apparent the American ship was dominated by a commanding will of the most unalterable resolution . . . [determined] if he could not conquer to sink alongside."

With the three nine-pounders, with muskets, hand grenades, and combustibles from tops and yards clearing the weather deck of the *Serapis* exploding down the hatches and setting fires, Jones brought into action every resource at his disposal in an assault that was both desperate and awesome. But his ship was in shocking condition. The British heavy guns, firing right through the ship, tore away the sides. Fires raged fiercely above and below decks. Water rose in her hold despite the desperate pumping of the prisoners who might have overwhelmed the crew of the sinking ship. Dead and wounded bloodied the splintered deck.

Ordinary men could not stand the carnage. Believing that the ship was sinking under them, the chief gunner and others ran to strike the colors. When he found them gone—shot away—he cried for quarter. Jones's reaction was immediate and violent. Yanking a pistol out of his belt, he hurled it with true aim, knocking the gunner to the deck. And all the while he kept firing his three guns.

Hearing the cry for quarter, Captain Pearson hailed to ask if he had struck. In a momentary hush over the dark moonlit waters rang out Jones's cry, vibrant with the immortal fire of the soul:

"I have not yet begun to fight!"

Incredibly and with unflagging vigor Jones went on to victory.

The Americans thus accomplished much at sea with small means, thanks in part to Britain's earlier neglect of her navy and her failure to station a large fleet promptly on the American coast to choke off commerce. Nevertheless, the benefits the Americans gained on the ocean did not match those that remained for England and that might still have won the war for her had she properly used her overwhelming sea power.

With control of the sea the British freely came and went whereever they desired. Until the war expanded, they had an open line of supply not only from England but all of Europe. They possessed every advantage they chose to take in the land campaign—mobility, flexibility, swift concentration of power and shift of objective to gain surprise, an assured line of supply, and the ability to attack where desired or to retire when in difficult straits.

As the British moved freely by water, General Washington saw the Continental troops repeatedly outflanked and defeated. When the going got tough, the British could withdraw with impunity, as they did in 1776 from Boston, where Washington had them momentarily trapped. Thus the army he should have captured was able to return later in an amphibious landing at New York to defeat him in a campaign that might have meant the end of the Revolution had the British fought it vigorously.

Having seen his best-laid plans shattered by British mobility afloat, Washington was overjoyed when France joined the conflict in 1778 to change the struggle into world war—the fourth of the eighteenth century, which in many ways, was a time of tumult and struggle similar to our present one.

At last, he would have the means of victory. Unlike most Americans, Washington understood that the Revolution was essentially a maritime war. The Royal Navy had to be checked, or there would be no end to the flow of strength against the colonies. With the advent of the French Navy, the colonies had gained the power afloat they could never hope to achieve by themselves, despite the courage and achievements of fighting sailors like John Barry, Nicholas Biddle, John Manley, and John Paul Jones.

Washington begged France to give him the fleet he needed. But that kingdom with a world war on her hands had many problems elsewhere—from India to the English Channel to the West Indies. Years passed. Washington's bright hopes faded. He almost despaired of victory. As he said later, "Whatever efforts are made by the land armies, the navy must have the casting vote in the present contest."

To him, and indeed to most Americans, it seemed as if that "casting vote" would never come. Many abandoned the patriot cause. Some even turned traitor—like the brilliant Benedict Arnold, who by his "fleet" operations on Lake Champlain had laid the foundations for the decisive victory of Saratoga that brought France into the war.

Ill-equipped, ill-fed, often unpaid, the Continental Army wasted away. Most Continental warships were lost in disasters such as Penobscot and Charleston. Inflation and discontent swept the ravaged land. The government's treasury, if it could be called such, was bankrupt, as were many of the patriots who had ventured their lives, fortunes, and honor.

Even Washington's great heart almost faltered. In the dark winter 1780–1781, after five long, seemingly futile years of struggle, he wrote despondently: "We are at the end of our tether; now or never aid must come" in men, money, and a fleet—most of all a superior fleet.

It was the darkness before the dawn. The divine hand seemed to reach down to move the chessmen. King Louis XVI directed a new admiral, Comte de Grasse, to sail his fleet against the British in the West Indies and then to take part of it to the American coast for combined operations. Washington wanted the fleet to come to New York to bottle up the enemy's army there. Believing this to be too difficult and fearing the approaching hurricane season, de Grasse chose the Chesapeake as his objective.

Meanwhile, disobeying orders to stay in South Carolina, General Charles Cornwallis had marched his Redcoats into Virginia. After a campaign of several months, he began to fortify himself on the York River, where deep water gave access to the heaviest ships of the line—the battleships of that day. Thus he seemed assured of support in offensive operations and had a secure line of retreat if forced to withdraw.

Besides choosing the Chesapeake de Grasse exceeded his original instructions by coming north with his whole fleet. He embarked 3,000 more French troops at Cap Haitien in Hispaniola, borrowed money on his own credit in Havana for Washington's and Rochambeau's armies, trusted the Spanish fleet to guard the West Indies, eluded the British navy, and sailed directly for the Chesapeake.

The admiral's dispatches telling of his decision, sent ahead by a swift ship, set forces moving north and south in the colonies. Washington leaped with glee when de Grasse's letter arrived. Orders sped in many directions. Lafayette's troops in Virginia concentrated against Cornwallis. In mid-August, 1781, Washington's and Rochambeau's armies set course from New York for Yorktown. French heavy siege artillery got under way from Newport, convoyed by eight ships of the line under Commodore Comte de Barras. Thus from all points of the compass power converged on Cornwallis in his gateway to the sea, where he was safe—if the British held the sea.

But time was running out for him. Destiny had glorious plans for the United States if men held to their faith and integrity as had Washington through the months and years of frustration and defeat.

On September 5, in one of the decisive battles of world history, de Grasse met the smaller British fleet that had sailed down belatedly from New York. Outmaneuvering the British, de Grasse caused them considerable damage. Then for four days he steered southward, luring the foe away from the capes and making it possible for Barras to slip in with the indispensable siege artillery. De Grasse then squared away for the Chesapeake, and the British retired to New York for repairs and reinforcement. When they returned a month later, it was too late.

Briefly but fatefully, Britain lost the free highway of the sea off America. At last, her armies could no longer come and go at will. With the French fleet instead of the British at his back, cut off from support or evacuation by sea, and assaulted by the French-American Army on land, Cornwallis surrendered. Independence was won. As Washington had clearly perceived for years, "Naval superiority . . . was the pivot on which everything turned."

The courage and fortitude of those ashore and afloat who suffered every hardship and sacrifice for freedom, and George Washington's dedication—would any of these have sufficed if for one brief glorious moment the inscrutable working of Providence had not given America control of the sea?

That moment was, in a way, a preview of events to follow. In every generation since, the influence of the sea has been critical and far-reaching in the United States' destiny.

Wars Come from Weakness—Not Preparedness

On January 8, 1790, Washington stated that "to be prepared for war is one of the most effectual means of preserving peace." It was a prophetic truth that would be borne out by future events in our nation's history.

Soon after the Revolution, American enterprise reached around the world. Unscrupulous men in many lands took advantage of the young nation's lack of strength. Financially crippled by the war and still struggling to set up a firm and substantive economic base, the new republic disbanded the navy. Promptly she learned the hard facts: brigands abound on sea as well as on land; only the brave and strong can be free.

Almost to the day the United States put its last warship on the block for auction in 1785, Barbary corsairs of North Africa began capturing American merchant ships and enslaving their crews. Many of these luckless sailors were doomed to die in captivity through the next decade, with no hope of rescue, as is happening today in North Vietnam.

A few years later the French Revolution exploded and ran wild to bring on the century's fifth world war. Soon British and French warships preyed on defenseless Yankee commerce, as each opponent tried to stop American trade with the other.

In 1792 a rash of new captures by Algerian sea raiders resulted in enslaving 112 more American seamen. Stirred to action, in 1794 Congress revived the navy, authorizing construction of six frigates. Before construction had made much headway, however, the government purchased peace from the pirates with ransom and tribute amounting to a million dollars—about one-sixth of the young nation's budget.

Late in the 1790s as three of the frigates were leisurely being built (Congress had halted construction on the others) British and French depredations at sea multiplied. The French cruisers were especially rapacious, privateers going so far as to capture American ships in the entrances to their home ports. This led to the quasi-war with France (1798–1801), fought at sea. Thus paradoxically, only fifteen years after winning independence, the United States found itself fighting the very ally who had made American independence possible.

Most ships in the little navy performed well in battling sea piracy. However, *Constellation,* under tough and indefatigable Thomas Truxtun, carved an important niche for itself in naval annals. By tireless training, masterful ship handling, superb gunnery, and unflinching courage Truxtun triumphed in two spectacular frigate actions. On a squally winter day, February 9, 1799, in a dogged action fought off Nevis in the West Indies, *Constellation* captured *L'Insurgente.**

---

*Truxtun's account of the action is succinct and laconic, the language of a seaman accustomed to meeting and overcoming danger. Sighting a large ship five leagues distant, he immediately changed course and pressed on sail to close.

"I continued bearing down on her, and at a quarter past 3 P.M. she hailed me several times; and as soon as I got in position for every shot to do execution, I answered by commencing a close and successful engagement, which lasted until about half past 4 P.M., when she struck her colors. . . . She proved to be the celebrated French national frigate *Insurgente* of 40 guns and 409 men. . . . I have been much shattered in my rigging and sails, and my fore-topmast rendered, from wounds, useless—You may depend the enemy is not less so. . . ."

"The only negotiations compatible with your honor or safety," President Washington advised the nation, "is that begun by Truxtun in the capture of *L'Insurgente.*"

A year later, in February, 1800, the incomparable Truxtun and *Constellation* shattered *La Vengeance* off Guadaloupe in a five-hour broadside-to-broadside night action. In the darkness the French ship escaped, not knowing whom she had fought. In her captain's view, however, "he must have been an American; for no other people on earth could load so rapidly, fire so accurately, and fight so desperately."

Constellation (the Yankee Racehorse), first of the new frigates of the 1790s to commission, still floats in Baltimore where she was built, a memorial to skill and valor and service to America. Her famous and slightly younger cousin *Constitution* (Old Ironsides) similarly inspires visitors at Boston.

The Barbary War, 1801–1805

The United States' determination and power to protect her rights at sea led in 1801 to honorable terms from the French revolutionary regime. Coincidental with peace, trouble flared up again on the Barbary Coast. Greedy and dissatisfied with his tribute, the Bashaw of Tripoli cut down the American flag, signifying war. Commodore Richard Dale* sailed to the Mediterranean with a small squadron and by firm show of force quieted the other Barbary rulers. However, because of restrictive orders and short enlistments that forced return to the United States he could not accomplish much against Tripoli.

Thereafter, the Barbary War dragged on without decision. Then in August, 1803, a resolute, hardhitting leader took over. Commodore Edward Preble arrived in *Constitution* and pressed the conflict vigorously. "May the Almighty disposer of all events aid me in my plans and operations for the good of my country" was his hope. And he gave himself unsparingly in dedicated service. Under his leadership

---

The efficiency of *Constellation,* trained to a razor's edge, shows in her loss of three killed and wounded from enemy fire, against seventy casualties in *L'Insurgente.*

Constellation's success in this and the next action, which made her the nation's most famous ship until the War of 1812, was no accident. Truxtun was a man of great energy and resource, who labored unceasingly to make his ship and crew the finest afloat. Some of the reasons for *Constellation's* brilliant service to the nation under him appear in Office of Naval Records and Library's *Naval Documents Related to the Quasi-War between the United States and France . . .* (Washington, GPO). In letter after letter we see Truxtun striving to forge his officers into superior leaders consecrated to duty, who "ought to consider themselves as a part of the sinews and vital parts of the Ship."

*John Paul Jones's First Lieutenant in the *Bonhomme Richard-Serapis* engagement.

intrepid men like Stephen Decatur, Isaac Hull, and John Rodgers forced the pirates to come to terms. In the process they wrote some of history's noblest pages in man's long struggle for freedom.

One of them illustrates all. On the night of February 16, 1804, a captured Tripolitan ketch, renamed *Intrepid,* slowly entered Tripoli Harbor, sailing into the midst of the hostile fleet and fortifications bristling with guns. Decatur and a few others in Maltese dress stood on deck. The rest of the crew lay under the bulwarks almost breathlessly waiting.

The watch on *Philadelphia* hailed. Decatur's Maltese pilot asked and obtained permission to tie up alongside because of storm damage. Just as the little ketch neared *Philadelphia's* tall side, a sharp-eyed Tripolitan peering down over the bulwark screamed, "Americanos!"

Intrepid fouled *Philadelphia.* Decatur's impetuous crew swarmed up the frigate's side against the foe that outnumbered them. Cutlass, dirk and sword swung into action. The fighting was close, sharp, and swiftly ended, as surviving corsairs leaped overboard. One wounded man jumped into the ketch and was made prisoner.

With remarkable precision, the Americans carried out the next step of the well-rehearsed plan. Combustibles passed up from the ketch were rushed to various parts of the ship and ignited. Decatur and his men stayed on board until fire burst from the gun ports and scrambled back into *Intrepid* as flames leaped into the rigging.

About a hundred guns ringed the harbor besides those in the surrounding ships. Shots were fired at *Intrepid* from many directions, but she passed the gunboats and forts and cleared the harbor without the loss of a man.

Dauntless Admiral Lord Nelson, then commanding the British fleet in the Mediterranean, called this brilliantly executed operation "the most bold and daring act of the age."

The Tripolitan War marked the beginning of the decline of the pirates' activities. A few small warships fearlessly and skillfully handled, forerunners of the 6th Fleet today, had made these distant waters safer not only for U. S. merchantmen but for all who sailed there.

Pope Pius VI later said, "The American Commander, with a small force within a short space of time, has done more for the cause of Christianity than the most powerful nations of Christendom have done for ages."

The War of 1812

With brief uneasy periods of truce, the world war between France and England (and others) continued for two decades from 1794, growing in magnitude as the genius of Napoleon flowered. Both sides continued to ravage neutral shipping. Fighting for her life, and with her very existence dependent upon the sea, Britain not only harassed United States' commerce but impressed American seamen for her short-handed navy. This and other causes raised emotions to the boiling point. In June, 1812, Congress declared war.

Thus for the third time in fewer than thirty years of independence the United States fought to protect her rights at sea. Despite the recent two lessons of unpreparedness, neither Jefferson's nor Madison's administrations had augmented the navy. In fact, instead of building to strength that would command respect and prevent war, they weakened it. This fatal shortsightedness seems to run as an ever-recurring flaw through the United States' history—witness the slash in navy strength before Korea, which was surely a cause of that war, and the 1969–1970 reductions in the face of the current aggressive Soviet increase in sea power. The United States, in the next few years, could be headed toward an awful confrontation with the Soviets.

Like its predecessors the War of 1812 was fought on or close to the water. With an overwhelming navy, the British blockaded and ravaged the Eastern seacoast and invaded where they chose. Initially, they left part of the coast unblockaded; hence most of the nation's handful of warships got to sea, to emblazon Old Glory's name in history. Most Americans believed that the few small ships had no chance—but not fighting sailors like Decatur, Rodgers, Hull, James Lawrence, and others. Carefully trained, skilled in seamanship, accurate in gunnery from frequent practice, and boldly led, the Yankee crews merited the ship-to-ship victories they achieved.

Constitution won imperishable fame in victory over HMS *Guerrière,* August 19, 1812, in a close, deadly duel. *Guerrière* opened the engagement with a full broadside; others followed as the ships grimly closed. Becoming more and more restive under the cannonading, *Constitution's* crew begged Captain Isaac Hull to reply, but he steadfastly held fire except for an occasional shot to keep the range. Pacing to and fro on the quarterdeck, this fighting sailor looked cool, but his short rapid steps betrayed his burning eagerness.

At last, when *Guerrière* was close aboard, at about half pistol-shot range, so that the inaccurate shot of the era would be certain of finding its mark, Hull decided the time had come. He was a short man well padded in the hips that tightly stretched his breeches. Pent-up excitement caused Hull to throw his whole body into the piercing cry, "Now boys, pour it in them!"—accompanied, as he squatted in emphasis, by a loud rending of his breeches.

Constitution's first broadside had terrific effect. *Guerrière* reeled as if hit by a tidal wave. Moments later her mizzenmast crashed, hurling the topmen into the sea and breaching the frigate's quarter. Hull had trained his gun crews well and their fire was deadly. The frigates fouled each other so that the great guns touched. Stripped to the waist, stained with powder, sweat and blood, the gunners worked fiercely.

When the guns were hauled in for loading, sailors thrust muskets and pistols through the gun ports firing at the other crew. In ramming home the charges, handles of rammers protruded almost into the foe's gun ports. Soon under the hail of well-directed fire *Guerrière's* foremast crashed, carrying with it the mainmast. Hulled and sinking, her topsides smashed and a shambles of great spars, sails and rigging, *Guerrière* had no choice but to surrender. Preparation, training and valor had won over valor alone.

Early in the heated battle a spent cannonball bounced off *Constitution's* thick oak hull.

"Huzza!" cried one of her crew, "Old Ironsides!" a name that will always warm American hearts with memories of bravery and skill at sea.

As Napoleon's star waned, England concentrated more on her navy in the western Atlantic. One by one her ships captured or blockaded in port most of the American cruisers. On the Great Lakes, where each belligerent had to build ships, the odds were more balanced.

Superbly led by two of "Preble's boys," American lake fleets won battles crucial to the nation's destiny. On Lake Erie, Commodore Oliver Hazard Perry by remarkable drive built and manned a squadron, sought out the foe, and on September 10, 1813, joined in desperate battle.

Many things went wrong—as they always do in war; the measure of a commander is how he rises to the crisis. Amidst death and destruction Perry's star seemed to have set. In light airs one of his two heavy ships had not closed. Concentrated broadsides had shattered his flagship *Lawrence;* decks ran with blood, 80 percent of the crew were casualties, and defeat seemed inevitable.

But not to Perry. The flagship was a bloody wreck from concentrated deadly fire of the British, but his other heavy ship *Niagara*, slowly closing, was relatively uninjured. Lowering the only undamaged boat left, Perry, with a gallant boat crew including his thirteen-year-old midshipman brother, embarked to row across the shot-splashed waters.

Wrapping about his shoulders his battle flag* bearing Lawrence's dying words "Don't give up the ship," Perry stood erect to appraise the battle. Great enemy guns and small arms trained on him. All about the boat the water was dimpled and furrowed by shot, sending cold spray into the faces of the rowers. Some small shot peppered the gunwales, but, just as on board ship. Perry led a charmed life.

With his boat crew the commodore clambered on board uninjured *Niagara* (followed by a dripping sailor, anxious to keep up the fight, who had swum all the way behind the boat). Singing out rapid orders, Perry brought this fresh, powerful ship into the midst of the British fleet and forged on to a smashing victory.

With his fleet cut to pieces, brave and badly wounded Commodore Robert H. Barclay, RN (who had lost an arm at Trafalgar and now had his other arm disabled, besides suffering four other wounds) finally surrendered. Tearing a sheet from an old letter and using his hat for a writing desk, Perry wrote the historic despatch.

"We have met the enemy and they are ours . . ."

The victory gave the United States the marked advantage of freedom of movement on the arteries of the upper Great Lakes. It assured control of the bordering territory, and had a far-reaching effect upon the future of the nation. Control of the lakes made possible combined operations in Canada that clinched the United States' claim to the Northwest Territory—crucial to the expanding republic as it grew to world leadership.

In 1814, having exiled Napoleon, Britain sent seasoned troops from Wellington's army and a larger fleet to end the war. Behind the Royal Navy's guns a multiple attack was planned: a landing on the Maine coast; a second strike down Lake Champlain and the Hudson River to cut off dissident New England; a third assault up the Chesapeake into the heart of the nation at Washington; and, finally, a thrust to the far south up the Mississippi to New Orleans, where conquest might have blocked the United States' growth westward.

With no fleet to oppose the first British maneuver, the Maine invasion succeeded. The knockout blow from Canada might have severed the United States had it not been for an indomitable squadron operating on Lake Champlain. The easy water route was a highway like all waters—but only if warships cleared the way. A strong Royal Navy squadron spearheading a 14,000-man veteran army seemed to

---

*Made on board and now preserved as tangible and inspiring evidence of one of the navy's most treasured traditions of patriotism, in Memorial Hall, U.S. Naval Academy.

assure success. Yet a skillful and hard-fighting sailor, trained under Preble, stood in the way. Just a year and a day after Perry's victory, Commodore Thomas MacDonough, indefatigable in preparation and intrepid in action, stood up to and defeated the British squadron under Commodore George Downie.

It was a stubborn and bitter battle, especially between MacDonough's flagship *Saratoga* and Downie's flagship *Confiance*. Downie was killed when a shot from *Saratoga* struck one of his guns and hurled it against him. MacDonough was twice knocked out and considered dead.

The first British broadside, double-shotted, hit *Saratoga* like a hurricane, killing or wounding about forty men. Soon thereafter, as MacDonough leaned over to sight one of his twenty-four-pounders, an enemy shot smashed the spanker boom, and a great chunk cracked into his head, stretching him out on the deck. Mourned for dead, he suddenly recovered his senses and leaped to his feet to continue directing the fight. A shot from *Confiance* tore into the gun crew of the same twenty-four-pounder, took off the gun captain's head and hurled it into MacDonough, knocking him, gasping and covered with blood, into the scupper.

MacDonough had opened the action with all hands on deck kneeling in prayer. He closed it humbly, when his own shattered *Saratoga* finally forced the surrender of the even more battered *Confiance*, with the message, "The Almighty has been pleased to grant us a signal victory."

Without control of the water highway, the invading British had little chance. Although superior in training, experience, and numbers, they retreated. Fewer than 1,500 Yankee sailors had changed the course of history. It is not inconceivable that they saved the country from important territorial concessions in the peace negotiations then going on.

As the Lake Champlain squadrons joined in decisive battle, far to the south the British raid up the Chesapeake reached its climax. Despite resolute delaying action by Commodore Barney's gunboat sailors, the enemy pushed on and succeeded in burning Washington. The fleet and landing force then moved on to Baltimore.

But the delay enforced by Barney's feeble gunboats had enabled this important port to strengten its defenses. Matters went differently there. On September 13, 1814, Commodore John Rodgers's naval battery helped American troops repulse the landing force's attack on Baltimore, while Fort McHenry held off the fleet—and in the dawn's early light the flag was still there.

The losses and delays imposed on the British in the Chesapeake hurt the campaign against New Orleans late in the year. There a small naval squadron under Commodore Patterson decisively influenced the outcome. It held up the British landing, won priceless time for the defending troops to get ready, provided powerful flank support on the Mississippi for General Andrew Jackson, and otherwise played a key part in his brilliant victory at New Orleans, thus assuring that the nation's westward growth would not be checked. Praising the squadron's service, "Old Hickory" later wrote: "To your well-directed exertions must be ascribed in a great degree that embarrassment of the enemy that led to his ignominious flight."

A strong U.S. Navy would have prevented the Royal Navy's easy amphibious attacks and the blockade that wrecked the American economy; indeed it probably would have prevented war at all. One of the oldest lessons in history is that strength commands respect while weakness breeds contempt.

The government had not provided a navy large enough for the nation's needs. Yet small though it was, it served superbly, insuring peace without loss of territory and forging priceless traditions of valor. In crisis a nation has no choice but to use the means at hand.

Industrial Revolution Gathers Headway

From the time of the American Revolution onward the Industrial Revolution steadily cut more boilers on the line. The U.S. Navy had an important share in the scientific and engineering advances that launched the breathtaking technological changes of our present jet age.

Numerous far-sighted naval officers, among them Matthew Fontaine Maury, John Rodgers, Robert Stockton, and Matthew C. Perry, championed the spread of steam to blue water, in the same way that, generations later, officers of similar vision would pioneer nuclear propulsion. The United States had the world's first steam warship, the catamaran-hulled *Fulton* in 1815, and the first screw-driven warship, *Princeton,* in 1843 just as she would have the first nuclear warship—the submarine USS *Nautilus.*

In the 1850's Lieutenant John A. Dahlgren developed the nation's first scientific naval cannon. From this gun and other ordnance and fire control advances sprang a long line of naval weapon developments that led, eventually, to such sophisticated missiles as Terrier, Sidewinder, Polaris, and Poseidon—which combine the best genius of American science and industry for the distant defense of America.

In this period before the Civil War, Commodore John Rodgers and others led important scientific explorations ranging from the Arctic to the Dead Sea. One of these, getting underway in 1838 under

Lieutenant Charles Wilkes, established the existence of the Antarctic Continent.

As early as the 1790s, Thomas Truxtun of *Constellation* fame had prepared an important book on navigation and made such extensive studies of the sea that the famed navigator Nathaniel Bowditch said that from Thomas Truxtun came "the knowledge we have of the Gulf Stream." The navy built steadily on this foundation, establishing in time the Naval Observatory in Washington. There Matthew Fontaine Maury gained renown for himself and the nation by his research in astronomy and in oceanography. His profound studies of wind and ocean currents made him world famous. The benefits he brought the world are epitomized on a monument to him in Goshen Pass, Virginia:

> Pathfinder of the Seas
> The Genius who first Snatched
> From Ocean & Atmosphere
> The Secret of their Laws ...
> Every Mariner
> For Countless Ages
> As he takes his Chart to Shape
> His course across the Seas,
> Will think of thee.
> His Inspiration Holy Writ. ...

These are only highlights of a multitude of nineteenth century naval accomplishments from the ocean depths into the heavens, which advanced science and technology and helped lay the keel for spectacular achievements in the twentieth century, such as Peary's discovery of the North Pole in 1909; Byrd's exploration into the Arctic and Antarctic; the nuclear submarine *Nautilus's* transit of the North Pole under the icecap; the larger nuclear powered *Triton's* submerged circumnavigation of the globe; the Polaris submarines' unseen patrols for freedom; and exploration into the ever-expanding frontiers of space.

These progressive commanders were men of many talents, including skill in diplomacy. In that generation, even as today, the navy often provided the visible, swiftly available, ready yet unobtrusive power that gives authority to negotiations. In those days the naval officer himself was also frequently the diplomat. Among several striking services they performed—including probably saving Hawaii from foreign annexation—none was more spectacular than the opening up of Japan. In 1854 Commodore Matthew C. Perry (Oliver Hazard Perry's younger brother) led his seven "Black Ships" into Edo, now Tokyo, Bay. With a shrewd mingling of knowledge, ceremonial splendor, determined power and finesse, iron-willed "Old Bruin" opened feudal Japan to the world.

These same men, employing the power of steam, had already helped win the Mexican War (1846–1848). The navy blockaded both coasts, neutralized strong points with gunfire, transported troops, guarded sea communications, and took a leading role in the joint operations that secured the long coast of California.

In the largest operation—an amphibious campaign beginning on March 9, 1847—the navy landed 12,600 troops with horses, artillery stores, ordinance, and munitions below Vera Cruz. The landing was oustanding in preparation, cooperation, and execution. Steam propulsion, which freed the force from the vagaries of wind and tide, sped every phase of the campaign: approach, landing, assault on the citadel under naval gunfire, and continuing support from the sea as soldiers and marines fought their way to the "Halls of Montezuma."

The increased speed, flexibility, and precision that steam gave to attack from the sea, when combined with sound operational techniques, cast long shadows ahead—to the combined operations of the Civil War that would preserve the Union—and much farther, to the invariably successful amphibious assaults that forged the outcome of World War II. Success in all these operations did not come solely from courage, skill, and bold leadership in good ships. The chain of achievement from that far-off day to the present has also rested on the mounting superiority sea-based power has gained over land-based power with each fundamental step of invention and technology. Together they have markedly increased all the age-old advantages of navies.

The Civil War

The swelling tide of sea power, aided by the advances of science and technology, accompanied the United States' rise to world leadership for the desperate crises of the twentieth century. Numerous technological developments came just in time to play an overwhelming role in the Civil War, which nearly destroyed but, in the unseen ways of Providence, at last firmly united the United States.

No war in history has surpassed the matchless bravery, fortitude, and sacrifice displayed by both sides in the desperately fought land campaigns from Manassas to Appomattox. No war has produced more brilliant and noble leaders than some of those men—from the North and South—whose names are enshrined in American hearts.

Nevertheless, without detracting in any way from the achievements ashore, study of the war in all its facets reveals that sea power overwhelmingly tipped the scales to victory for the North.

Small though the federal navy was at the outset, it promptly gave the North control of the sea with the mighty advantages this brings to all operations, such as:

(a) Facility of movement, because of range, carrying capacity and speed of ships, which provides flexibility in both strategy and tactics;

(b) Quick change of objective or adjustment to emergencies, omnipresent in war, to counter disaster and win victory;

(c) Speed of attack to achieve surprise;

(d) Ease of concentration and almost irresistible power to overwhelm behind the massed big guns of ships;

(e) Assured flow of logistics and reinforcements—while making these requirements more difficult for the opponent;

(f) Ability to withdraw if trapped ashore near navigable water;

(g) Freedom to import war materials from overseas nations while denying imports to the foe.

Through the four years of the war we see all these factors strengthening the North and working against the South to defeat her—from combined operations on the western rivers to amphibious assault and blockade of the long southern coast. The South had no navy to start with and was never able to create a strong one. Hence her offensive operations were subject to serious limitations in maintaining adequate supply lines. Her defenses were frequently outflanked and penetrated by attack from the water. Year after year she suffered a succession of irreversible disasters on the Atlantic Coast, in the Chesapeake tidal region, the Gulf, and the Mississippi River and its tributaries.

The first disasters, counterbalancing Manassas and other Confederate victories, took place on the coasts of the Carolinas in 1861. Next came those on the Cumberland and Tennessee Rivers, then on the Chesapeake. In fact, Grant's final triumphant campaign was founded on the federal navy's control of the Chesapeake, the Potomac, and the James.

The North's maritime strategy included (a) blockade, (b) amphibious assault, (c) severing the South along the Mississippi, and (d) combined operations.

The Blockade

The Union blockade, which steadily strangled the industrially deficient South, began weakly with a few ships, but the numbers steadily multiplied. In time more than 450 ships served in the coastal blockade that cut off commerce in and out of Confederate seaports. Desperately short of munitions and industry, the South starved—while the industrially powerful North increased her superiority by importing war material as needed from any part of the world.

Amphibious Assault

This facet of the Union's offensive operations began in August, 1861. Flag Officer Stringham's warships bombarded the forts at Hatteras Inlet into submission as Ben Butler's troops went ashore, wet and bedraggled, through the booming surf. Follow-up amphibious and combined operations took over most of the North Carolina Sounds and closed the back door to Norfolk, helping to insure its fall.

On 7 November, Flag Officer S. F. DuPont struck below Charleston to capture Port Royal Sound as a central base between Hampton Roads and Key West for blockade and assaults against the coast. In succeeding years other ports would fall and innumerable destructive raids large and small would cruelly wound the South causing much loss of sorely needed resources and containing large numbers of troops often gravely needed by Lee. Early in the war, in fact, General Robert E. Lee lamented a truth that would produce setbacks throughout the Confederacy on coast, sound, or river.

"Wherever his fleet can be brought, no opposition to his landing can be made. . . We have nothing to oppose his heavy guns."*

The assaults had other important results—increased effectiveness of the coastal blockade and, perhaps most serious, the wide dispersal of Confederate strength to try to combat them. How much difference dispersed troops and ordnance might have made if they had been concentrated on the main battlefields east and west!

Severing the South

Disaster for the Confederacy quickly began to loom on the Western Rivers, though few wise heads perceived it soon enough. With sound foresight, under hard-driving Commander John Rodgers and followed by equally iron-willed Flag Officer Andrew Hull Foote, the North forged a river fleet of wooden and semiironclad gunboats.

The wooden craft, quick conversions of river sidewheelers, promptly

---

*This and other Civil War quotations used may be found in the Naval History Division's *Civil War Naval Chronology*. Washington, GPO 1961–1966, published in six parts and now republished as a single volume. The chronology contains a wealth of information and an abundance of illustrations.

took control of the Ohio and upper Mississippi. This control of the main highways of communication and transportation extended the North's operations, cramped those of the South, and was an important factor in helping to keep Kentucky and Missouri in the Union. Had the situation been reversed with the South in control, the whole character of the war would have changed—perhaps sufficiently to have saved the South from defeat.

That "inland sea power" would have a significant influence in the fortunes of war became dramatically evident in February, 1862. As the month began, the Confederate lines extended far up into Kentucky, anchored on the "Gibraltar of the West," at Columbus on the Mississippi just below the Ohio River junction. However, through the vigorous use of water-based power, the situation changed almost overnight.

Foote's gunboats convoyed General Grant's army up the Ohio in a swift move that covered in hours what would have taken as many days on the quagmire roads. Spearheading Grant's attack on 6 February, the ironclads forced the surrender of strategic Fort Henry on the Tennessee. A few days later they helped to take Fort Donelson on the Cumberland, with its army and mountains of munitions and stores in the Confederate depot upstream soon falling to the invader. The "impregnable" fortifications at Columbus, which had seemed destined to resist for years, were abandoned along with irreplaceable ordnance.

Gunboats drove south on the Tennessee and Mississippi. Buttressed and aided by their mobility and the firing power of their big guns, Union land forces forged on to victories at Shiloh and Island Number 10.

Meanwhile, the Union Fleet built up at the mouth of the Mississippi. Then, like a hurricane bursting in from the sea, it struck. In the mid-watch darkness that began 24 April, Flag Officer David G. Farragut, in a wild melee against ships and forts, drove past the bastions guarding the approaches to New Orleans.

The next day the largest and wealthiest city in the South—its principal shipping and cotton export center—surrendered to a fleet manned by fewer than three thousand men mounting big guns the defending Confederate armies could not match. Loss of New Orleans and the ironclads building there was a blow from which the South never recovered. It assured the way to the sea for the great midwest and the irretrievable division of the South.

In a gallant and desperate battle staged on the high river bluffs at Vicksburg, the Confederates managed to delay the fatal severance.

But on 4 July 1863, besieged by land and water and lacking naval strength to combat the federal warships striking from north and south, the stronghold surrendered.

"The Father of waters," wrote President Abraham Lincoln, "again goes unvexed to the sea."

The South's fate was sealed.

Victory had come through wise employment of total military strength in combined operations. As Grant correctly said: without the Navy "the campaign could not have been successfully made with twice the number of men." Happily for the future of the Union this truth was deeply ingrained in Grant from the days he began operations behind Foote's gunboats. He would soon put that experience to the ultimate test in the East against the genius of Lee.

Combined Operations, Virginia.

As the foregoing events cruelly wounded the South on the Atlantic Coast, in the Gulf, and along the western rivers, similarly fatal maritime operations weakened the Confederates in the Chesapeake arena of conflict.

Here from beginning to end, except for one brief stirring ironclad interlude, the federal navy's dominance brought the North's armies matchless advantages. In 1862, supported by heavy navy guns and with assured logistic lifeline by water, General McClellan's army forced the Confederates back on all fronts bordering the Chesapeake and its rivers. Norfolk fell, with its major navy yard, and McClellan almost captured Richmond. Checked there, out-generaled by Lee, and threatened with annihilation, McClellan saved his army by withdrawing under the powerful navy guns of the squadron on the James.

The control of the Chesapeake for support, concentration, freedom of operations and logistics never ceased to aid McClellan's successors in victory or defeat. Even in the closing months of the war, General Grant benefited daily from the mobile power of naval guns. They enabled him to move troops quickly by water, to shift fronts, change bases, pour in supplies, and outflank Lee. Without the mass transport, flexibility, overwhelming naval gunfire support and ease of concentration afforded by control of the water, the war in the East might have ended in a stalemate instead of Lee's surrender at Appomattox.

Innovation

Trying to break the ever tightening noose of sea power, the South turned to ironclads and other innovations. In the fall of Norfolk

Navy Yard to the Confederates early in the war, the Union Navy also lost several ships, the best being the fine new steam frigate *Merrimac*. She was set afire and sunk, but the Confederates salvaged and converted her into the ironclad *Virginia*.

Steaming directly from the navy yard into battle under Flag Officer Franklin Buchanan*, *Virginia* scattered the Union's strong blockading squadron, sank frigates *Cumberland* and *Congress,* in which Buchanan's brother directed one of the batteries, and withstood the concentrated fire of many guns without serious damage. As the tide ebbed, to avoid going aground, the victorious ironclad retired for the night to make repairs, planning to complete the destruction of the blockading fleet the next morning. Through the night telegraph reports swept across the divided nation, raising wild hopes in the South and terror in the North.

Yet at midnight the Union's "cheese box on a raft" arrived, having nearly foundered on the tow down from New York, where she had just been completed. The next morning, as *Virginia* stood out and headed for her prey, she saw between her and the great wooden warships the curious little *Monitor*. Hour after hour the two strange antagonists pounded each other in this classic first battle between ironclads. It was a draw; but the furious cannonade of iron against iron swept around the world. It heralded to all nations the end of the age of wood and sail, the blossoming of a new era of iron and steam.

The Confederates also successfully developed various types of mines (called torpedoes), sinking or damaging some forty Union vessels—presaging their extensive use in the twentieth century. They constructed torpedo boats—termed "Davids" in the South's hopes they might be giant killers—lineal ancestors of the modern destroyer. And they built crude submarines. C.S.S. *H. L. Hunley* was converted from a boiler at Mobile, Alabama, and shipped to Charleston to attack the blockading fleet. With men on cranks for engines, she sank twice in the course of operations, losing all or most of her crews. Yet new volunteers came forward, true to their heritage of valor and patriotism. On the night of February 17, 1864, though she went down with all her crew, never to be recovered, *Hunley* sank U.S.S. *Housatonic*—another first in history and an omen of a giant new force destined to revolutionize naval warfare.

Both sides employed balloon reconnaissance from ships—distant ancestors of the aircraft carrier and of the mighty wings of naval

---

*First Superintendent of the U.S. Naval Academy.

air power that, along with submarines (like Polaris types), bring navies ever increasing advantage over less mobile forces ashore.

All these new developments caused losses to the North. But they could not begin to counterbalance the inexorable pressure of the blockade, the irresistible power of attack from the sea, the burning fire of warships striking up and down the inland arteries, the swift and overwhelming impact of heavy guns in combined operations.

The Civil War is revered in American hearts as a stirring clash of armies filled with deeds of valor and inspiration. It is this, of course. Yet if a man stands offshore where he can view the South's terrible sense of need that could never be met afloat, he cannot fail to come away with the sobering knowledge that America's destiny may well lie in the great waters.

The need for her to control the sea is at least as desperate as in those far-off gallant years. Nothing can take the place of superior sea power; and there is little chance of developing it if it is not on hand before war breaks out. Grave warning has been issued to the United States today. Will the mass of her citizens comprehend too late the imminent peril in the Soviet rush toward maritime supremacy?

3

World Struggle for Survival of Freedom

I$_N$ helping to preserve the Union and preparing the United States for the responsibilities of leadership in the twentieth century, sea power played a role that cannot be overstated. Characteristically, however, scarcely had the Civil War ended when the United States abandoned naval supremacy as a foundation of strategy; this action would have brought disaster had an aggressor such as the Soviet Union and not Great Britain ruled the waves.

Appropriations declined, the navy dwindled, and construction virtually stopped. This came at a time of swift change in science, engineering, technology, and thus in warship development. Out of this restless reaching for the future came the mighty battleship, the effective and deadly submarine, the long and powerful reach of aircraft carriers, and the amphibious assault force.

The Dawn of Trident Sea Power

The invention of the internal combustion engine and advances in electricity, machinery, metallurgy, and many other fields contributed to revolutionizing world navies. In America, however, public apathy and lean appropriations checked progress. Nevertheless, a number of officers took the lead in new developments. Lieutenant Bradley Fiske (later Rear Admiral) made important contributions in electricity and the "wireless." Fiske experimented with electronic communications years before Marconi first successfully communicated via wireless. The principles of one of Fiske's patents—radio control of torpedoes—today enter into the control of all pilotless objects, including guided missiles and satellites.

Beginning in 1879 the navy sent a succession of officers overseas for formal education in shipbuilding, marine engineering, and other technical fields, laying the foundation for our modern navy. Perhaps the most famous of these was Albert A. Michelson.

Following graduation in 1873 from the Naval Academy and a tour at sea, Michelson returned to the Academy as an instructor. Backed by Commander W. T. Sampson (a leader in ordnance and later distinguished in the Spanish–American War), Michelson conducted experiments in the speed of light that have entered into man's exploration of the atom and the infinity of space. With a few dollars' worth of equipment, his ingenuity, and midshipmen assistants, he measured the speed of light more accurately than ever before.*

In 1873, the year of Michelson's graduation from the Academy, Captain Stephen B. Luce and other officers formed the Naval Institute as an unofficial forum to stimulate discussion in strategy, tactics, gunnery, engineering, ship construction, and other fields of naval science. A decade later, again under the leadership of Luce, the Naval War College began its noted careeer at Newport—the first of its type in any navy.

Commodore Luce headed the War College initially and had Captain A. T. Mahan ordered there on the staff. From Mahan's lectures evolved his great work *The Influence of Seapower Upon History*, which became world famous and probably had more impact upon navies than did any other book ever published.

In the 1880s regeneration of the physical navy began when Congress authorized construction of three cruisers with advanced armament and armor to be of high quality steel of American manufacture. Hence resurgence of naval construction was an important aid to the growing U.S. steel industry, whose production would undergird America's spectacular industrial growth during the 1900s.

New warships came off the ways with steadily improved engineering, gunnery, and fighting performance. Novel small types joined the fleet as well as heavy ships such as armored cruisers and the evolving battleship. The self-propelled torpedo, introduced soon after the Civil War, was becoming formidable. In 1890 the "new navy" commissioned the small, fast torpedo boat USS *Cushing* (named for the leader

---

*Michelson was sent overseas for study in Berlin, Heidelberg, and Paris. During the course of his education, the navy allowed him to resign to concentrate on physics, for which he became the first American to win the Nobel Prize. Einstein stated that without Michelson's work his theory of relativity would have been "an interesting speculation." Michelson credited the navy for his basic training and opportunity.

of the night attack in 1864 that sank CSS *Albemarle* with a "torpedo" lashed to a spar projecting from the bow of a launch and rammed against the enemy).

Many claimed that the torpedo boat spelled the end of large fighting ships, that at last the will-o-the-wisp of a cheap and easy means of controlling the sea had been found. This, of course, was a chimera, like President Thomas Jefferson's gunboats. Soon navies produced the "torpedo boat destroyer." USS *Bainbridge,* commissioned in 1902, initiated this type for the U.S. Navy. Successive designs would bring larger, faster, more powerful destroyers, capable of carrying out a myriad of duties inshore or on the high seas, besides destroying torpedo boats. Highly versatile, Jack of all trades and good in all, this type would prove invaluable a few years later in the bitter battle against undersea titans.

The outbreak of the Spanish–American War in 1898 thus found the United States with a modern if small navy. The war's objective was the liberation of Cuba, but the first result was to reach across the Pacific to spread freedom there. On 1 May 1898 Admiral George Dewey brought the steel navy into Manila Bay for its baptism under fire. His "You may fire when ready, Gridley" to his flag captain in *Olympia* (now preserved in Philadelphia) initiated a decisive victory that made the United States a Pacific power.

Halfway around the world in the Caribbean, Admiral Sampson's fleet landed marines in Guantanamo Bay, covered the landing of a 17,000-man army that advanced on San Juan Hill and Santiago, and on 3 July 1898 defeated Admiral Pascual Cervera's fleet. These victories won control of the seas and assured an early end to the war.

The United States had world responsibilities, which President Theodore Roosevelt well understood. During his tenure especially, the nation increased the size and quality of its fleet to meet the new demands. The battleship grew in power and effectiveness. Speedy cruisers slid down the ways. In 1900, the year before Roosevelt became president, the navy commissioned its first submarine, USS *Holland.* A decade later the Navy Department began to integrate the crude bamboo and cloth airplane into the fleet. Even then men foresaw its specific application for improving the navy's ability to control the sea and assault the land.

In September, 1910, Captain Washington Irving Chambers, able and far seeing, was assigned to handle aviation matters in the Navy Department.*

---

*Captain Chambers was cited by the Aeronautical Society as the "first to demonstrate the usefulness of the airplane in navies."

Two months later, on 14 November, scout cruiser USS *Birmingham* made the world's first launch of an airplane from a warship. Soon, on 18 January 1911, followed the world's first landing on a ship, this time USS *Pennsylvania*. The ship's skipper, Captain C.F. Pond, exultantly exclaimed, "This is the most important landing of a bird since the dove flew back to the ark!"

Having demonstrated the feasibility of handling planes afloat, the Navy Department now purchased its first planes. With its experienced shipbuilders and experts in a broad range of engineering and technological fields, the navy was uniquely fitted to adapt planes to the complex requirements of ship operations, and indeed to develop and build planes.

In 1912 at Washington Navy Yard Lieutenant Theodore Ellyson made the first catapult launch. Three years later the first catapult launch from a moving ship occurred from USS *North Carolina*. In 1912, also, Lieutenant John Towers, flying from Annapolis, remained aloft six hours, ten minutes and thirty-five seconds to set a world endurance record for seaplanes and the U.S. record for all types of planes—thus beginning a series of records and firsts naval aviators have continued to the present.

Likewise in 1912, naval officers pressed forward with innovations such as an automotic pilot, airborne radio, and torpedo attack methods. In fact, for some years the navy had set the pace in America in various technical fields, including radio communications, where the impact on naval operations was early recognized. Throughout the first decades of the century the navy led the way in promoting advances in radio research and development and manufacture on the course that would bring the United States to world leadership in electronics.

In this same period brilliant naval officer-engineer Lieutenant Jerome Hunsaker established the nation's pathfinding course in aeronautical engineering at MIT—long the prime training source in this field for army, navy, and civilians.

By this time, on the eve of World War I, the submarine, still an unknown instrument in war, had steadily progressed in reliability, size, and effectiveness, though still small and not designed for extensive cruising. The 700-mile passage in 1913 of a five-boat squadron shepherded by surface ships from Guantanamo Bay, Cuba, to Panama stood out as a milestone of potential distant service.

When war broke out in Europe in 1914, the U.S. Navy had accepted over thirty submersibles. The latest ones—G, H, and K classes—displaced about six times the tonnage of *Holland* (SS-1), but still had a normal surface displacement under 400 tons. They could dive twice as deep—to 200 feet—cruise nearly twice as fast on the surface, and boasted crews up to two officers and twenty-six enlisted men, against one and six in *Holland.*

The early submarine skippers included Ensign Chester W. Nimitz, of whom the nation would hear much more, and Lieutenant Arthur MacArthur, Jr. (brother of Douglas and said by his friends to be even more capable), who died on active duty as Captain, USN.

Neptune, with his uplifted trident, represented to the ancients the all-pervading influence of the sea in human affairs. Now in the depths, on the surface, and in the sky, the true trident of sea power took shape. In 1914 shadows of giant new strength, still in its infancy, cast ahead with import none could fully gauge.

World War I

The submarine in the first year of the war quickly demonstrated its potent possibilities. Germany entered the conflict with a smaller undersea fleet than any other major naval power. German and British subs both scored early successes but the most profound effect upon world thinking came on 22 September 1914, when the U-9 sank in quick succession three aging British cruisers.

Consequently, naval powers speeded submarine development and construction programs—and that of ASW vessels even more, since the surface hunter needs a considerable superiority in numbers. By the end of the war the United States had commissioned and had on the ways approximately five times as many submarines as in 1912. Of these, twenty E-, K-, L-, and O-class boats operated overseas.* Some of the latest class building, the S-boats, would serve with credit in action during World War II.

For the United States, submarines were a small part of a tremendous shipbuilding program needed to gain victory. A few battleships and cruisers were laid down before 1919. But the main construction effort went into destroyers, subchasers and other ASW vessels, minecraft and other auxiliaries, and a host of merchant ships to sustain the vast flow of troops, supplies, and munitions that poured into France.

The U.S. Navy's surface fleet supported Britain's magnificent war

---

*One L-boat attacked by two German subs had the unusual experience of watching a torpedo fired at her by one foe miss and sink the other. Mistaken identity caused another, the L-10, to take a depth-charge drubbing by a U.S. destroyer. When he safely surfaced and identified himself, the enraged sub skipper recognized his Naval Academy roommate on the destroyer's bridge.

effort by safely convoying to Europe some two million American troops (without the loss of a soldier enroute) and mountains of munitions and other materials to help turn the tide to victory. Destroyers were an important factor in this monumental achievement. U.S. battleships operated with the British Grand Fleet as guardians against major surface raids on the vital arteries of sea communications. The Mine Force laid almost sixty thousand U.S. mines in the North Sea as a submarine barrier.

Ashore the marines won imperishable fame at Belleau Woods and elsewhere by their gallant fighting.

When the United States entered the war, naval aviation had made long strides though, like its counterpart ashore, it had not yet reached the point of decisive influence on warfare. However, U.S. naval aviators did play a growing role in combating the other newcomer undersea. From less than three score planes in 1917, the navy's inventory mounted past 2,100. Their pilots logged about 3 million miles on flying missions (some 800,000 being overseas), attacked enemy submarine bases, other military targets ashore, and twenty-five German submarines.

Over 40,000 officers and men served in naval air. Some of them, working with industry, developed a "flying bomb." This pilotless, remote-controlled airplane was the next step after the granddaddy of guided missiles—the torpedo. It could take off unmanned and be directed to target with bomb load but did not become a useful weapon before the armistice. Between the wars the navy continued work on remote control, equipped the ex-battleship *Utah* as an unmanned, highly maneuverable and speedy target ship, and employed drone planes for antiaircraft gunnery training and development.

The navy also developed giant NC seaplanes for distant overwater cruising. Although not ready by the time war ended, in the spring of 1919 one of them, NC-4, completed the world's first crossing of the Atlantic by a plane. Commander A. C. Read, the pilot, flying via the Azores, landed in Lisbon harbor 27 May 1919. Thus even the modest planes of World War I began to show promise of making sea-based power more significant than ever in shaping the fate of nations.

The airplane, like the submarine, brought new duties to the flexible and versatile destroyer—a workhorse in the complex and increasingly potent navy. During the war antiaircraft machine guns went into them (as well as other ships) and later 3″ AA guns (though lacking suitable fire control). Thus began what would become deadly AA batteries many years later. To combat the submarine—learning from

British experience—the United States equipped destroyers with hydrophones and depth charges. In this fashion they began to achieve the capabilities that would make them so effective in the three-dimensional struggle of World War II.

Dream World—Peace through Disarmament

The United States ended World War I with the largest fleet in the world in commission or building—including over one hundred more destroyers than she has in 1971, when the ASW problem is many times greater. Wisely maintained and used in world affairs, this fleet might have averted the tragedy of America's involvement in war against Japan.

Such strength was especially called for from America because the war had shattered the social, economic, and political order that had, in general, prevailed among the great powers. Out of the wreckage sprang the maniacal extremes of fascism and communism that respected only the laws of power. Then, as in the case of Vietnam today, the popular clamor was for "the boys to come home." Men convinced themselves that disarmament would insure lasting peace— a self-delusion that never dies in America.

The United States initiated the Washington Conference, 1921–1922, and promptly offered to dispose of fifteen capital ships under construction, plus an equal number of predreadnaughts, in a wholesale abandonment of her need for a strong two-ocean navy. The Washington Treaty of 6 February 1922 assigned capital ship strength in a 5-5-3 ratio for the United States, Great Britain, and Japan, with smaller ratios for France and Italy. Other nations scrapped mostly older ships and building plans. Japan, for instance, scrapped one new and eight old capital ships. She also demanded and got U. S. agreement to strengthen no bases west of Pearl Harbor.

As a consequence, this partly unilateral disarmament by the United States (as occurs today with respect to the U.S.S.R.) and soon a severe limitation of the annual budget shrank the navy at exactly the wrong time. The United States had forged to the forefront as the leader of freedom. She and other free nations gravely needed the binding sinews of the sea to entertain any hope of deterring despotism, already gathering force in Eurasia.

Despite the handicap of these lean years and the inadequate force that ultimately and inevitably led aggressors to attack, the navy initiated vital transformations. Significant advances were made in ship construction, electronics, gunnery, guided missiles (the government's first small steps in atomic energy looking toward nuclear propulsion), and better submarines and aircraft.

In 1921 Congress established the Bureau of Aeronautics at the request of the Navy Department. The next spring the Navy commissioned its first carrier, USS *Langley*, a converted collier. USS *Saratoga* and *Lexington*—converted from unfinished battle cruisers and commissioned in 1927—augmented America's sea power at a time when extremists claimed that aircraft had ended the usefulness of navies. What disaster would have beset America had this false thinking prevailed!

Fortunately, instead of abolishing carriers, during the lean 1920s and 1930s the navy integrated aviation even more closely into the fleet. Past experience had demonstrated that the more a new weapon goes afloat and is woven into existing capabilities, the greater becomes its value. Impressive technical and operational progress included the radial air-cooled engine and dive bombing that would play a decisive part in the forthcoming world struggle.

Air entered increasingly into the navy's readiness training—in scouting and spotting, offense and defense against surface and air attack, amphibious assault, and ASW. As aircraft each year flew farther, higher, and faster, the navy solved its unique problems of taking planes to sea, thereby better serving the nation's needs.

Fleet operations with carriers demonstrated the shape of things to come. During war games in 1928, *Langley* struck Pearl Harbor in a surprise attack—with flour bombs. In fleet exercises of early 1929 the new big, fast carriers *Saratoga* and *Lexington* proved outstanding in offense. *Saratoga's* wide end run around the Galápagos Islands caught the defenders by surprise and "destroyed" the Panama Canal, blocking passage from the Caribbean of part of the defending fleet. Admiral W. V. Pratt called this "the most brilliantly conceived and most effectively executed naval operation in our history." *

Yet regardless of the evidence of the revolutionary importance of seagoing aircraft, Congress squeezed the appropriation money. In 1928, the Navy Department requested funds to construct five carriers—and eventually got one, the small *Ranger* (named for John Paul Jones's frigate that received the first foreign salute to the Stars and Stripes), commissioned six years later.

---

*"*Sara*" would execute a similar brilliant surprise attack against Pearl Harbor in 1938 war exercises. The attacks are well covered by Norman Polmar in his outstanding *Aircraft Carriers*, N.Y., 1969 and Eugene E. Wilson in his profound *Slipstream*, 2nd ed., 1965 and in *The Navy's First Carrier Task Force*, USN Proceedings, Feb., 1950, pp. 158–169.

Fortunately for America, as *Ranger* built, two men who would be Titans in reviving America's sea posture assumed key positions in the government. In 1931, Congressman Carl Vinson became Chairman of the House Naval Affairs Committee. In 1933 Franklin Delano Roosevelt took office as president. Despite public apathy, reflected in Congress, naval buildup got underway—as a byproduct of the National Industrial Recovery Act. In 1934, with funds from the Public Works Administration (PWA), the nation laid down *Yorktown* (CV-5) and *Enterprise* (CV-6), famed "Big E" of World War II.

As related hereafter, other ship construction followed, but despite the drive of Roosevelt and Vinson, it was not enough. Even as late as 1937, with imperialism engulfing the Far East and Europe, futile dreams of peace without power bemused America. Appropriations that year gave the navy a budget of only half a billion dollars supporting fewer than one hundred thousand men operating undermanned ships.

Two more carriers slowly grew on the ways—*Wasp* and *Hornet*. Both were commissioned after war broke out in Europe, and *Hornet* just before Pearl Harbor. This handful of ships, adding the enormous reach and hitting power of landing fields speeding with the fleet, brought new dimensions to the fleet's historic virtues of mobility, flexibility, and swift concentration of power. What a difference it would have made had there been more of them! Yet these few carriers—so desperately needed against Japan's ten carriers—would help to turn the tide from national disaster in a courageous performance all Americans should treasure and honor.

Similar construction programs were launched on other types. Some cruisers and destroyers were laid down before *Yorktown* and *Enterprise* as the U.S. gradually built up to treaty strength. In fact, aided by WPA funds, the president and Carl Vinson greatly benefited the nation by special attention to renewal of the destroyer fleet. Shipyards began sixteen new destroyers a year, on the average, from 1934 until 1939. This was a fraction of the number needed and that later sped from the ways after the storm broke, but enough to avert even worse setbacks than those soon to come.

In 1937 the United States laid the keel of her first new battleship in nearly twenty years. USS *North Carolina* would commission in the spring of 1941, along with her sister ship *Washington,* just in time for the tremendous service demanded of them and eight successors laid down from 1939 on.*

---

*The sixteen-inch guns, with radar incorporated into their superb fire control equipment, had astonishing accuracy. The writer observed *North Carolina* hitting a

The new "battlewagons" and carriers complemented each other in the carrier task force just as do the line and backfield of a football team. Much faster than their predecessors, the new battleships could maneuver at high speed with the carriers. The tough, heavyweight BB could hit hard with her sixteen-inch guns and massed antiaircraft batteries, and take more punishment than any other type—and, like all else in life, war demands the ability to take it as well as to dish it out. Formidable, majestic, and tremendously potent, the new battleships were well nigh invincible when united with the carrier. Together with accompanying cruisers and destroyers, these two large types sailed as the greatest concentration of power man had ever produced.

After the first two battleships, none completed, shook down, and trained until mid-1942, when other new ones began to join the fleet.* They and the new carriers that commissioned during the war, the stream of new cruisers, destroyers, submarines, amphibians, and other types, insured victory at sea, which, in turn, made victory possible ashore. What a difference it would have made in history had construction speeded up only two years earlier.

While integrating airplanes into America's sea arm and developing the carrier task force into a potent fighting group, the navy rushed ahead with procedures for setting up a solid defense against air assault. The best defense, of course, is to destroy the attacker at the source; the next best is to meet the planes in the air with defending fighters before they can launch bombs or torpedoes.

Improvement in radio resulted in more effective control of planes in the air. Discovery and development of radar by the navy made possible distant detection of attackers and assisted in guiding our own fighters to meet them. Since radar was just being introduced into the fleet when Japan struck, it took time to achieve the maximum benefit from this remarkable technological advance. But it soon became increasingly important, not only in air but also in nearly all other naval employment.

From 1935 on radio-controlled *Utah* played a double role in preparing the navy for the forthcoming crisis. She provided the aviators

---

fast-moving target the size of a van with the first shot at a distance of fifteen statute miles. Each ship's twenty-five-inch, 38 caliber guns, and in time scores of 40mm. and 20mm. machine guns bristling from every cranny, gave them the most awesome gun air defense. Four states have wisely preserved their valiant name ships as shrines to valor and service—*North Carolina* in Wilmington, *Alabama* in Mobile, *Massachusetts* at Fall River, and *Texas,* her World War I namesake in Houston.

*Eight more were completed and served well during the war. In order of commissioning they were: *South Dakota, Indiana, Massachusetts, Alabama, Iowa, New Jersey, Wisconsin,* and *Missouri.*

with a swift, maneuverable target that boasted all the realism of war except defensive gunfire. Hence, the navy's dive bomber pilots became the best in the world. At the same time, *Utah* conducted fleet training schools on board for AA gunners, working bugs out of weapons and giving large numbers of gunners concentrated firing experience.

The U.S. Navy's five-inch, 38 caliber batteries and associated fire control equipment constituted the best heavy antiaircraft system in the world, ashore or afloat. As radar began to enter into the target fire control solution, these guns became increasingly effective. Unfortunately, because of budget restrictions, only part of the fleet carried the five-inch, 38 caliber type when war came and effective AA fire control radar was still on the way.

The pinched budget limited procurement in many fields, including suitable amphibious assault craft, and was a factor in the torpedo deficiencies that bedeviled submarines particularly early in the war. From the early 1920s the navy and marines did conduct large-scale and realistic amphibious exercises. Reports pointed out the requirements for specialized assault craft, from large attack transports to assault boats and amphibians. A few experimental landing craft types, including even the forerunner of the amphibian tractor (LVT), appeared. In 1933 the Marine Corps formed the Fleet Marine Force. Integrated with the fleet as a complete combat force, like the ships themselves, it was always ready to go on call.

With this background of experience and organization, a board of marine and naval officers at Quantico (an outstanding training center) put into print standard doctrine in the *Tentative Manual for Landing Operations* that joined the large body of fleet publications for every type of naval operation.

In its essentials, the manual proved sound, as did the Fleet Marine Force and concepts of gunfire and air support when war put them to the test. The principal deficiency was in assault craft and ships, which began to come off the production line only when spectacular German successes shocked the nation awake from the illusion of peace without effort. Then at last, citizens were able to comprehend again what John Adams had long ago stated: "Liberty is won by those willing to defend it."

Though the nation's lack of foresight left her sorely unprepared when World War II erupted in September, 1939, foundations for victory at sea had been laid. Had the United States appropriated funds for a larger navy soon enough, it seems certain Japan would not have dared to take the Pearl Harbor gamble. A few hundred million dollars more expended through each year of the 1930s could have saved tens of billions in the 1940s—and, more importantly, could have averted the dreadful toll of human lives, suffering, and catastrophic world dislocation that continue to darken civilization.

World War II

Centuries before Christ the incomparable Thucydides set down the first passages of a history that still has no peer. He began writing at the onset of the Peloponnesian War because it would be "great and memorable above any previous war." These same words might be applied to World War II.*

On 7 December 1941, the sun shone brightly in the late forenoon as USS *Saratoga* (CV-3) berthed at the Naval Air Station in San Diego. We on the flight deck had just begun to double up the lines, dreaming in the sun of soon being with our loved ones, when suddenly the bull horn near us on the forecastle blared out "Now hear this . . ." At the first word, from premonition or urgency of tone, my heart sank. "Now hear this, *Japan has bombed Pearl Harbor.*"

In that instant the world turned upside down. Never would it be the same again for any of us. Plans for days in port went overboard. All that day and all night we labored feverishly, taking on our own and extra planes for Pearl Harbor, fuel, munitions, and stores. Boats raced to and from the ship. In any moment that could be snatched men tried to reach families by telephone. It was a madhouse. Yet everything eventually fell into place, and we sailed at dawn.

In some such manner as this war came suddenly and devastatingly to all Americans, especially to those in ships and ashore west of Midway

---

*Were this chapter multiplied a thousandfold, it could not do justice to the massive outpouring of human effort, dedication, and valor that marked this greatest of struggles—for war brings out the best in man more than the worst. The hundreds of books written about these tumultuous years include several fine series that cover the United States' participation in the sea war. The best are Rear Admiral Samuel Eliot Morison's graphically written fifteen-volume *History of United States Naval Operations in World War II*, and Captain Stephen W. Roskill's notable four-volume *The War at Sea.* The latter, designed to record the British Navy's outstanding service, is also filled with information on the U.S. Navy's operations—as is Morison's series on those of the other contestants.

To these we should also add the U.S. Marine Corps' formidable series, *History of U.S. Marine Corps Operations in World War II.* Vice Admiral Friedrich Ruge, first head of the German Navy after the war, has written a group of splendid volumes from the German viewpoint. The U.S. Army's monumental series on the war is replete with the influence of the sea. This applies likewise to the British Military History Series.

We could mention scores of other superb accounts of individual battles and campaigns. A bibliography of selected works, published by the Naval History Division of the U.S. Navy Department in Washington, can guide readers to accounts of almost any phase of naval operations in World War II.

with no time to arrange their personal affairs. It was like the sudden ending of life, crossing the last horizon into infinite seas with no time to prepare, as indeed it was for many at Pearl Harbor and others in the Pacific who would never see their families again.

Saratoga dramatically entered Pearl Harbor after a high-speed run amidst the roar of planes, the streaming smoke of destroyers dashing to and fro, and the giant geysers and underwater shocks from plane and ship depthcharging suspected submarine contacts (though more likely at a surprised school of fish).

Inside the entrance we met a scene of carnage. Proud warships lay awash or askew in drydock. *Oklahoma* lay capsized, bottom up, as did my old and beloved ship *Utah*. The shattered remnants of *Arizona* projected above the oil-streaked surface. Large grains of powder for *Arizona's* fourteen-inch guns sprinkled the ground—thrown a great distance when her magazines exploded without detonating all the powder bags. The stench of fire and destruction still hung in the air.

It was a monstrous and treacherous attack, launched under the cover of negotiations in Washington. It shook souls and brought sorrow, but not defeatism. Rather, in the navy one met a spirit of determination, a fierce concentration of effort to pick up the pieces and go after the enemy.

This spirit matched the remarkable conduct of those in the stricken ships, struggling on 7 December against explosion, fire, and destruction without warnings. As an officer on one of the ships reported, the attitude of the men "was marvelous; there was no panic, no shirking nor flinching, and words fail in attempting to describe the truly magnificent display of courage, discipline, and devotion to duty of all."*

Not enough could be done at first for want of means. Even the outbreak of war in Europe, 1 September 1939, did not awaken enough Americans into understanding that aggression knows no bounds to ambition. Slow increase in military strength did proceed, yet nine months later when the Germans suddenly drove to the Channel coast, the U.S. Navy still had only about 150,000 men.

The fall of France and Dunkirk at last alarmed Congress and forced it to take strong action. Bills in rapid succession called for the "Two-Ocean Navy" that the country had abandoned eighteen years earlier. The 271 new fighting ships authorized included eleven carriers. But none of the latter could possibly be built and ready for action short of three years, and most would take longer. As Admiral Harold R. Stark said, "You can't buy yesterday."

---

*Volume 3 of Samuel Eliot Morison's fine series, *The Rising Sun in the Pacific*, p. 107. One excellent volume with many personal accounts of survivors is Vice Admiral Homer N. Wallin's *Pearl Harbor: Why, How, Fleet Salvage. . . .* GPO, 1968.

Hence when Japan struck, she could risk the gamble because of U.S. weakness. With much of the American fleet knocked out at Pearl Harbor, Nippon could proceed on a realistic timetable of expansion into the South Pacific and Southeast Asia. Despite the fact that Europe had been consumed by war for more than two years, the U.S. was still far from ready. Right up to the time of Pearl Harbor a high percentage of Americans believed that the best way to avoid war was to avoid preparation for war.

As President Truman said, in approving the 1945 Navy Court of Inquiry on Pearl Harbor, "The country was not ready for preparedness. Every time the President made an effort to get a preparedness program through the Congress, it was stifled. Whenever the President made a statement about the necessity of preparedness he was vilified. . . I think the country is as much to blame as any individual. . . [for] Pearl Harbor."

Ships, guns, planes, tanks, and the millions of trained men needed by America could not spring up overnight. Thus one can understand how some Japanese leaders convinced themselves that the surprise attack was a decisive victory, that soft Americans would not undertake a prolonged uphill struggle and would accept a negotiated peace.

Actually, the attack was Japan's greatest blunder. It unified the United States as nothing else could have. Even those who had blindfolded themselves could see the light. It made possible a concentrated outpouring of strength, though the price was bitter and high. Americans must ponder, however, how slim their chances for recovery and counterattack would have been had the Japanese war lords possessed the vast capability and resources the Kremlin wields today.

Atlantic Battle Won Makes Victory Possible in Europe

Perceiving Germany to be the more powerful and dangerous opponent, the United States gave first priority to the defeat of Hitler. From September, 1939, President Roosevelt had taken increasing defensive action in the Atlantic. The Neutrality Patrol of warships and patrol planes began to operate off the East Coast, from Newfoundland to the Guianas, thus covering the Caribbean and the flow of essential raw materials such as petroleum and bauxite.

For the first year and longer Nazi submarines did not imperil shipping in the waters of the Western Hemisphere. Land-minded Hitler not only entered the war with a small submarine force (forty-nine operational craft) but also for some time did not press construction. Through the first fifteen months of the war Germany lost thirty-one submarines, and her building program had not even replaced these. At the end of 1940 she had only twenty-two operational U-boats.

The fall of the low countries and France in May, 1940, adding a long open coastline for submarine and air bases closer to British shipping routes, enabled even this handful of submarines to become very effective. Had Hitler promptly concentrated his attention on submarine warfare, along with supporting planes, he might well have cut the Atlantic lifeline to the British Isles in that critical year of 1940 and won the war.

As it was, the few submarines, supplemented by air attacks and magnetic mines, inflicted such heavy ship losses that Britain's position became precarious despite brilliant efforts by her navy.

In this crucial period President Roosevelt instituted a "short of war" policy to prepare against the Nazi menace and to help save Britain. This fully involved the navy. American officers joined the British Navy to learn war lessons direct. A naval mission was established in London. Staff conferences of the military forces of both countries would follow later in Washington.

On 2 September 1940, England and the United States entered into the famous destroyer-naval base deal that gave the island kingdom fifty of the old four-stack destroyers in exchange for U.S. ninety-nine-year rights to naval, air, and military base sites from British Guiana to the Bahamas. Britain threw in as a gift base rights in Bermuda and Argentia, Newfoundland.

Far outmoded by the advances of more than two decades since their design, and many of them long laid up, the old destroyers were, nevertheless, lifesavers. A broken sword is better than none. In the hands of Britain's intrepid sailors the old four-pipers served magnificently until British, Canadian, and U.S. shipyards could produce the large fleet of escorts needed for victory.

In the spring of 1941 Lend Lease began, and the United States extended the Neutrality Patrol eastward to cover Greenland and the Azores. In July, after the Nazi steam roller swept into the U.S.S.R., the U.S. Marines replaced British troops in Iceland, arriving in a task force of twenty-five ships. The U.S. Navy now began to escort convoys there. In September the hard-working destroyers joined in the escort of convoys bound for Britain, shepherding the merchant ships to the escort ocean exchange area some six hundred to seven hundred miles from North Ireland.

On 17 October USS *Kearny* (DD-432), newly built and much tougher than the old destroyers, was torpedoed, but she controlled the damage and reached Iceland. The last day of the month USS *Reuben James* (DD-245), of World War I vintage took a torpedo that apparently exploded the forward magazine and blew off the entire fore part of the ship aft to number 4 stack.

Actually, when war broke for the United States in December, the Atlantic Fleet just kept doing what it had begun—except much more. Allied war strategy called for a holding action in the Pacific while giving first priority to the European theater. Large numbers of U-boats now coming into commission threatened to bring the collapse of overseas operations. There was no easy solution. The convoy system, with intercept of U-boat radio and controlled routing to avoid subs known to be prowling certain areas, helped greatly. Better ASW equipment and new weapons like the "hedgehog" (forward-throwing depth charges) brought added effectiveness. So did radar. Aircraft added their speed and long vision, both for protection against air raids and for search and attack on submarines.

Yet the main solution lay in more ASW ships and planes. There was desperate need for more of everything—yesterday. New units were coming off the line but not fast enough. The months following Pearl Harbor were dark in the Atlantic as well as the Pacific. In the first six months of 1942 U-boats sank more than 3 million tons of shipping. The pattern continued through the year with especially heavy losses from air and submarine attack on the northern convoys to the U.S.S.R. during the long summer days. The allies lost some 8 million tons of ships to all causes in 1942.

In 1943, however, the tide turned. More and more escorts accompanied convoys. As additional ships became available, it was possible to form special escort support groups that could rush to the aid of a convoy under attack. Far ranging escort and patrol aircraft equipped with radar made it increasingly hazardous for U-boats to surface in much of the ocean—and with limited underwater range the submarines had to run most of the time on the surface.

As Admiral Donitz pointed out in his memoirs, the submarine of World War II was still *a surface vessel that could dive*. Nuclear power, however, has made the submarine a true *underwater* boat with a revolutionary advance in effectiveness.

Now, too, the airplane began to go to sea with the convoys. Escort carriers, initially conversions of merchant ship hulls, provided convoys with their own planes for search and attack. When more of these jeep carriers became available, with escorts to screen them, special hunter-killer groups could be dispatched to known or suspected areas of U-boat concentration.

The ship-airplane team won the Battle of the Atlantic,* but only

---

*Much of America's share of the credit for this victory goes to Admiral Royal E. Ingersoll. Sagacious and experienced, he made the right estimates and correct decisions. He seemed almost able to read the U-boat commanders' minds, just as the fine organization he set up to route convoys and protect them from submarine attack often read their position through radio intercepts.

after awesome losses, and after the United States had embarked on an all-out effort to produce the means to do the job. Before American and British production took effect, the Germans came perilously close to winning the war in the Atlantic. It is sobering to realize that she came this close from a slow start with few submarines—less than one sixth of those under the Russian banner today.

While combating the submarine, the United States and Britain boldly went on the offensive against the Nazi armies within a year after Pearl Harbor. In November, 1942, even as the Battle of the Atlantic still seemed to hang in the balance, the allies launched a multipronged amphibious assault into North Africa. General Dwight D. Eisenhower was C-in-C (Commander-in-Chief) Allied Expeditionary Force, and Admiral Sir Andrew B. Cunningham, RN, Allied Naval Commander. Two British Naval Task Forces struck into Algiers with some 80,000 British and American troops mounted in England. Rear Admiral H. Kent Hewitt, USN, commanded the Western Naval Task Force that launched General George F. Patton's 35,000-man army in three widely separated landings on Morocco's Atlantic coast after outstanding preparation and safely escorted passage from Norfolk, Virginia. Ship gunfire and naval air strikes preceded the landings and supported the soldiers ashore.

These far ranging transoceanic assaults denied northwest Africa to the Axis and provided air, sea, and land bases for the next operation. After major fighting in North Africa, in July, 1943, a mighty amphibious force of over 1,400 ships landed nine allied divisions in Sicily. Vice Admiral Hewitt's cruisers and destroyers of the Western Naval Task Force played an outstanding part in the victory by repeatedly knocking out enemy tank and infantry assaults with gunfire, in General Eisenhower's words, "devastating in its effectiveness."

Then followed the fall of Mussolini, landings on the Italian peninsula at Salerno in September, where naval gunfire again was essential to victory for the hard-fighting troops for days after they landed. The German commander reported that the warships "with astonishing precision and freedom of maneuver . . . shot at every recognized target with overwhelming effect."

Later came the tough Anzio struggle, the fall of Italy, Normandy, and the final irresistible onslaught from the sea in southern France to speed the collapse of the Nazi armies. The Normandy landings were, in a sense, the reverse of Julius Caesar's conquest of Britain two thousand years earlier. The allies launched the assault at short range from England but this was possible only because of the long buildup of troops and enormous stocks of munitions and supplies brought, in large part, across the Atlantic from America, through a submarine gauntlet now held in check.

More than two thousand ships and craft of the U.S. Navy joined those of the Royal Navy and allies in the torrent of force hurled against the Nazis entrenched in Normandy. Intensive minesweeping and bombardment opened the way. The Underwater Demolition Teams plunged in, many giving their lives under fire to breach a way through the obstacles and beach mines. Then the amphibious craft sped to the beach under cover of air and naval gunfire.

After the troops stormed ashore on D Day, that fierce 6th of June, 1944, destroyers close inshore—risking grounding and sinking from enemy fire—exchanged salvos pointblank with the short batteries. Battleships and cruisers laid their deadly and precise fire far inland, miles beyond the beachheads. Field Marshal Gerd von Rundstedt stated from the shock of experience, "The fire of your battleships was a main factor in hampering our counterattacks. This was a big surprise both in its range and effect."

Less than a year later, after much sanguinary fighting ashore, came V-E Day to overjoy the Allied world. Most Americans remember best the battles and campaigns ashore in this giant struggle to overthrow Hitler. Names like Casablanca, Sicily, Salerno, Normandy, the Battle of the Bulge, and the Rhine Crossing stand out as remarkable feats of planning and valiant execution. Yet, in analyzing these epic land successes, one would do well to recall that the sea figured overwhelmingly in all of them.

Not only amphibious assaults, but also the long follow-up campaigns ashore—ground and air—depended on power afloat that began in the shipyards overseas, extended across thousands of miles of perilous ocean routes and joined in the spearhead of naval might on the distant shore. Every type of warship, merchant vessel, naval plane, and landing craft entered into the projection of America's total power overseas both for assault and for all following operations.

The Pacific—Where Uncommon Valor Was a Common Virtue

Allied war strategy (as mentioned) called for a holding action in the Pacific in order to concentrate on defeating Hitler. Yet strong leaders such as Admirals E. J. King and Chester W. Nimitz and General Douglas MacArthur refused to "sit on their ditty boxes" while Japan consolidated and expanded her large early gains. These able men knew that even with meager means much can be accomplished by astuteness, skill, and boldness. As soon as possible they turned to the attack, and history records no more desperate battles than those from Midway to Okinawa.

When a nation holds the sea, it has the ability to marshal rapid concentration of amphibious force and then, spearheaded by the fleet, to strike with speed, surprise, and momentum. This the Japanese did after Pearl Harbor.

As 7 December 1941 dawned over the Hawaiian Islands, Japan already possessed greater naval capability than that of the combined U.S. Pacific and Asiatic Fleets—one more battleship, eleven more cruisers, more destroyers, submarines and amphibious vessels, and ten carriers to America's three.* Before that fateful morning had ended Japan's superiority had become overwhelming.

Thus the Japanese military at the helm had a free hand to carry out their plans for expansion. Exploiting their control of the sea, they captured Guam and Wake and swept in rapid amphibious assaults through the Philippines, Southeast Asia, and the South Pacific. The heroic opposition they met from Wake to Corregidor to the desperate sea battles of the Java Sea and Sunda Strait in Indonesian waters can never be fully related and will always be understated. Indeed, no writer can do justice to the outpouring of the human spirit in service to freedom in all this globe-encircling struggle of World War II.

In the few pages available here, it is possible only to touch on some highlights of the drama of combat, the valor, the resourcefulness, the nobility, and sacrifice even to death of men fighting from land and sea. Many fine books have been written in broad or detailed perspective dealing with segments of this dedication to America's future. It is the writer's hope that these pages may lead readers to some of these stirring accounts so that posterity may better understand its debt to those who served so nobly in pursuit of the American dream of liberty and dignity of man.

In the first months of the Pacific War the few ships available to the allies in the Far East, like the small forces ashore, fought heroically against the Japanese juggernaut. They even snatched victories, as in the intrepid attack of Commander Paul Talbot's four old four-pipers at Balikpapan on the night of 23 January.** The powerful western Japanese attack group steaming from the Philippines to Borneo and

---

*One of these, *Saratoga*, had just completed yard overhaul in Bremerton, Washington, that included installation of her first radar with its huge "bed spring" antenna and 1.1-inch machine guns. Both of these had many bugs to work out, and the ship was not worked up in other ways, to reach full efficiency, always necessary after any length of time in overhaul.

**USS *John D. Ford, Paul Jones, Parrott,* and *Pope.*

south landed at this important oil center about halfway down Makas-
sar Strait. There in the mid-watch early on 24 January, the four old
destroyers drove into the midst of the far superior Japanese force, sent
four transports and a patrol vessel to the bottom, damaged others, and
escaped almost unscathed—a clear-cut victory over great odds.

Except for submarines, which conducted a steady war of attrition
against the Japanese, by the end of February most of the allied naval
forces in the Far East had been sunk or forced out of action. Yet even
as the enemy expanded, Admiral Nimitz's small fleet began to strike
back by means of submarines and carrier task force raids against
enemy-held islands.

The first assault was directed westward across the Pacific via air
attack and cruiser-destroyer bombardment against Japanese-held positions in the Marshall Islands, halfway on the long sea stretch from
Oahu to Guam. After other raids farther along the road to Japan, on
18 April 1942, Admiral William "Bull" Halsey launched Lieutenant
Colonel James H. Doolittle's sixteen B-25 army bombers from USS
Hornet something over 600 miles from Honshu for a raid on Tokyo
that shook Japan.

These raids affected Japanese morale, but her military forces continued to expand to the south, threatening Australia. Admiral Nimitz's
carriers sped to this distant area and entered into the fray. In late
February, 1942, *Lexington's* planes won a marked victory over land-
based attackers. The next month she and *Yorktown,* operating in Rear
Admiral Wilson Brown's task force, struck the Japanese hard as they
moved in amphibious hops down eastern New Guinea.

The Defensive Offensive—Coral Sea and Midway

Next followed two critical battles, both significant, one a turning point
in history. Japan's plans called for extending her conquests far to the
south and east, drawing the smaller U.S. fleet into mortal battle to
annihilate it, and then behind a vast perimeter from the Aleutians to
Samoa to consolidate these acquisitions in a mighty sea empire that
would endure beyond the United States' will to engage.

The next step to the south called for Japan's occupation of the
southern Solomons and Port Moresby in Papua, opposite Australia.
These would provide good harbors for the Nippon fleet and air mastery of the Coral Sea. In early May Rear Admiral F. J. Fletcher, with
a task force built around two carriers, met and checked the Japanese
in the first naval battle in history in which on each side the airplane
afloat and not the big surface gun delivered the offensive blows.

The Japanese lost the light carrier *Shoho,* suffered severe damage to the new attack carrier *Shokaku*, requiring long repairs, and much of the air group of *Zuikaku*, the other Japanese carrier in the battle. Admiral Fletcher lost a tanker, a destroyer, *Lexington*, and almost lost *Yorktown*. The Japanese occupied Tulagi, opposite Guadalcanal, but the Port Moresby invasion force turned back.

Tactically the Japanese won the Battle of the Coral Sea, suffering less loss. But strategically the Americans triumphed, though it may not have seemed evident at the time. Japan's thrust to the south was checked. Even more important, the battle had influence of far-reaching import on the decisive action that would soon follow far to the north.

There an avalanche gathered to descend on Midway and the Aleutians under forceful Admiral I. Yamamoto. American Intelligence indicated enemy intentions and the approximate time schedule, yet some of Admiral Nimitz's small staff thought the Japanese were putting out false information to draw the U.S. Pacific fleet to the north while the real attack cut the lines of communication to Australia. Therefore, equally important as breaking the code was Admiral Nimitz's courageous moral decision to concentrate for the northern blows.

He realized, of course, that even if his decision turned out to be right the odds facing his forces left little room for confidence. Admiral Yamamoto assembled every ship that could be spared: eleven battleships, ten carriers planned but two did not sail,* twenty-two cruisers, sixty-five destroyers, twenty-one submarines (and midgets), some seven hundred planes, and numerous auxiliaries, including transports (those for Midway bearing five thousand troops).

Against this armada Admiral Nimitz could marshal only three carriers, eight cruisers, fifteen destroyers, twelve submarines, two hundred thirty-two carrier planes, and one hundred twenty-one army, navy, and marine planes packed on Midway as the fateful day neared. His old battleships of World War I design were too slow to operate with the carriers or against the Japanese fast battle force, and new ones were not yet available to him.

Admiral Nimitz rushed his carriers back to Pearl Harbor from the South Pacific. Admiral Halsey's Task Force 16, with accompanying cruisers and destroyers, arrived on 26 May, replenished, and sailed north on the 28th. To his sorrow Halsey remained behind, hospitalized, while Rear Admiral Raymond Spruance replaced him. As the task force sped north, Admiral Spruance's signal to the ships covering

---

Shokaku and *Zuikaku*, which, like *Yorktown*, with energy could have been readied.

plans for the operation contained these words that were more portentous than even he could have realized:

The successful conclusion of the operations now commencing will be of great value to our country.

Yorktown arrived at Pearl on the 27th. Having been at sea continuously for more than three months, her crew and air group needed time for rest and overhaul of planes and equipment, but there was no time. Her battle damage would have ordinarily required three months for repair, but working around the clock and completing only repairs essential for battle, the Navy Yard had her ready for sortie on 30 May. The carrier, with two cruisers and six destroyers, comprised Task Force 17. Admiral Fletcher, Senior to Admiral Spruance, was in overall command.

The two task forces met northeast of Midway in the late afternoon of 2 June. It was just in time—indeed, the hand of Providence seemed to direct events throughout this historic and decisive battle. The Japanese submarines, scheduled to be in position between Oahu and Midway by 1 June to detect ship movements and attack, did not reach the area until 3 June. Early that same morning PBY search planes out of Midway sighted part of the enemy's occupation force approaching from the southwesterly sector. In the afternoon B-17s bombed from high level without damage to the force.

Protected by the cloud cover of a low pressure front, the Japanese carrier striking force under Vice Admiral C. Nagumo, approaching from the northwest, was not sighted though the Japanese heard search planes buzzing overhead. Yamamoto, with the main body built around seven battleships, followed farther to the west out of range.

That busy afternoon of 3 June the Japanese Aleutian Strike Force bombed Dutch Harbor, inflicting damage, covering the forces that occupied Attu and Kiska, and hoping to lure the Pacific Fleet in that direction and away from Midway. Instead, Admiral Fletcher maneuvered northeast of Midway as Admiral Nagumo converged, neither aware of the other. At midnight the two forces were approximately 200 miles apart with their fateful confrontation hours away.

At dawn on the 4th, Admiral Nagumo launched the first wave of 108 planes. Soon a PBY reported the great flight approaching Midway, 150 miles distant, and another spotted and reported the carriers. Every plane on the island that could fly headed for the enemy task force, except the 27 fighters that remained to defend against the Jap attack. They and the AA batteries put up a good defense, shooting down many planes, but 17 of the marine fighters were lost and 7 more severely damaged.

The Midway based B-16s dropped their bombs on the carriers from high level, with no damage to either side. The marine dive bombers and army and navy torpedo planes gallantly bore in to close attack but also registered no hits and, without fighter protection, lost more than half their number. Midway had shot its air bolt. Nagumo surged on unchecked. Yet the sacrifice of the land-based planes had not been in vain. Part of the carriers' second strike group carried torpedoes should U.S. warships be sighted. Expecting further Midway air attacks, the Japanese began to strike these below to rearm with bombs for another Midway assault.

Even as this began, the American carriers were launching their attack groups, and a Japanese search plane soon afterward reported sighting ships to the eastward. Nagumo decided to shift plans again to attack them, but to accept the delay as he recovered the first strike planes and retired to the north while refueling and rearming them.

Just as he finished, the first American carrier planes arrived. The Japanese turn to the north had confused the American air groups, who searched on different courses. Thus when the Japanese carriers were finally located and attacks were made they were not the coordinated bomber-torpedo plane strike with fighter cover as had been planned.

Torpedo planes of *Hornet* and *Enterprise* reached the target first and though they lacked fighter protection, heroically roared in to attack. Wildly maneuvering, the carriers avoided the torpedoes. Their fighter cover dove to attack and with the ships' AA fire shot down all but four of the slow, obsolete attackers.

At this fateful juncture, a few other intrepid men decided the course of history. Again noble sacrifice had not been in vain. The carriers' radical maneuvers to avoid torpedoes had prevented their launching planes. Just as the carriers *Akagi* and *Kaga* recovered and started to launch, *Enterprise* dive bombers screamed down like a bolt out of heaven. With the carrier fighter cover pulled low by the torpedo planes, the dive bombers had a field day. *Akagi* and *Kaga,* their decks loaded with planes, burst into flames and explosions from the hits. They never recovered.

During this same period *Yorktown's* air group worked over *Soryu* nearby and soon she joined the other two Jap carriers as flaming torches, reversing the fortunes of the battle, and changing the whole prospect of the war.

Nagumo's fourth carrier, *Hiryu,* out of sight to the north, eventually inflicted severe damage on *Yorktown** in two separate attacks before she was found and, in turn, knocked out by *Enterprise* dive bombers.

---

*Admiral Fletcher's flagship. With her communications knocked out, he passed overall tactical command to Admiral Spruance with his undamaged carriers. On the

Unable to control the fires and explosions, the Japanese sank *Hiryu* the next morning.

That night Yamamoto sought surface action. Spruance shrewdly estimated the Japanese admiral's intentions and frustrated them by retiring eastward. With overwhelming carrier and pilot casualties, Yamamoto finally called off the Midway operation and withdrew, suffering the loss of a heavy cruiser and damage to other ships in carrier air attacks. Few battles in history have had greater impact. Never again could Japan harbor any realistic hope of winning the war.

Midway broke the back of Japan's carrier air power. The road was still uphill for the United States as a penalty for her unpreparedness in the 1930s, and the next months would be especially rough ones. But the odds against her had been slashed. Midway won precious time until America's industrial might could produce the ships, planes, and weapons required to win the war.

The Offensive Begins—Guadalcanal

Now began the long, slow, bitterly fought task of pushing the Japanese back. The carriers' long range punch repeatedly struck the foe behind his perimeter. Under their far-ranging protection, Admiral Nimitz projected a series of overwhelming amphibious attacks that have no parallel in war.

In the drive, many types of ships besides carriers served their unique roles. Cruisers and destroyers provided indispensable AA and ASW (destroyers) screens for carrier and other task forces, fought many night actions in restricted waters, and supplied continuous fire support in amphibious operations. Minesweepers led the perilous way to many a beach, clearing a route through minefields. The new battleships racing at high speed and bristling with AA batteries brought massive addition to the strength of carrier task forces, and their sixteen-inch guns hit distant targets with deadly accuracy. The old battleships supplied the same potent punch in amphibious assaults against hardened fortifications.

The fleet could not have operated without efficient service of various auxiliaries, such as ammunition ships (which when they exploded took all hands), reefers, tankers, and others. In addition, numerous different ships and craft developed for the complex, specialized tasks required in an amphibious assault, such as escort carriers, assault transports and cargo ships, LST and LCI, rocket craft, control vessels, landing craft for tanks and personnel, amphibious tractors, and tanks. In any operation the submarine played a key role, always endangering

6th a Japanese sub dealt a mortal blow to *Yorktown* and the valiant destroyer *Hammann* alongside trying to save her.

the foe, penetrating his inmost seas to disrupt and destroy the lifeline of shipping, sinking key warships and over 55 percent of Japan's large merchant ship losses that brought ruin as her economy ground to a halt.

Admiral King's inflexible determination to get started with offensive operations in the Pacific to keep the Japanese off balance, whatever the requirements in the Atlantic, led to the first amphibious assault, coming only two months after Midway. Brilliant and tough Rear Admiral Kelly Turner commanded the attack force while calm and imperturbable Major General A.A. Vandegrift headed the marines. Driving into Guadalcanal-Tulagi on 7 August, the attack caught the Japanese by surprise. The marines easily gained their first objectives; but then came disaster.

The invasion was a bold gamble to begin with, since the Japanese Navy was still much larger than the U.S. Pacific Fleet. This superiority increased when, on the night of the 8th, a strong, well-handled striking force surprised Turner's weary fighting ships during the mid-watch. Torpedoes and gunfire sank four cruisers, with little damage to the attackers, though an American submarine sent heavy cruiser *Kako* to the bottom as the enemy force retired.

The Japanese commander did not follow through and attack the still partly loaded amphibious ships off the landing beaches. Their loss could have turned the defeat into total catastrophe. As it was, in the weeks ahead the marines and navy held on at Guadalcanal only by a thread, and at times it seemed this would snap.

The following four months witnessed desperate fighting on land, sea, and in the air—seven knock-down and drag-out important naval battles, ten or more pitched land battles, and daily air, naval, or land skirmishes. It was a series of near Thermopylaes that has no parallel in the history of warfare.

Marines, joined in mid-October by a regiment of the army's fighting Americal Division (and in late November by others), and sailors fought from foxholes and trenches often half-filled with water. Marine, navy, and army pilots rose from the air strips now enveloped in dust, now slithering in mud from the frequent tropical rains, often taking off while the Seabees filled craters from enemy air or naval bombardments that never let up for long. Daring auxiliaries or small warships (often without protection) ran the gauntlet of air, submarine, and surface ship attack. Some didn't make it, but enough got through to maintain essential supplies, munitions and fuel. The navy suffered heavy losses operating to protect and support the fighting forces ashore. These included carriers *Hornet* and *Wasp* and serious torpedo damage to *Saratoga*.

The losses would have been more severe—probably overwhelming—had not new battleships arrived to lend their weight to the struggle. In the first carrier actions supporting Guadalcanal operations, the Battle of the Eastern Solomons, 24 to 25 August 1942, *North Carolina* (BB-55) paid for herself several times over when the intense AA fire shot down a formation of Japanese bombers that had broken through the Combat Air Patrols and might have mortally damaged the priceless carrier *Enterprise.*

Three weeks later a Japanese submarine torpedoed *North Carolina,* but the damage control party sealed off the great hole promptly and the tough ship continued to operate at high speed. When she sailed to Pearl Harbor for repairs, *South Dakota* (BB-57) took her place on the firing line protecting *Enterprise.* In the Battle of the Santa Cruz Islands, 26 to 27 October, the battleship's bristling AA batteries helped save *Enterprise.* However, lacking the massed AA protection a BB provides, *Hornet* was repeatedly hit and ultimately lost.

Wasp had been sunk by a submarine in September while supporting a convoy with reinforcements for Guadalcanal, which stout-hearted Admiral Turner nevertheless pushed through. *Saratoga* was still undergoing repairs from a submarine torpedo hit suffered some weeks earlier, so Admiral Nimitz had left for the whole Pacific only *Enterprise,* famed "Big E." She had received some bomb damage at Santa Cruz, but the capable naval constructors at Noumea promptly repaired it.

Desperate as were the other battles afloat, ashore and in the air, none surpassed the series of night surface actions, large and small. Some the U.S. won, some she lost, and both sides suffered heavily. The greatest of these came in the series of engagements that has come to be called the Battle of Guadalcanal, 12 to 15 November 1942.

Having failed in piecemeal attack and reinforcement, the Japanese decided to send in massive reinforcements supported by a powerful fleet, including battleships, to drive the Americans into the sea. The first wave approached down the Slot on the 12th to subject those ashore to the deadly harassment of heavy gun bombardment.

At the same time Admiral Halsey, who had recently taken command of the South Pacific, based at Noumea, had dispatched army and marine reinforcements to Guadalcanal under the command of Admiral Turner. Despite a fierce Jap air raid, most of the troops had been landed when coast watchers reported the approach of the strong bombardment force, centered around 2 BBs. Undaunted by the odds, Turner's escort commanders, Rear Admirals Daniel J. Callaghan and Norman Scott, charged into the jaws of death with their cruisers and destroyers.

It was a dreadful nocturnal melee, with cruisers and destroyers firing almost pointblank into the mighty battleships. Both American admirals lost their lives, as did many courageous men under them. All their ships were sunk or damaged, but they had accomplished their mission. The enemy had also suffered heavy loss, including the shattered BB *Hiei,* which was finished off the next day by planes she had not been able to destroy on Guadalcanal and by the air group from *Enterprise* as the latter roared up from Noumea, still repairing battle damage. Even more important, the gallant Americans had blocked the bombardment that could have knocked out our shore-based planes that were destined to play an important role in the days that lay immediately ahead.

Guadalcanal had been saved, but only temporarily. The large enemy troop convoy was headed for the island. Ahead of them, with no ships to bar the way, two cruisers bombarded the entrenched Americans on the night of the 13th. Following the transports came a strong covering force. The next day *Enterprise* and Guadalcanal aviators sank a retiring cruiser and a majority of the transports—only four reached the beach to debark troops but never got away.

Nevertheless, on came the covering force composed of a BB, five cruisers and nine destroyers under Vice Admiral N. Kondo, intent on at last completing the fatal big-gun assault.

However, the battleships screening *Enterprise* in Rear Admiral T. C. Kinkaid's task force had now reached the area. Admiral Kinkaid detached them to meet the new threat. Thus, as the Japanese sped toward Iron Bottom Sound, daring Rear Admiral W. A. Lee, commanding the last surface force of any consequence in the South Pacific—the new battleships *Washington* (flagship) and *South Dakota,* plus four destroyers—rushed in to oppose them. The fate of American troops dug in on Guadalcanal may well have rested on his success or failure.

Another desperate night battle ensued. Lee's four destroyers were sunk or knocked out. *South Dakota* was hit and put out of action, though not critically damaged. *Washington's* devastating fire wrecked the Japanese battleship *Kirishima.* Alone but undismayed and without supporting ships or protecting destroyers, Lee in *Washington* chased the remaining Japanese ships north until long past midnight.

This crucial series of naval actions meant the beginning of the end of the struggle for the steaming malaria-filled jungles of Guadalcanal. Victory was assured, though much additional fighting ensued before the island fell.*

---

*In early December Major General A. M. Patch, USA, relieved General Vandegrift. Two months later, at the end of Japanese resistance, General Patch received

The Sea Road Back

Considerable time has been devoted to this first year of the Pacific War because it was decisive. Space permits only brief mention of the heavy fighting and vast campaigns thereafter that eventually led to Tokyo Bay.

By 1943 Japan's high tide of advance had begun to recede. Now followed a succession of amphibious assaults, night naval battles, skilled air operations and much deadly combat up the Solomons (in which able Captain Arleigh Burke, brilliantly handling his destroyers, became known as "31 Knot Burke").

The U.S. Army, Navy, Marines, and Allied fighting men will always remember names such as New Georgia, Munda, Kula Gulf, Kolamban-gara, Vella Gulf, Vella Lavella, Choiseul, Bougainville, Empress Augusta Bay, St. George Channel, and other names as they furrowed these dark and dangerous waters toward the Bismarck Archipelago. There, Rabaul in New Britain and Kavieng in New Ireland, to a lesser degree, were major enemy fleet, air and military bases.

While Admiral Halsey's amphibious and striking forces chewed up the Solomons and struck Kavieng and Rabaul by air, General MacArthur's forces pushed up through eastern New Guinea taking Salamaua, Lae, and Finischafen opposite New Britain by October. At the end of the year they moved into the eastern part of New Britain.

Behind the United States' growing sea power, Halsey's and Mac-Arthur's amphibious forces now occupied Emirau Island north of Kavieng and the Admiralties northwest of Rabaul. Thus, this great Japanese overseas base with its garrison of 100,000 men and vast stores of supplies and munitions was sealed off from its homeland and left to die on the vine.

The great task in the South Pacific and the first in the South-west Pacific had been completed. Now Admiral Nimitz and General MacArthur could fix on the distant objective. The next stage of the war likewise rolled forward in two giant amphibious prongs.

General MacArthur took the southern route, operating behind the spearhead of his 7th Fleet and under the security seaward of Admiral Nimitz's powerful forces—for all operations fell into a coordinated plan in the broad strategy directed by the Joint Chiefs of Staff in Washington.

The 7th Fleet consisted mostly of American ships (augmented

---

a message something like this from Admiral Halsey: "Having sent General Patch to do a tailoring job on Guadalcanal, I am surprised and pleased at the speed with which he removed the enemy's pants to accomplish it."

when necessary from main forces in the Pacific under Admiral Nimitz), but also included Australian and certain other Allied warships. From November, 1943, on the fleet operated under Admiral Kinkaid, one of the U.S. Navy's finest commanders, the 7th Fleet Amphibious Force, commanded by Rear Admiral (later Vice Admiral) Daniel E. Barbey, projected MacArthur's troops in a succession of short amphibious hops. These amounted to some 50 separate actions, large and small, in the course of the war. They were so well-executed and invariably successful that throughout the Southwest Pacific Admiral Barbey became known as "Uncle Dan, the amphibious man."

The landings ranged along the north coast of New Guinea from Hollandia (April, 1944) to Sansapor (July, 1944) thence on 15 September to Morotai in the Moluccas (Spice Islands), bypassing neighboring strongly held Halmahera Island. For these operations, besides his land-based air under General Kenney, General MacArthur's sea flank was covered by Admiral Nimitz's fast carriers than ranged far and wide destroying Japanese ships and aircraft.

They operated as Task Force 38 if under Admiral Halsey's 3rd Fleet or as Task Force 58 if under Admiral Spruance. Whether serving in either fleet, their commander was the hard hitting veteran Vice Admiral Marc A. Mitscher, whose support included Vice Admiral Lee's powerful new battleships. In advance of Hollandia, as Task Force 58, the fast carriers struck enemy island bases from Truk to Palau. Then they turned their avalanche of explosives loose on the objective areas before and after the landings.

As the Solomons campaign prospered in 1943, and as growing strength permitted, Admiral Nimitz gathered forces for a parallel drive to MacArthur's southern thrust. It would steer closer to the ultimate target—Japan—and at the same time support and ease MacArthur's operations. Before beginning the Central Pacific attacks, the army and navy (Vice Admiral Kinkaid operating in the far north) cleared the Japanese from the Aleutians. Amphibious forces struck Attu, 11 May 1943, and in July went ashore standing up on Kiska from which the enemy had secretly withdrawn. Included in the Aleutian Operations was the naval engagement of the Komandorskis shrewdly fought by Rear Admiral C. H. McMorris.

To command the 5th Fleet* in the Central Pacific drive, Admiral Nimitz selected Admiral Spruance, who had been his chief of staff since Midway and was now replaced by Admiral McMorris. In late summer Admiral Turner was brought north to head the 5th Fleet

*Until after the Kwajalein operation called the Central Pacific Force.

Amphibious Force, and teamed with Major General (later Lieutenant General) Holland M. Smith, USMC, heading the Expeditionary Troops. Admiral Mitscher commanded the fast carrier striking forces and Admiral Lee the fast battleships. Surely no fleet ever sailed under a more seasoned and capable group of leaders.

This team handled all the great Central Pacific amphibious thrusts. The first came in November, 1943, not long after MacArthur's forces captured Finischafen in eastern New Guinea and those of Halsey had invaded Bougainville to the east. The Gilbert Islands, just north of the Equator and east of the International Date Line, were the first objective. Admiral Nimitz desired to capture the airfield there and to establish bases for aircraft preparatory to the next move westward.

From the north out of the Hawaiian Islands steamed Admiral Turner, as always choosing the point of danger nearest the enemy. His Task Force included troops of the 27th Army Division led by Major General Ralph C. Smith and scheduled to land on lightly defended Makin Island. Turner swung south of the equator, and northeast of the Ellice Islands paralleled Rear Admiral Harry W. Hill's Tarawa attack force. Assault troops for this strongly fortified and well-garrisoned island were the 2nd Marine Division (Major General Julian C. Smith in command), mounted in New Zealand and the New Hebrides. Other groups proceeded separately, including the several escort and fast carrier task groups.

Thus, from widely separated points and on various courses, the Pacific Fleet's forces struck the Gilberts like a typhoon on 20 November 1943, while planes from the fast carriers blasted distant Japanese airfields to thwart air attack.

Makin, with its few defenders, fell to the 27th Division without much loss. Erratic tides and almost impregnable defenses made Tarawa one of the most bitterly fought contests in the marines' gallant history. Some 980 died in its conquest, along with 29 sailors. Through the sinking of the escort carrier *Liscome Bay* off Makin by a submarine and other casualties, naval losses approached those of the fighting troops ashore.

Now the navy sailed irresistibly on through Micronesia. Massive attacks smashed into the Marshall Islands in early February, 1944. Preceded by prolonged pre-invasion bombardment of unprecedented magnitude, amphibious assaults that have been termed near perfect against strong resistance conquered the huge Kwajalein Atoll in short order. The 4th Marine Division swept over fortified Roi and Namur islands to the north, while the 7th Army Division conquered stoutly defended Kwajalein Island to the south.

Speeding up the schedule by more than two-and-a-half months the amphibians promptly steamed northwest several hundred miles to take Eniwetok Island that same month, under the shield of the fast carriers that overwhelmed the enemy's air reaction. This swift advance established a new ball game. The pace on the road to Tokyo quickened.

In June, while MacArthur's troops leapfrogged along New Guinea far to the south, Spruance and Turner surged into the Marianas, landing on Saipan 15 June. The large islands of this chain, pointing north to Japan, and providing airfield space for the army's heavy bombers to hit Tokyo itself, were a vital link in Japan's inner defense perimeter.

The Japanese had heavily garrisoned and well fortified the island, but as had happened from Tarawa on, the Americans' swift advance caught the enemy off balance with additional guns, mines, and other defenses still not in place. It was another demonstration of the virtue that sea power provides—to hit fast and deeply with penetrating effect.

The Japanese fought fiercely ashore and promptly struck back by air and sea in the far-spreading Battle of the Philippine Sea.* This confrontation cost the Japanese three carriers and two oilers sunk, four carriers and other ships damaged, and 476 planes lost, including shore-based ones, against superficial damage to Spruance's fleet and the loss of 130 planes, most lost from running out of fuel as the courageous carrier pilots flew past the point of no return to strike the distant retiring Japanese forces.

In late July, 1944, Turner's amphibians drove ashore on Guam and Tinian** and soon secured them. Development of the islands as a major naval, air, supply and staging base complex proceeded around the clock. By autumn the B-29s transferred from China began bombing the Japanese main islands. The long trip to Tokyo over Japanese island chains without fighter escort caused the bombing to be carried out from maximum altitude, reducing accuracy. Likewise, damaged planes and those low on fuel often ran into trouble and were lost at

---

*TF 58 consisted of seven CV (Bunker Hill, Enterprise, Essex, Hornet, Lexington, Wasp, Yorktown), eight light carriers, CVL (Bataan, Belleau Wood, Cabot, Cowpens, Langley, Monterey, Princeton, San Jacinto), seven new BB (Alabama, Indiana, Iowa, New Jersey, North Carolina, South Dakota, Washington), twenty-one cruisers (from Baltimore to San Francisco to Wichita), and fifty-six DD (from Anthony to Wadsworth). This juggernaut was a far cry from the three CV, eight cruisers and fifteen DD Fletcher and Spruance brought into action at Midway two years earlier. For flexibility of operations the force was divided into Task Groups, three of which were commanded by men the writer knew well and admired as bold fighting sailors: Rear Admiral J. J. Clark, Rear Admiral J. W. Reeves, and Vice Admiral W. A. Lee.

**Rear Admiral Harry W. Hill directed an especially well conducted landing on Tinian.

sea. As a result, the decision was reached to capture ugly Iwo Jima in the Bonins.

Late in August Spruance departed in his flagship *Indianapolis* for Pearl Harbor to plan and assemble amphibious forces for the operation. The fighting ships now became the 3rd Fleet under Admiral Halsey. Thus the horses remained the same, but with a new driver.

In daring, far-ranging forays characteristic of him, Halsey tore into the Philippines and elsewhere with his fast carriers, preparing for the mid-September landings of his forces in elaborately defended Pelelieu* among the Palau Islands and MacArthur's on Morotai. Meeting weak enemy air resistance, Halsey proposed speeding up the offensive, bypassing Mindanao, like Rabaul, and striking a third of the way up the Philippines at Leyte on 20 October. By tireless exertion this landing date was met.

The powerful Central Pacific and Southwest Pacific prongs now converged on the single objective of Leyte Gulf. With their guns scarcely having time to cool, old battleships and other of Nimitz's ships joined MacArthur's assault forces. Halsey's carriers hit shipping, aircraft and shore facilities from Formosa to Mindanao. Admiral Kinkaid still commanded the 7th Fleet, while veteran and durable Lieutenant General Walter Kreuger directed the invading troops of the 6th Army. Thus on October 20, 1944, General MacArthur strode ashore a few hours in the wake of the assault waves fulfilling his promise as he left Corregidor: "I will return."

Again the Japanese responded with an all-out fleet effort that resulted in a series of widely separated engagements that have been called the greatest naval battle of history. Submarines, surface vessels from PT boat to battleships, aircraft carriers, and planes ashore and afloat entered the fray. Except for mines, they employed every type of naval weapon large and small, from long to pointblank range. In the night action of Surigao Strait the old BBs** from the Central Paci-

*The plans also included an assault on strongly held Yap and lightly defended Ulithi (for a fleet anchorage) but Yap was wisely bypassed.

**Of the eight old BB in the Pacific Fleet, six participated in the assault on Leyte and in the night battle of Surigao Strait: *California, Maryland, Mississippi, Pennsylvania, Tennessee* and *West Virginia*. After completing other duties, the remaining two, *Colorado* and *New Mexico,* also joined the 7th Fleet and were among the OBB that fought their way up the kamikaze sea road through Japanese-held islands to Lingayen, north of Manila in early January, 1945. The remaining five of the total of thirteen OBB that served the nation so well were in the Atlantic Theater. These were *Arkansas* (The "Ark"), *Idaho, Nevada, New York,* and *Texas.* Following Normandy and the Southern France landings, the Navy transferred all five to the Pacific, where they served with the battle-scarred OBB veterans there in the Okinawa assault. Thus both "The Ark" and *Texas,* that commissioned before World War I began, endured to deliver smashing blows from their great guns to help end World War II.

fic, as well as cruisers and destroyers, virtually annihilated one prong of the enemy's fleet converging on the landing area. Far to the north, in the Battle off Cape Engano, Admiral Halsey with his fast carriers and battleships inflicted heavy casualties on a Japanese fleet that had lured him away from San Bernandino Strait.

Through the uncovered strait the powerful central enemy force of battleships and cruisers—though it had suffered severely from submarine and air attack—pressed through undetected and steered south for Leyte Gulf.

However, as the Jap fleet neared the objective, it encountered such magnificent resistance from the air groups of the slow escort carriers supporting the American operations and a handful of "Small Boys" (DD types) that the Japanese admiral turned back at the moment the prize seemed to be in his grasp. The United States' naval history records no more heroic actions than in this desperately fought engagement against overwhelming odds.

With the Japanese fleet terminated as a major menace, all eyes and ships' prows turned north. In the Philippines under the shield of carrier aircraft and warships MacArthur pushed up through the heart of enemy-controlled islands for an amphibious landing in Lingayen Gulf. Despite heavy kamikaze attacks, Vice Admiral J. B. Oldendorf steamed up the long, hard route to Lingayen with the bombardment and fire support force of battleships, cruisers and destroyers. They arrived at the objective on January 6, 1945, and stayed there against all attack, bombarding Japanese position for three days in advance of the arrival of the U.S. landing forces.

In February, 1945, Spruance, at the helm again on the battle line with Task Force 58 under Mitscher, sped to within sixty miles of Honshu, Japan, and conducted heavy air strikes on the Tokyo area during the 16th and 17th. These were preliminary to the assault on the gloomy island of Iwo Jima on February 19. Planned for early January, the operation had been delayed because MacArthur's Luzon campaign required the presence of Nimitz's warships longer than scheduled.

Okinawa and the Surrender

Now the might of America gathered in a giant armada of some 1,500 ships and headed for the enemy's vitals. On April 1, behind the shield of the fast carriers—interposed between Japan's home airfields—and under the guns and planes of the attack force, the largest long-range amphibious assault in history descended on Okinawa.* Kamikazes

---

*The enemy offered little resistance at the beach itself, though trenches, underground passageways, fortified caves and tombs honeycombed the shoreline and

from Japan began to swarm against Turner's attack force as it swept into position offshore. With large numbers reserved in Japan for this crisis, they would become a grave and costly problem in the coming days, but "Terrible" Turner and his gallant sailors, marines, and army did not waver. The fleet had come to stay.

Okinawa sealed Japan's doom. In the campaign the carrier fighters and ship guns destroyed some 5,000 enemy aircraft. Fast carrier task forces raided Japan at will and battleships bombarded the coast. The atomic bombs at Hiroshima and Nagasaki merely stamped "finis" to what was already certain. They did prevent the invasion of the home islands, which was planned but not necessary because of the United States' control of the sea and air that strangled Japan.

Ships filled Tokyo Bay on September 2, 1945, for the surrender ceremonies. These took place appropriately on board Admiral Hal-

---

inland reaches of the green island. For days beforehand Rear Admiral W. H. P. (Spike) Blandy, one of the ablest men ever to serve America, had coolly stood offshore with his bombardment force and subjected the formidable fortifications to the precise gunfire for which he was noted.

Losses during this phase must have been a factor in the Japanese decision to pull back from the shore. The approach of Turner's armada with added gunfire and air support, along with memories of pulverizing blows in earlier American assaults, may have influenced the decision. By avoiding severe beach losses, the Japanese commander could hope to delay the invaders in a prolonged land campaign. Thus kamikazes, submarines, and surface ship raids would have a chance to decimate the fleet offshore. This was undoubtedly a controlling cause. Regardless of the reasons, the troops dashed ashore standing up.

In Rear Admiral L. F. Reifsnider's flagship, *Panamint,* in which the writer sailed, Major General R. S. Geiger, commanding the marine half of the landing, estimated it would take about a week to capture Yontan Airfield, less than two miles from the landing beaches. Considering the known defenses, this seemed a reasonable estimate. With their customary élan and only light opposition, the marines captured the field long before noon that same day. When I asked General Geiger what he thought about that, as we watched proceedings from the bridge, he exultantly replied "It's the damnedest April Fool I've ever seen."

Those wishing to read more deeply about the fascinating story of sea power's influence upon America's development to world stature will find a large number of selected works in the Naval History Division's *United States Naval History, A Bibliography,* Washington, GPO, 1969, 5th ed. The best single history covering the navy's service up to World War II is Dudley W. Knox's *A History of the United States Navy,* rev. ed., N.Y., G. P. Putnam's, 1948.

The best source for World War II is Samuel Eliot Morison's *History of United States Naval Operations in World War II,* Boston, Little, Brown, 1947–1962, 15 vol. The work was done under and with support of the navy but is not an official history; the author had full leeway to express his views and there was no censorship. The Naval History Division and its predecessors have published documentary collections or works such as *The Dictionary of American Naval Fighting Ships,* Washington, GPO, 1959—five volumes so far published, which are the very keel of history. The Division has also published a number of illustrated summary brochures—such as "The United States Navy, Keeping the Peace," Washington, GPO, Rev. 1968—that give a bird's eye view of the field covered. These are listed in the bibliography and available, as is it, from the Government Printing Office at a nominal sum.

sey's flagship *Missouri,* for without victory at sea no victory could have been won. The storm-beaten and war-scarred warships that had breasted far seas, the battle-tested sailors manning them, and the planes zooming overhead gave visible evidence of what is needed to check aggression.

This naval strength did not come easily or quickly. For the second time in scarcely a generation, by the grace of God and the sacrifice of many brave men, the United States had been given time to prepare while others held the line. Never again would she have this time. And as certain as storms, aggression would come again. The struggle to preserve the freedoms Americans enjoy—freedoms dearly bought by men before them—has no end. Each generation must be ready to defend them. Each has a charge to keep.

Too few of those wildly celebrating VJ Day understood these truths. Otherwise they would have kept the strength needed, and there would have been more chance for President Roosevelt's ringing words broadcast to the Filipinos at the time of the Leyte Landings to come to pass:

> . . . we renew our pledge. We and our Philippine brothers in arms—with the help of Almighty God—will drive out the invaders; we will destroy his power to wage war again, and we will restore a world of dignity and freedom —a world of confidence and honesty and peace.

5

War Won—Peace Lost

Man's troubled history unfolds few periods in peace-time as significant in shaping the future as the so-called years of peace 1945–1950. In the subsequent decades of unrest, tension, and conflict, the United States has reaped the results of the decisions of the American people and their leaders.

When Japan signed the Instrument of Surrender on board USS *Missouri* in Tokyo Bay on 2 September 1945, few realized that this apparent end was in reality the opening verse of the opening page of a turbulent chapter in history.

The United States now had the inescapable role to lead world freedom, that could be exercised only by the sea. How would she accept the role? Would she maintain the strength the leader must have, make the sacrifices, wisely meet the responsibilities of leadership? Would the wisdom include maintaining a navy strong enough to carry out obligations certain to come in all the seas of the world, as had Britain in the nineteenth century?

The Demobilization Frenzy

Her first steps in 1945 were not encouraging. National demand to "bring the boys home" turned into almost a frenzied demobilization. Planes, ammunition, jeeps, and other items were dumped in the ocean. Combat ships joined others in "Magic Carpet," a gigantic troop lift. In a few months the United States had almost wrecked its mighty war machine—demobilizing at a rate twice that of World War I, when need for postwar strength was far less pressing.

Some politicians and newspaper pundits condemned the services for not demobilizing faster. Others, as if praising the nation, compared her demobilization achievements with those of the U.S.S.R. One writer noted happily, "In Korea a few American troops are next door to as many as 500,000 Russian troops."

An attack at the very heart of the nation's power to lead occurred in a bitter struggle to scrap naval aviation, the navy's large capital ships, and its marines—in fact, to reduce it to a convoy-transport service. Led by a few men, the assault gained the support of the majority of Americans, easily deluded by the chimera of cheap security.

In the past, weapons like the torpedo, submarine, and airplane had made navies "obsolete." The panacea this time was the atom bomb. Carried in long range planes, it insured peace in our generation; and for all time to come, the theory ran, it would do away with ordinary wars. We did not need marines or amphibious assault ships because amphibious warfare, which had just performed so brilliantly in helping save freedom, had become outmoded by the technological magic and awesome might of our nuclear arsenal. Even widely respected military men such as General Omar Bradley publicly stated that we would not again see large scale amphibious assaults.

Nor would there be any requirement for aircraft carriers and accompanying battleships with their powerful main batteries and overwhelming antiaircraft fire. Atomic bombs would demolish fleets along with airfields and bases. Moreover, the U.S. Navy had no other fleet to combat anyhow. Thus, while public demand continued to reduce all military expenditures, the pressure was particularly hard on the navy. Suddenly the world's leading nation no longer needed a strong sea power—even though ocean highways still spread from her shores to all continents, world commerce multiplied, and the United States became ever more dependent on raw materials from overseas markets.

Fortunately events moved too fast for the United States before she could destroy her sea strength and thereby herself. A strong core of the fleet remained for the critical duties of peace. Less spectacular than war, they are, nevertheless, equally vital. If the navy's existence and rapid shifts to points of crisis can check aggression, prevent war, or limit it, then it has, indeed, well served the nation and mankind.

Opportunities for this kind of service came thick and fast. The Communists' unchanging design to win the world made itself clear in many quarters. The Allies had won the war but not the peace. The U.S.S.R. took over shattered Europe wherever her armies controlled land areas—obviously following a plan developed before Germany's surrender and callously violating agreements. In Churchill's words, uttered in a speech at Fulton, Missouri in March, 1946: "From Stettin in the Baltic to Trieste in the Adriatic, an iron curtain has descended across the continent."

Following the ancient imperialist expansion to the south, the So-viets fanned civil war in Greece, put pressure on Turkey for large concessions, including bases on the Straits, and refused to withdraw troops from Iran.

Trouble in the Middle East

During World War II Britain, the U.S.S.R, and the United States had moved considerable forces into Iran to maintain the flood of munitions and supplies that an endless stream of ships brought into the Persian Gulf as the lifeblood of the Soviet Army. As had been mutually agreed, after peace Britain and the United States withdrew, but not the Soviets, who thus extended their long record of deceit and broken pacts. Be-sides failing to evacuate their troops, they set up the puppet "republic" of Azerbaijan in Iran's northwest province.

Now in March, 1946, scarcely six months after the surrender on board USS *Missouri,* Stalin's next aggression maneuver seemed to threaten a renewal of world war. When Iran moved against the puppet regime, the Soviets dispatched reinforcements and armored units rum-bled toward Teheran and the Turkish border. Iran brought the breach of international agreement before the United Nations Security Coun-cil, which voted against the U.S.S.R.. The United States and others also strongly protested Russia's move.   *IS IT RUSSIA OR SOVIETS? MAKE UP YOUR MIND*

To meet this and other crises in the Middle East, the United States backed up its protest with the one thing aggressors respect—visible force. Before the Security Council vote President Truman despatched USS *Missouri,* majestic symbol of victory, to the Mediterranean. The cruiser *Providence* and destroyer *Powers* on station in that historic sea became *Missouri's* consorts, and in early April they sailed east to Constantinople.

Ostensibly they came on a good will mission to return the remains of the Turkish ambassador to the United States, who had died months before. No one, including the Soviets, failed to grasp the visit's deeper significance. West European newspapers noted the importance of the arrival of this powerful ship in relation to Soviet ambitions to domi-nate the Dardanelles—an aim as old as Peter the Great. Through the Straits and Iran she had her eyes fixed on the fabulously oil rich Middle East, route to the Mediterranean and Indian Ocean and key to continents.

In menaced Greece influential observers clearly saw the import of the visit. A Greek newspaper commented:

> Russia knocks threateningly at the land gates of Turkey. America knocks at the sea gates . . . saying "Don't be afraid, I'm here."

Another writer noted that this evidence of America's vast power, pro-

VERRY VAST INDEED, 3 SHIPS

jected over five thousand miles from her shores, came not for aggression. Neither did it come to serve expansion or ambition for international domination but "is at the service of . . . peace, justice, right, and equality."

Even as USS *Missouri* steered for the Mediterranean, the Soviets reached an agreement with Iran to withdraw their forces in six weeks "if no unforeseen circumstances occur." With U.S. manifest strength backing skilled Iranian negotiating, none did. Neither did the U.S.S.R. increase pressure on Turkey. Azerbaijan is still the only place along their frontier that the Soviets have backed out of a successful coup.

Greek elections in March had strongly rejected the Communist-dominated left. So the Communists sought to gain by subversion what they had lost in fair election. Again *Missouri* helped sway events. Shortly after her Istanbul visit, she made a courtesy call to Greece. Standing in from over the horizon, the battleship bore not only her own formidable power but the symbol of U.S. purpose backed by strength men could see. The U.S. Charge d'Affaires pointed out the noted battleship's influence:

> Its special significance for Greece was fully appreciated and enthusiastically welcomed by the Greek Government . . . [and] people . . . Nor was it lost on the Greek Communist Party or on the Russian Embassy in Athens. The visit contributed in substantial measure to calming local apprehension regarding the security of Greece and, together with recent elections, was an important factor making for a recent marked improvement in Greek morale.

Communists ceaselessly intrigue and probe. USS *Missouri* had sailed away when conditions again seemed ripe to the Soviet leaders to stir the pot. They renewed demands on Turkey for a share in control of the Dardanelles—the usual tactic of the Bear in getting its nose under the tent. Likewise, as Greece prepared for a September referendum on the return of the monarchy, through the Ukraine in the United Nations the Soviets charged that the Greek policies threatened peace. Urged by Defense Secretary James Forrestal, President Truman decided to send a stronger squadron to the Mediterranean. Warned of the possibilities of war, Truman declared that it was just as well to find out now, as in five or ten years, whether the Soviets moved toward world conquest.

On 28 August, the United States released news of a planned courtesy visit to Greece in early September, just after the referendum, by the powerful new aircraft carrier *Franklin D. Roosevelt*. The cruiser *Little Rock* and five destroyers would accompany her. The referendum took place without serious incident, providing for the return of the king. On 5 September *Franklin D. Roosevelt* and the rest of the squadron entered these historic waters that had witnessed the ebb and flow of empire after empire since Salamis, where the Greek fleet changed the course of civilization thousands of years ago.

Out of these beginnings grew the U.S. 6th Fleet. It cruises in the wake of other American squadrons that have sailed there now for nearly two centuries bearing American power and purpose for peace, freedom, and the dignity of man.

This fleet with its far reaching air arm has become a continuous silent, flexible deterrent to overt Soviet takeover in this area so long sought by Russian rulers. At the time Walter Lippmann accurately wrote:

> The Red Army which dominates eastern Europe and could not be removed by a diplomatic frontal attack, can be outflanked in the eastern Mediterranean.

The "Truman Doctrine" further promoted stability in Europe. It provided massive economic aid to Greece and Turkey just as, on a broader scale, the Marshall Plan and other aid helped friend and foe restore the ravages of war. Never has a nation given so much so unselfishly to so many. The President declared that the aid program to Greece and Turkey was "frank recognition that totalitarian régimes imposed on free peoples by direct and indirect aggression, undermine the foundations of international peace and hence the security of the United States."

Blocking Soviet Imperialism

The United States fleet in the Mediterranean, which guaranteed a free sea so that the Truman Doctrine could work and block Soviet imperialism, soon faced another challenge. Italy scheduled elections for April, 1948. Months beforehand the Communist Party started a campaign to control the elections through the familiar method of riots and coercion. Well engineered, noisy demonstrations swept the north. Perhaps they were designed to prepare the way for a coup. A fortnight before the election Italian police seized thousands of rifles and a small mountain of ammunition on a Yugoslav ship intended for Communist use in the election.

Meanwhile, for months 6th Fleet warships had operated off Italy showing the flag and paying good will visits, which were now stepped up. The Soviet Union had strongly protested the ship visits, thus indirectly acknowledging their important morale effect in strengthening resistance to terrorism and ambitions of the Bear from the North.

Steaming thousands of miles from the United States, our warships had now dominated events great and small in the cause of freedom. Admiral Alfred Thayer Mahan's words regarding the British Fleet's influence on Napoleon's ambitions could be applied with little change to the Soviets: "These far distant, storm-beaten ships upon which the Grand Army never looked stood between it and the domination of the world."

Stalemated by the U.S. 6th Fleet that same April, 1948, the Soviets began the Berlin blockade. The Allies responded with the famous Berlin Airlift flying in 2.5 million tons of food and supplies. The airlift, in turn, was made possible by "Operation Sealift." Across the lifelines of the seas the Allies controlled sped U.S. Navy tankers, other auxiliaries, and merchant ships. At Bremerhaven they unloaded the quantities of food and supplies needed for a great city.

They also brought over 2 million gallons of aviation gas for the airlift planes that included two outstanding squadrons of naval patrol planes from the Pacific. United States arms overseas, including air, must depend on control of the seas to operate. Foiled by air and sea, the Soviets lifted the blockade, May 12, 1949. Time and again, firm strength has caused them to cut bait.

Thus, after the first sweeping takeovers, Soviet expansion had been checked in the West. Encouraged, the United States and European allies formed the North American Treaty Organization (NATO) in 1949. To be an organization at all, it was imperative that freedom of ship movement be maintained across the Atlantic. This demanded control of the sea by a navy of unchallenged superiority.

Even though these victories based on such a navy came to pass, checking communism without firing a shot, incredibly they made very little impression on American minds. Still domestic attacks were marshalled against aircraft carriers and other elements of the fleet. Still the government slashed the navy, as too many Americans and their leaders seemed to live in a fool's paradise of wishful thinking.

While the United States weakened the force that had played a key part in checking the Soviets in Europe and the Middle East, the Soviets turned to fish in the troubled waters of Asia. They looked to China particularly, which, for most of this century, had suffered the ravages of external and internal wars, leaving the nation in a state of economic shambles and political unrest. There they found unprincipled leaders eager to accept Communist support in intrigue, subversion, and rebellion. They also found, as in any nation, larger numbers of men of principle—especially youth—who could be deluded by propaganda appealing to their emotions and misguided ideals.

Thus, as the West made sound progress but let its margin of seapower dangerously narrow, disaster of the utmost import took shape in the East. The Soviets do not concentrate on one area but look at the world as a whole. Tentacles of subversion dart in and out, seeking soft spots. They retreat when confronted with strength, leap out and coil around the heart where there is weakness. They follow the single goal—to win the world—which every Soviet leader from Lenin on has steadily proclaimed.

Long ago Chiang Kai Shek said, the Japanese are "a disease of the skin but the Communists of the heart."

The Soviets saw China as the real prize in the struggle for the world. After stripping the industrial machinery from Manchuria for her own use, the U.S.S.R. gave every support to the Chinese Communists. She and Communists in the United States, including infiltrators in the government and universities, also pushed the propaganda campaign that deluded so many Americans. They hailed the Chinese Communists as dedicated patriots—"agrarian reformers"—fighting for freedom and the dignity of man.

A number of Americans in government, colleges, and journalism, whether purposely or not, served the Communist goals—like Owen Lattimore of the Pacific Institute and Johns Hopkins University, who, it has been said, as much as any man, misled the United States about the true character of the Chinese Communists, resulting in the loss of China. The U.S. Senate Internal Security Subcommittee labeled him "A conscious, articulate instrument of the Soviet conspiracy."*

The United States failed as sadly in the East as she succeeded magnificently in the West. After VJ day, she did use the fleet to land small occupation forces in North China, and later to bring one of Chiang Kai Shek's armies from the south into Manchuria. Not appreciating what the Communists engineered, thereafter the United States failed to support the Nationalist government against them. We lost China—even though one of our indirect reasons for becoming involved in the bloody Pacific War was to save China from the clutches of Japan.

By the end of 1949 when the Nationalist cause was lost (and Mao was liquidating millions of civilians who would not go along with him), our navy was not large enough to cope with the world duties demanded of the United States. Was this one of the reasons for the United States' fatal course in the Pacific? Did the weakened fleet destroy our will to be firm? Not enough ships remained to handle problems in Europe and Asia at the same time. Did it thereby become easy to rationalize that the Communist takeover in China was inevitable

---

*Report of the Committee of the Judiciary, 82nd Congress, 2nd Session, Hearings. Internal Security Subcommittee, Washington, GPO, 1952, p. 218. This entire document is a revealing lesson of what may be happening today as Communists cleverly manipulate public opinion.

and not significant enough to cause us serious concern? Had the United States backed the Nationalists to the hilt, would she have had Korea, Vietnam, and perhaps darker trails approaching over the horizon?

The Soviets Opt for Sea Power

As the United States fatefully abandoned Mahan's concept of the influence of sea power, the Soviets, ironically, adopted it. Our country's success in using its maritime power to avert chaos and strengthen small nations' morale to resist subversion had become stamped like a branding iron in Stalin's mind. Sometime about 1950 when the Soviet naval buildup and United States slashes had already greatly narrowed the margin between the two navies, Stalin decided to go ahead with his next bold maritime leap forward.

Having augmented his forces to protect the coast, he now initiated a long-range plan to construct swarms of medium range submarines and sizable surface fleets that could begin to reach out into neighboring seas such as the Mediterranean. If the United States could range across the world with mobile power to influence international events, why should he not follow suit?

He already had a broad foundation on which to build. In the last year of World War II, as the Soviets regained territory, they rehabilitated shipyards and began constructing warships for coastal and offshore defense. To avoid delay, they built from designs at hand. On VJ day in 1945, the Soviet Navy had 85 to 100 warships of destroyer escort size and larger, about 240 submarines and 500 to 600 small vessels such as coastal patrol boats and minecraft. A number of these, including 1 cruiser, 28 frigates, and numerous minecraft and other small ships had come from the United States. By late 1950 this navy had increased by 50 percent or more to total 300 to 350 submarines, over 15 cruisers, perhaps 115 destroyer types, 400 to 500 patrol craft and PT boats, and a similar number of minecraft, other auxiliaries, and amphibians.

United States Cuts Back

What happened to the United States fleet in these same five years? After the first wholesale cut at the end of the war, other reductions followed regularly. The Secretary of Defense's office, envisioned as a small coordinating staff by James Forrestal, its first occupant, ballooned in size. With the mounting increase in overhead, red tape, and civilian control beyond the point of sound balance and judgment, the maritime view became submerged.

Forrestal's successor, Louis Johnson, and Secretary of the Navy Francis Matthews, who took office in May, 1949, made additional heavy cuts in the navy. They particularly concentrated on carrier and other capital ships, marines, and amphibious forces. In the spring of 1949, Secretary Johnson canceled construction of the great carrier *United States.* In August, he ordered the phased reduction of attack carriers in operation from eight to four, and air groups from fourteen to six. The number of USMC squadrons was cut in half.

The miasma of cheap salvation in the atomic bomb became so strong that many so-called experts urged complete elimination of the carrier and amphibious forces, including the marines, and all battleships. The argument advanced was that since the U.S.S.R. had no carriers, why should the United States bother with any? The atomic bomb had ended the feasibility of amphibious assault, so why waste money in that sector? Thus, the United States progressively weakened herself in naval areas where she had outstanding superiority over the Russian Navy—forces all important in maintaining world stability and hope for peace.

While unsuccessfully resisting disastrous reductions, naval leaders happily were able to continue research and development essential for the swift-changing technology of our time. Under Fleet Admiral Chester W. Nimitz, Chief of Naval Operations from 15 December 1945 to 15 December 1947, the navy, after years of preparation and repeated requests, was permitted to initiate nuclear propulsion. In less than a decade this would result in the phenomenal success of USS *Nautilus,* the world's first nuclear warship.

Progress continued to be made in many other fields: in naval aviation that included a patrol plane capable of setting a world distance record that lasted into the 1960s; in ship designs of all types; in antisubmarine technology; in antiair and other guided missile development where the navy had long been in the forefront; and in a wide range of basic research, the navy taking the lead in contract support with universities and other laboratories.

Nevertheless, construction slowed almost to a standstill; ships were decommissioned by budget edict, great numbers went to the scrappers, the fleet dwindled—and with it the power of the United States to keep the peace.

As the Soviet Navy increased 50 percent or more, the size of the United States Navy was cut about 85 percent. The VJ day total of over 5,000 ships of patrol size and larger (not counting the smaller landing vessels) had been slashed to 671 in June, 1950. The battleships that had contributed so magnificently to the fast carrier task forces and to the United States' overwhelming amphibious victories had suffered almost complete elimination. The 13 old battleships, powerhouses of the amphibians, had all been decommissioned, and more than half had been scrapped. The 10 high-speed new battleships that had ranged with the fast carrier task forces to the shores of Japan itself against all opposition had dropped to one in commission. Thus the United States had cut her battleship fleet by 95 percent.

Aircraft carriers also had suffered severely, even though they were the backbone and principal capital ships of the fleet. The twenty heavy far-ranging attack carriers that had spearheaded the long drive to victory had dropped to seven and would soon go down to four. Light and escort carriers, essential to antisubmarine warfare and amphibious assault had melted from seventy-nine to eight.

Shrinkage in other vessels had brought them to or below comparable Soviet types. For example, the hard-hitting cruiser force had dwindled from 73 to 13, and minecraft from 611 to 56. In these categories the Soviets then had probably 18 cruisers and more than 150 minecraft.

The 738 versatile destroyer types, of which there were never enough to meet demands from all points of the compass, now claimed only 136 in commission. This figure is particularly shocking considering that the U.S.S.R. possessed approximately 350 submarines, compared to under 50 operating German submarines at the start of World War II.

Over 85 percent reduction in the U.S. Fleet in fewer than ten years! What joy this must have brought Stalin as he surveyed his growing fleet and shipyards humming with new construction. What satisfaction he must have felt over the virtual disappearance of the U.S. Navy in the far Pacific where "The fleet that came to stay" was now a ghost fleet. What peace of mind he must have gained to hear top American politicians say that the United States should further cut military strength and that we could not maintain power in South Korea—where the United States evacuation had left a vacuum. How confident Stalin must have been, therefore, in late June, 1950, with China under the Communist belt, over the success of his next probe to destroy an oasis of freedom on the sea fringe of the iron curtain.

6

Disaster from Lack of Foresight

Power flows into a vacuum. The United States' leadership could not have more studiously laid plans to bring on the Korean War than by its actions in the ancient Hermitage Kingdom and on the oceans from 1945 to 1950. On the other hand, no nation could have more carefully planned to take over the peninsula than the U.S.S.R. UNITEDSTATES OF SOVIETREPUBLICS

Stalin began preparing for a power grab in Asia promptly after Germany's fall, ordering massive shifts of men and munitions to the Far East. Then, less than a week before the Japanese surrendered, he sent Soviet troops sweeping down into Manchuria and Korea. He was so eager to gain Korea that he entered this strategic peninsula not only by land but by a series of amphibious envelopments. The atomic bomb had opened Pandora's box.

The Allies looked to a just peace after surrender; the Soviets to expansion with all the spoils they could grasp. They stayed on course for a goal that has never varied—world Communist rule. In 1945 and later they made fearsome progress, winning vast territory and putting a quarter of the world's population under Communist domination.

Russian imperialism had reached for Manchuria and Korea through generations. The Peace Treaty provided for Manchuria's return to Nationalist China. On the surface Stalin accepted this, but he made certain the opposite would occur by turning over huge stores of Japanese munitions to the Chinese Communists. He also stripped the industrial and mining machinery from this great province both for Soviet use and to increase the economic and political chaos that favors

Communist takeover. Neither did the Soviet troops evacuate that rich land; after all, at Yalta the allies had recognized the U.S.S.R.'s "preeminent interest in Manchuria."

Korea was divided "temporarily" at the 38th parallel, with Soviet troops holding the north, Americans the south. They would remain just long enough to help Korea get back on even keel and ready for self-government. When the time seemed propitious, the two halves would become a "unified, free and democratic Korea." The Communists, however, have a different definition of the word "democratic" from that used in America.

Propaganda and the emphasis in the news on the valiant Russian soldier had developed a dangerous illusion in the United States that the U.S.S.R. had dropped the cold war of communism. Therefore, it was easy to rationalize that Russia's troops should occupy these Japanese conquests to help shape democratic governments. This might apply to the man in the street, but certainly not to informed leaders who had constant evidence both in Europe and Asia of the real Soviet intent.

Neither should our leaders have failed to realize that the United States could do nothing overseas for herself or her allies, or the cause of freedom, without solid means of getting there and the strength to stay. Seldom has history recorded greater lack of foresight. Given the charge of world freedom, the United States did not face up to it in the Far East with vision and strength.

In the American sector, with generous aid, the industrious Koreans made rapid progress in readying themselves economically and politically for self-government. In the north, under the iron grip of the Soviet Army and the small Communist Party they made progress, too—but for war instead of peace.

Realizing that the citizens would not willingly unite under Communist rule, Stalin blocked all the U.S. and UN efforts even to discuss unification. He prepared for decision by force—the only way the Communists have taken over any country.*

In 1948 an international commission came to Korea to supervise national elections. This they accomplished in the south, but the Communists wouldn't even let them cross the border. The duly elected government under Syngman Rhee took over in Seoul. The Communists refused to recognize him and countered by setting up a puppet figurehead calling himself Kim Il Sung. Full page advertisements in the *New York Times* in 1969 touted him as a great and noble leader.

---

*Except recently in Chile, where the electoral system made it possible for the Communist minority to elect their candidate.

Now the two powers withdrew occupation troops but with different goals. The Americans were glad to get out; in this time of deep cutback both the Joint Chiefs of Staff and the U.S. State Department rationalized that Korea had "no great strategic importance" and publicly stated that the Pacific defense perimeter stopped at the Korean Straits. The U.S. left for defense in South Korea little more than a militia force and some small naval vessels suitable largely for coast guard duties.

The Soviets still sought the unification they wanted. So they trained and left in North Korea, with full equipment of tanks, artillery, and planes, an army of perhaps a quarter million men, including reserves, and a small navy. Training missions continued to develop and add to the forces up to 25 June 1950. In the spring a few weeks earlier, Moscow through *Izvestia* announced to Communists everywhere that unification of Korea was expected to occur that summer in time for national elections on 5 August.

After withdrawing, the United States did return a small military aid cadre and slowly built up the South Korean forces but provided no heavy fighting arms. By June, 1950, South Korea had a tiny navy and an army in name of about 90,000 men. But it lacked tanks, combat planes, and medium and heavy artillery. The Soviets left behind power for aggression; the United States left a vacuum.

Propaganda, Communist infiltrators, deluded liberals, and false economy helped to shape the United States' tragic errors. The nation took a fatal course indeed when she abandoned the maritime strategy upon which she had grown great for the demonic strategy of the atomic bomb and the threat of mass destruction. This made the other errors easy, especially that of false economy. For the fiscal year starting 1 July 1950, the president and his leading assistants decreed a defense budget limit of 13 billion (cutting all services but especially the navy, which saw its aircraft carriers reduced from eight to four, and the marines slashed to two skeleton divisions)* beyond which the nation would go bankrupt—only to spend many times this amount after June, 1950.

Aggression into Weakness

Suddenly on a sleepy Saturday evening, June 24 (East Coast time), a fateful message shattered Washington's dream world—INVASION.

---

*For fiscal year 1950 the Defense Department programmed a total Fleet Marine Force of 6 infantry battalions and 11 aviation squadrons. Moreover, no Defense Department programming after World War II even recognized the existence of the Marine divisions.

No one in the United States could anticipate that the Communists would pour into South Korea that June like a torrent through a collapsing dike. Yet had Americans not rationalized, they would have known that the vacuum left in South Korea and the virtual withdrawal of the navy from the far Pacific could only spur the Communists to attempt a takeover.

President Truman made a great and wise decision to oppose the aggression—thus reversing the United States' course and apparent intentions. More foresight, or at least prudent reaction to the growth in Soviet power, would have made this decision unnecessary. A few billion dollars more in the late 1940s would have saved scores of billions in the 1950s, not to mention untold anguish and the greater cost of lives that included more than 33,000 Americans.

The decision to commit naval and air forces was made in Washington the evening of the 26th (the 27th in Korea). Using tanks, planes, and artillery in support of the massed infantry, and amphibious landings down the east coast, the enemy torrents had already swept deep into the south along three main lines of attack. With their vast superiority in numbers, in experience (many battle-hardened veterans of service with the Chinese Communists), and in arms, nothing in South Korea could stop them.

Could enough help from overseas reach there in time? If so, troops and arms could come in sufficient quantity only by sea. President Truman's decision to dispatch aid would stand up only if the United States could control and use the sea. She could do this only if no navy of consequence blocked the way, for the once mighty U.S. Navy in the far Pacific had vanished. Little more than its shadow remained in Vice Admiral A.D. Struble's 7th Fleet, which boasted one aircraft carrier, *Valley Forge,* the cruiser *Rochester,* eight destroyers, four submarines, and five auxiliaries. Where once powerful task forces ranged, these few ships must now cover the thousands of miles of coastline from Sakhalin to Singapore—like having one squad of policemen for all of New York City.

Supplementing these ships, General Douglas MacArthur's navy, under Vice Admiral C. T. Joy, Commander Naval Forces Far East, added the five-inch AA cruiser *Juneau,* four destroyers, one submarine, one British frigate, some minecraft, and, on temporary assignment, one each of five amphibious types*—faint echo of Terrible Turner's (Vice

---

*This small Amphibious Group One, under the command of Rear Admiral James H. Doyle, had recently arrived in response to General MacArthur's request for navy and marine experts to train his occupation forces in amphibious warfare. The amphibious instruction had just got underway when war came.

Admiral Richmond Kelly Turner) amphibious force that roared into Okinawa with more than 1,200 ships.

The Communists' multipronged drive quickly captured Seoul, the capital of South Korea. On the rugged east coast the invaders leaped south in small, unopposed amphibious landings. The one that met opposition could have been decisive. On the day of invasion the South Koreans' only offensive fighting ship, a little PC, intercepted northeast of Pusan an armed steamer with 600 invasion troops and, after a running fight, sank it. Pusan, the only port available for bringing in sufficient reinforcements and arms, was then defenseless. Had the North Koreans taken it this first day of invasion they might well have won the war before the United States entered.

When the United States decided to act, two days later, Admiral Joy dispatched what little force he had to help. Fortunately naval units have among their attributes long endurance and the ability to react swiftly.

Streaming through the night, early on the 28th *Juneau* began investigating reported enemy landings near Pusan. Then she proceeded up the coast, and on 29 June her guns began to rake the onrushing east coast invasion prong with devastating fire. Troops ashore have always especially dreaded naval gunfire because of its accuracy, volume, high-terminal velocity and sustained blows.

Soon other ships joined, including three from the British Commonwealth. Supporting the outnumbered defenders, this handful of ships blocked any further amphibious landings down the South Korean coast and markedly slowed the Communist advance.

In the weeks ahead other fighting ships would arrive, including more fine vessels from the British Commonwealth. Through the war they would serve magnificently in close support of infantry; in knocking out enemy troop concentrations, tanks and artillery; in disrupting the coastal line of communications, caving in tunnels, wrecking trains and truck caravans.

Early on 2 July *Juneau* with HMS *Jamaica* and *Black Swan* fought the only engagement of the war with the little North Korean Navy. They sank three out of four PT Boats, two out of two gunboats, and later ten trawlers loaded with ammunition convoyed south during the night by the warships.

The Sea's Controlling Influence

Sea power made many other contributions in that savage conflict. Americans think of the Korean War as hardship and death in the bitter hills ashore. It was certainly all of this. Yet every foot of the struggle forward, every step of the bitter retreats, the overwhelming victories, the little battles, the withdrawals and last-ditch stands had their seagoing support and overtones.

The spectacular achievements depended on amphibious power—the irresistible capability of the twentieth century scientific navy to overwhelm land-bound forces at the point of contact. It was America's undeserved fortune that this amphibious capability, though mutilated in the immediately preceding years, nevertheless had remnants that, by improvisation, residue of expertise, dynamic leadership, and tireless labor still rose superbly to the need in Korea. Had the Communists waited even a single year more, it seems certain the weakening of the U.S. Navy by deliberate political decision would have gone past the point of no return.

The need for amphibious lift came quickly. Late on 30 June General MacArthur received authority to commit U.S. troops as well as the navy and air force. For occupation duty in Japan he had four understrength divisions, composed in considerable part of young, incompletely trained recruits and without heavy tanks. Promptly he moved the first of these—the 24th Infantry Division—by available shipping across to Pusan, with advance units going in by air. The 25th would soon follow, and then the 1st Cavalry in a landing over the beaches at Pohang, the northeastern anchor of Allied resistance.

Other troops that could be scraped together in the Pacific and the United States thousands of miles away would follow. Unhampered use of the sea gave MacArthur the immense advantage of easy and swift transport of large bodies of troops and millions of tons of munitions, fuel, equipment, airplanes, food, and other supplies. Without the sea lanes he would have had no chance at all. As in all important wars that have affected America's destiny, this one also hinged upon a maritime strategy.

More spectacular and decisive use of amphibious capability than at Pohang would come later. Meanwhile, the value of naval forces that government leaders had battled fiercely to whittle down became vividly clear. To delay the enemy, General MacArthur initiated air as well as ship attack on the invader's lines of communications. The Air Force concentrated on those around Seoul and North Korea's capital, Pyongyang, striking at road and railroad centers. However, the bombers based in Okinawa had nearly a two thousand-mile round trip to hit these targets. The fighters in Kyushu had about half this round trip which gave them limited endurance north of the 38th parallel and little more south of it. Hence the North Korean bombers that had struck the South Koreans with such demoralizing effect still had relatively free rein.

Aircraft carriers that could get in close were desperately needed. Only two stemmed the troubled waters of the Far East, USS *Valley Forge* and HMS *Triumph,* a light carrier. After the United Nations Security Council vote of military assistance, British Commonwealth warships in the area under Rear Admiral Sir W. G. Andrews, RN, joined the U.S. Navy bringing a measurable addition, besides the carrier, of two light cruisers and seven destroyers/frigates. These and the rest of Admiral Struble's force might be needed in the Formosa Straits, where the Chinese Communists threatened invasion. Or they might face the greater problem of Soviet entry with aircraft. In addition, submarine-undersea contracts had already been reported. Nevertheless, on the evening of July 1, Admiral Struble's Task Force 77 (two carriers, two cruisers, and ten destroyers) departed from Okinawa for the Yellow Sea.*

Not long after *Juneau* and her consorts polished off much of the little North Korean Navy, Task Force 77—with one eye on the Soviet fleet nearby to the north, reached its launch point in the Yellow Sea in the early dawn on 3 July.

In a real sense, it had steamed into the mouths of the Bear and the Dragon. Only one hundred miles to the west lay Mao's airfields in Shantung. Stalin's air base at occupied Port Arthur was a swift two hundred miles to the northwest. With wary fighter cover over the force, twenty-one Fireflies and Spitfires from *Triumph* smashed the important airfield installations at Haeju.

In the heart of the enemy land thirty-six Corsairs, Panthers, and Skyraiders from *Valley Forge* roared in over Pyongyang. Shooting two Yaks out of the sky and destroying nine planes on the ground, they also shattered the hangars and fuel storage tanks. Later strikes that day hit the railroad marshaling yards in the capital. These knocked out locomotives, other rolling stock, repair facilities, and breached one of the bridges across the river. That ended air trouble from these areas for some time and hampered the enemy's flow of logistics. Also, it may well have deterred the Soviets from committing more planes to the conflict.

General MacArthur and Admiral Struble had larger dimensions to consider than the Korean War itself. As these solid blows landed, they had to project how the Soviets would react with their many submarines, powerful air force and armies. There was the further problem of the Communist Chinese, ever threatening across the Formosa Straits. Meanwhile, the carrier task force retired to the base at

---

*Carriers USS *Valley Forge* and HMS *Triumph;* cruisers USS *Rochester* and HMS *Belfast;* eight U.S. destroyers and two British destroyers.

Buckner Bay, Okinawa, about halfway between the Straits and Japan. Here it could move freely in any direction.

On July 5, the weak advance detachment of the 24th Division gallantly met the enemy but was overwhelmed by superior numbers well equipped with tanks and artillery—there was no provision for close air support as in navy-marine operations. Successive elements of the division met the same fate as they fought to gain time. Along with the 24th Division the 25th also took a pounding against heavy odds. In the savage route at Taejon, which fell on July 20, Major General W. F. Dean, commander of the 24th, was captured.

Their brave sacrifice and the air force and navy's attacks on lines of communication slowed the foe. Underway by sea from all directions, reinforcements steadily flowed into Pusan. But the Communist hordes pressed on. And the problem for the U.S. and its South Korean allies was whether the necessary material and men could be brought on the scene swiftly enough to prevent the Communists from overrunning the country.

Pusan Perimeter—Backs to the Wall

By late July the invaders had swarmed across all of South Korea except a shrinking perimeter around Pusan—long to the northeast, paralleling the sea and narrow to the west. To the northeast, the weary defenders with ship gunfire and air support had checked the Communist advance along the east coast, near Pohang. To the northwest, advancing up to twenty-five miles in some sectors during the last week of July, the enemy burst over the mountain wall into the Naktong River basin, surging towards Pusan. To the southwest, they were scarcely thirty miles away. Grimly the tired allied troops fought on. Then at a critical juncture late on 2 August, a navy task group with the First Marine Brigade, commanded by Brigadier General E. A. Craig, arrived from San Diego, California, nearly six thousand miles away.*

The ships had scarcely lost weigh when embarkation began and continued through the night. At 0700 the next morning the brigade rushed to the front. Lieutenant General W. H. Walker, USA, commanding within the perimeter, hurled the Marine Brigade and part of the 25th Infantry Division against the enemy's south flank in a well-designed spoiling attack. The Brigade's tanks led the van. Its observation and air support planes flew overhead from the escort carriers *Sicily* and *Badoeng Strait,* under the command of Rear Admiral R. W.

---

*General Craig's brigade consisted of a reinforced Marine infantry regiment and Marine Air Group 33 (MAG 33).

Ruble, which had arrived to base the marine squadrons. Coordinated artillery fire and close air support by Marine Air Group 33 flying from the "Jeep" carriers gave the marines ability to blast opposition out of the way.

Yet as the army-marine task force knocked the enemy off balance in the Masan area (coveted by the Imperial Russian Navy half a century earlier), a crisis developed to the north. Surging across the Naktong in force, the Communists threatened to burst down the river road into Pusan.

Accordingly, on August 13, the Marine Brigade was rushed back from Masan and hurled into the Naktong breech alongside tired troops.

The battle uphill against the entrenched and more numerous enemy on "No-Name Ridge" was a charge into the impossible. The understrength marine battalion leading the attack, on 17 August, suffered 142 casualties out of its 240 men in a few hours. But great bravery, buttressed by coordinated artillery and marine air support from the carriers, could not be checked. One example of the navy-marine system of close gunnery and air support illustrates thousands of similar incidents that have so brilliantly served the nation:

The next morning, held up by a heavy machine gun nest less than a hundred yards ahead, the marines called for help from the air. Under ground control, a dummy run, a target marking run by MAG 33, and a strike were completed within nine minutes, and a 500-pound bomb, deposited squarely upon the nest, eliminated this obstacle and panicked enemy troops.*

Unable to stand up to this kind of fighting, the enemy recoiled and fled across the river. Artillery and fighter planes from the Jeep carriers concentrated on the crossing point. The muddy Naktong ran red. Powerful bomber and fighter bomber strikes from USS *Philippine Sea* blasted enemy troop concentrations and supply dumps west of the river, completing the shattering defeat.

Its task brilliantly completed, the Marine Brigade would now get a rest. On August 20, it went into reserve to the south awaiting the arrival of the rest of the 1st Division and preparing for one of the masterful battle strokes of all history. The brigade's withdrawal was none too soon to suit either its able commander, Brigadier General E. A. Craig, USMC, or General MacArthur. From the beginning the Supreme Commander had a different operational plan in mind for the brigade than the fight at the Pusan Perimeter.

History of Naval Operations: Korea by James A. Field, Navy Department, Washington, 1962, p. 152, an indispensable book for study of the Korean War.

The Bold Sea Plan

Even in the first frantic days of the war, great commander that he was, MacArthur had looked beyond a dogged defense. Victory comes from striking blows, not just turning them back. Even in the deepest straits, a leader must find the foe's Achilles heel and attack.

The Communists' principal lines of communication centered in Seoul and radiated from there southward. Well understanding the incomparable benefits of maritime strategy, which had stood him in such good stead in World War II, the general planned a lightning amphibious assault far behind the enemy lines to cut his lines of communication and then to put him in a pincer between two nutcrackers.

Not appreciating the Communists' strength and momentum, early in July MacArthur contemplated landing the 1st Calvalry Division on the west coast. Events swiftly frustrated this hope as he was compelled to throw every available man into the perimeter to try to check the Communist steamroller.

Nevertheless, the general held to his purpose. The formation of the Marine Brigade cheered him. It was just what he needed; he had earmarked it to land in Japan to prepare to lead the amphibious end run. But with the threatened collapse of the perimeter he had unhappily diverted it there.

His reluctance would have been greater except that other marines were coming. After the promise of the brigade, he promptly asked JCS for a full marine division to spearhead the "decisive stroke." This was impossible without wrecking Fleet Marine Force, Atlantic, and calling up reserves. Like the rest of the navy the marines had been cut deeply. Their two understrength divisions did not suffice for the needs of the troubled Mediterranean-Middle East let alone the Pacific.

The brigade had been organized in record time from men currently available on the West Coast. Then ships had been assembled and loaded with equipment and planes, and the troops embarked and sped across the Pacific. However, no margin remained for the rest of the division. As conditions worsened in Korea, President Truman authorized calling up the Corps' reserves, and on July 20, the Joint Chiefs of Staff (JCS) authorized the move to Korea of the rest of the 1st Division for November or December.

General MacArthur shot back an urgent request for arrival by 10 September "to accomplish a vital stroke." Miracles of effort continued by the navy and marines to meet this "impossible" deadline.

Despite opposition at every level, including JCS, the general would not waver from his plan. With his ability to move a large force easily and swiftly by ship, he saw a golden opportunity in this wide end run, especially if it could be made soon before the foe prepared. But perhaps no amphibious operations in history presented quite the problem of this one.

First was the short time to get ready. Both the marines and the army had difficulties. However, special ones confronted the navy, which had to take troops into treacherous waters, land them on the far shore at the precise moment, and keep them secure with support and supplies. Ships had to be found and configured for amphibious duties, detailed plans developed for every participant—from carrier, cruiser, lead gunfire support destroyer, transport and on down through every spitfire little craft to the landing boats in the transports. In addition, navy beach parties, "Seabees," and others ashore had to fit into the schedule.

A steady flow of munitions, rations, gasoline, black oil, and supplies of every sort had to be underway even before the assault. Intricate training of many types had to be conducted—with no time to do it. Nothing is as complicated in the affairs of men as large scale amphibious assault, which requires coordination of every ship, boat, plane, and man. At the same time, if successfully executed, nothing concentrates such overwhelming jet force. The question was: could they succeed, could they do all this with only weeks to go?

In the second place, of all the possible landing sites on the west coast, Inchon, the port of Seoul twenty-five miles west-southwest, offered the rewards of swift capture of the capital and severance of enemy supply lines where they were most vulnerable. At the same time it presented the greatest hazards. The Attack Force would have to approach through a long, tortuous channel. It and the harbor could be easily mined—the planners would have got more gray hairs had they known that in the weeks before the assault Soviet mine and naval technicians reached North Korea in large numbers. At many points shore batteries could enfilade the channel, which gave little sea room for maneuver. Tremendous tides, like those in the Bay of Fundy, raced in and out, leaving broad flats of impassable ooze on the ebb.

Instead of prolonged and continuous bombardment in advance, the gunfire support ships would have to retire with the ebb. The landing "beaches" were impassable mud flats at low tide and, for two of them, lofty sea walls at high tide. The assault had to be made at spring tide, when the moon's gravitational pull raised the flood to maximum height, since the LSTs needed twenty-nine feet for beaching at Inchon. September's spring tides of 31.2 feet ebbed and flowed on the 15th. The next—only 30 feet—in late October, was too late because of the imminent onset of the Korean winter. It was already August 28 when the JCS approved the concept.

On September 15, the spring tide reached its height of 31.2 feet at 0659. This would have been just right, giving the troops all day to push ahead while the beached LSTs unloaded in good light as the tide ebbed and flowed during the day. But the long approach through restricted waters would thereby have to be made at night. What about mines and ships sunk in the channel? What of those amphibians with no radar? Slow, single-screwed, and cumbersome, they would have to breast currents up to seven or eight knots, close to the actual speed of the slower ones. A slight error in navigation or a ship sunk by gunfire or mine could bring disaster to all.

Evening high tide fell at 1919, thirty-seven minutes after sunset. Allowing daylight approach, this reduced the navigation hazards. On the other hand, it gave the enemy all day to move in troops and strengthen defenses. Landing in twilight, the troops and beach parties would have the perils of darkness as well as the enemy to contest.

In the words of Admiral Doyle's communications officer, Commander Monroe Kelly, "Make up a list of amphibious 'don'ts' and you have an exact description" of Inchon.*

Perimeter Crisis Again

After its defeat on the Maktong in August, the enemy relaxed pressure to lick its battle wounds and recoup. Despite the navy's need to prepare for Inchon, its guns and planes and the air force's planes continued to hammer the Communist supply lines. They caused much damage, yet because of the small number of ships and planes involved massive aid continued to reach the North Koreans from the U.S.S.R., primarily by night. More troops poured down from the north. On the night of August 31, the storm broke. All around the perimeter the greatest disaster yet threatened as powerful Communist assault columns drove back the allies.

On September 1, when the magnitude of the attack became clear, messages flashed. Far up in the Yellow Sea, Task Force 77 launched strikes early that morning against railroad bridges and marshaling yards in the Seoul-Pyongyang complexes. These attacks served a double purpose of reducing pressure on the perimeter and preparing for Inchon. Other flights were in the air when the emergency call for

---

*From Colonel Robert D. Heinl, Jr.'s *Victory at High Tide, The Inchon-Seoul Campaign,* Philadelphia, 1968, J. B. Lippincott, p. 24. This brilliantly written and researched volume has no peer for the Inchon campaign. It was indispensable for this chapter.

assistance came. Immediately responding by shift of rudder, as is the way of ships on the countless highways of the ocean, the Task Force immediately swung to the southeast, recalled flights in the air, built up speed to twenty-seven knots, and began hitting the enemy along the perimeter.

Repeated strikes through the day much injured the invader, despite deficient communications and air control. The next day, with navy controllers in charge, strikes went well, shattering troop concentrations, destroying tanks, trucks, and barges.

Meanwhile, the Marine Brigade again dropped preparations for Inchon and hit the trail for the Naktong bulge. Here the situation was even more critical than before. By September 2, nearly two North Korean divisions had crossed the river and advanced toward Pusan. Intense fighting followed. With the marines in the forefront, the Eighth Army first stopped, then drove the invaders back. By the evening of 4 September, the marines had reached the hill from which eighteen days earlier they had launched their attack to crush the first Naktong bulge. Late on the 5th, as they drove to complete the job, orders recalled them. The crisis had eased; Inchon D-day approached; as amphibious spearhead on Red Beach, the Brigade would leap out of the frying pan into the fire.

Inchon

Rumbling along through the mid-watch to Pusan, the fighting 5th Marines had no rest ahead. For weeks as they served the nation, valiantly helping to save the perimeter, ships had been converging on the Far East from many points of the compass and from as far away as the Mediterranean with troops and supplies for Inchon.

Now the movement to the objective was beginning, and the 5th Marines were just coming out of the last desperate fight. They had no time to rest up, to indoctrinate replacements fully, to line up needs carefully for the military masterpiece against tremendous odds that Inchon became. Even as they wearily approached Pusan during the early hours of the 6th, the first echelon of the attack force—small, slower ships—finished preparations and sailed that day.

For that matter, however, none of the complex force had time to get fully ready. Few of the ships had amphibious experience. Most of them had not even been together. The assault had to be made before winter and before the enemy built up defenses and mined the approaches. It was a case of scramble and heave, improvise, jury rig, and rush to battle to "do the best you can with what you have," as Admiral E. J. King was wont to say.

The navy and marines, usually on sparse budgets for the demands on them, were used to such conditions. Strengthened by the training from World War II, they knew how to put together the intricate puzzle of amphibious assault. They could improvise to meet the many difficulties and unknowns. Yet seldom, if ever, have they had to meet demands like Inchon. It would be difficult to find in history an operation that equaled it in problems.

Thus, as the first echelon got underway from Japan on the 6th, every responsible commander knew that only superb performance and the grace of Providence could ensure success. The top ones included Vice Admiral A.D. Struble, USN, commanding the Attack Force; Rear Admiral James H. Doyle, Attack Force Commander; Major General O.P. Smith, Commanding General 1st Marine Division and Landing Force Commander; Major General E. M. Almond, USA, commanding X Corps. In the practice of amphibious campaigns, he was to assume command of operation ashore once the beachhead was secured. Many other leaders in all services would also play key roles. Failure by any one might have ended in failure for all.

During the ensuing days other components of the Attack Force sailed. Steadily the different groups converged on Inchon at carefully fixed speeds. Typhoon Jane screaming over Japan on 3 September had caused much damage and hindered final preparations. Then on the 10th her sister fury, typhoon Kezia, was spotted, approaching at a speed calculated to hit Japan on the 12th or 13th. The assault shipping with the First Marines was scheduled to sail from Kobe on the 12th.

Redoubling efforts, the hard working crews and troops telescoped the schedule and sailed early on the 11th into mountainous seas. As the amphibians plunged and wallowed through the raging storm, buffeted by winds up to ninety knots, they suffered much damage. Had Kezia headed on toward Inchon, it would have shattered the armada, but in the will of Providence it curved to the east.

For weeks the attack and escort carriers had repeatedly struck roads, railroads, transportation centers, and electric power stations from Kunsan some one hundred miles south of Inchon to Pyongyang, a similar distance to the north. Far East Air Force planes had served well with strikes around Kunsan as part of the deception plan that included air attacks, ship bombardment and raids on several west coast points, with emphasis on Kunsan.

On the 10th the escort carriers completed preliminaries, before retiring to replenish for the assault, with a blazing au revoir of napalm on Wolmi Do, Inchon's fortified island connected to the city by causeway. This burned off the vegetation on the landing side with "presumable discouragement to the garrison."

Now the fast carriers stepped up their precision attacks to close off land approaches to Inchon. On D-1 the escort carriers *Sicily* and *Badoeng Strait* would rejoin to concentrate the power of the four U.S. carriers on the objective while HMS *Triumph* hit Kunsan to keep the foe guessing.

On September 13, the advance bombardment group steamed up the tortuous channel. Following six U. S. destroyers came four cruisers —USS *Toledo* (Rear Admiral John M. Higgins, USN), *Rochester,* wearing Admiral Struble's flag, HMS *Jamaica* and *Kenya.* Panther jets from the fast carriers orbited overhead. Approaching on the last of the ebb, the ships would have a flooding tide for the bombardment. At Anchor, stemming it, they would be heading out without having to maneuver in narrow waters.

At 1145 came the chilling cry "Mines!" There on the port bow of *Mansfield,* the leading destroyer, watched seventeen ugly black Soviet contact mines. One destroyer remained behind to destroy them by gunfire while the rest held their course to bombardment stations, some less than one thousand yards from the island fortress—air photographs had revealed over one hundred guns and strong points on the island and Inchon waterfront.

As the cruisers anchored downstream and the destroyers steered into pointblank range, powerful ADs roared in from the fast carriers offshore and in screaming dives released their bombs on the island. Just before 1300 the destroyers began slow, deliberate fire to flush out the enemy's masked guns, many hidden in caves. Soon they took the bait and a maze of red-gold gunflashes rippled over the island. Projectiles tore into several of the anchored destroyers.

For an hour they blasted back, knocking out many strong points, miraculously at a cost of only one dead and several wounded. Now the eight- and six-inch guns of the cruisers took up the fire and continued until late afternoon with one break for another fast carrier air strike.

On the 14th, with the remaining targets largely pinpointed, cruisers, destroyers, and carrier aircraft worked over the enemy all day. Wolmi Do looked like "it had been shaved." Fortifications around Inchon were shattered. The shore lay silent as the ships retired for the night. The destroyers alone had fired almost as many five-inch projectiles as hit Omaha Beach in the Normandy landings

That night, in accordance with the plan that had evolved to use both tides, the bombardment ships with eight others entered Flying Fish Channel. "It was after midnight" and "dark as the inside of a cow's belly." Behind the leading destroyers came three fast destroyer transports (APD). With an LSD they carried the 3rd Battalion, 5th Marines—commanded by Lieutenant Colonel Robert Taplett—formidable victors in the perimeter. Astern of them lumbered three rocket ships (LSMRs), then more destroyers and Admiral Doyle's command ship, *Mount McKinley,* packed with top brass starting with General MacArthur. Last came the four veteran cruisers.

By first light the destroyers had reached their familiar bombardment stations close inshore. Marine planes from the escort carriers opened a spectacular day roaring across Wolmi Do with the wham of bursting bombs, the rippling crack of five-inch rockets, the staccato burst of 20 MMs. At 0520, with the Wolmi Do landing set for 0630, the signal that had set valor underway on many a gallant beach fluttered to the flagship's yardarm: "Land the Landing Force."

Boats clattered into the water, marines went over the side, destroyer guns trained out. At 0540 the sharp crack of their guns and distant boom of the heavy batteries of the cruisers downstream shattered the silver dawn. General Lemuel C. Shepherd, Commanding General Fleet Marine Force, Pacific, veteran of many landings, observed, "I have never seen any better shooting. The entire island was covered with bursting shells."

At 0615, "with a tremendous hiss and swoosh and thunderous roar" two rocket ships on the northern flank launched the first of 2,000 five-inch rockets to smother the rear of the slopes facing the beach. The other LSMR steamed slowly across the boat lanes, smothering the beach defenses with a hail of fire. The control vessel hauled down the signal flag. With a roar the first boat wave took off for the beach at full throttle.

At 0628 the ships checked fire, and two squadrons of Marine Corsairs from the escort carriers roared in blasting the defenders. Now the boats grounded, the ramps went down, the green clad marines leaped out, crossed a low sea wall and with Corsairs plowing up the dirt ahead raced into the charred, pitted island amidst "smoke, dust, and devastation."

As the final bombardment reached its awful crescendo in the minutes before H Hour, the first waves headed for the shore. The crash and thunder of ship guns ceased briefly, only to be replaced for the final short dash by the screaming roar of marine Corsairs and navy ADs. Support was so close that the boats "were pelted with spent 20mm empties."

The dazed garrison offered little resistance. Within half an hour the American flag waved over the island's highest hill. Scarcely an hour later the battalion commander proudly broadcast to the flagship, "Wolmi Do secured."

When mopping up ended before noon, the marines counted up their losses—amazingly only seventeen wounded.

Observing from the flagship with increasing elation, General Mac-Arthur sent his historic message to the fleet, "The navy and marines have never shone more brightly than this morning."

Thus went the morning tide; the hardest was yet to come in the twilight flood tide landings on the mainland. The defenses there had already much attention. Now the carriers and gunfire support ships concentrated on them. A holocaust of explosives seared Inchon's hills and waterfront all that long day. For their part, the fast carriers sent strikes on a twenty-five mile radius inland to halt reinforcements.

The transports and LSTs stood in on the afternoon tide, and as H hour of 1730 approached, boated their troops. Bombardment and plane attack intensified until "the whole area for miles was obscured by smoke and debris and burning fires."

While the sun settled low in the west, more than five hundred landing craft churned offshore in the roiled waters. The wild scene became even more lurid when clouds darkened the waning day and rain squalls struck the milling landing craft. Through rain, smoke, fires and mist loomed two of the principal objectives—Observatory Hill and Cemetery Hill.

On Wolmi Do the victorious marines prepared to cross the causeway to assist in the capture of Inchon. The other two battalions of the battle-tried 5th Marines crouched in their boats ready to assault Red Beach north of the causeway. Simultaneously two miles to the south, the 1st Marines, hastily reactivated and rushed to the Far East with scarcely any time for training, waited in amphibian tractors (LVTs).

The Red Beach sea wall "seemed as high as the RCA building." The boats rammed into and held themselves in place with engines ahead slow while scaling ladders banged against the heavy stone wall. Marines scrambled "up and over" in smoke, havoc, and enemy fire. Most defenses had been knocked out, but enough remained to make this no walkover.

Nevertheless, the battle-experienced marines pressed ahead working their way through the town and to the top of the dominating high ground in the final dim light of day and blackness of early evening. Support from afloat continued as they drove inland—air support for over an hour, call fire including starshells through the night.

At Blue Beach mortar fire met the incoming waves and knocked out one LVT before ships' guns knocked it out. Smoke rolled down on the amtracs lumbering along at full waterborne speed of under four knots. Mingling in the gloom with rain squalls, bursting rocket and shell from the ships and the thickening twilight, it formed "an impenetrable mustard-colored haze" over beach and boat lanes. Nevertheless, the first waves crossed some two miles of shallows and landed exactly on schedule.

Without sufficient control boats and with an unexpected cross current setting the slow amtracs to the south, considerable confusion and dispersion resulted for the ensuing waves. But things go wrong in battle, especially so in the incredibly complex details of an amphibious assault. A measure of the true mettle of a fighting unit and of its leaders is ability to adjust rapidly and overcome difficulties on the spot. This the 1st Marines did, and they advanced inland to their D-Day objectives before midnight.

As the first waves hit the beach, LSTs, with the indispensable beans, bullets, vehicles, and fuel headed in and landed at H + 30 minutes. Large, slow, unwieldy, jammed with dangerous combustibles such as ammunition and gasoline, they would ordinarily have come in later, but time and tide would not delay. Mortar, machine gun, and rifle fire plunged into them. Gas ran on deck from punctured gas drums. Ammunition trucks caught fire, but sailors and marines dashed in to quench the blazes.

The plan provided eight LSTs for this first supply attempt in hopes that six would survive. Miraculously, through valor, hard work, astute leadership and good fortune, all eight got in. Through the dark intertidal night, working under brilliant floodlights, the crews and navy and marine parties ashore furiously unloaded. On the dawn tide of the 16th the eight empty LSTs retracted and nine more slid in. So it went for the next several days, the masterful follow-up matching the intricacy of the landing, carefully worked out and brilliantly executed.

In those tense days, supported far inland by naval gunfire and all the way by marine and navy carrier planes, as is their habit, the marines drove on hard, giving the foe no chance to recover his balance. In two days they captured Kimpo airfield, halfway to Seoul to the northeast. Repeatedly repelling enemy counterattacks and storming fortified positions, by the 19th, when the 7th Army Division (landed later by schedule) began to join the front lines, they had reached the outskirts of Seoul's suburbs.

The capital would fall on the 28th after heavy fighting as the enemy poured in reinforcements from the north. Meanwhile to the south, as the 8th Army drove out of the perimeter, the North Korean armies collapsed. Thus in less than a month after the last grave threat to Pusan, an almost overnight giant strike from the sea had turned a war nearly lost into complete rout of the enemy. Inchon was a perfect example of America's need always to hold the sea and of the terrific power that can be concentrated into a massed amphibious attack from it.

General MacArthur truly said, "The amphibious landing is the most powerful tool we have. To employ it properly we must strike hard and deep."

Much else would follow these first three dramatic months of the war. General MacArthur's forces penetrated far to the north in the next few weeks, some reaching the Yalu River border with Manchuria. Then suddenly disaster struck. On November 25, massive Chinese Communist armies, pouring across the border, hit hard at the dispersed and separated American spearheads. Unready for the surprise assault, and with its flanks exposed, the American advance in the west was hurled back with heavy losses.

In this phase the navy and marines distinguished themselves again. The marine division had reached Chosin Reservoir high in the rugged mountains of the north. On "orders from above," they had begun to strike west through almost impassable terrain to link up with the 8th Army when the Chicoms hit.

Surrounded by an overwhelming force of more than sixty thousand men and cut into groups by road blocks, the marines refused to panic. Calling in carrier air support they closed up. Then behind fighters, dive bombers, artillery, and tanks, taking their casualties, prisoners, and equipment with them, they fought their way through freezing weather and blinding snowstorms down the long bitter trail from Chosin to Hungnam. There they were safe. As historian Field wrote, "Again in touch with the friendly sea all things were possible."

One of the epic marches of history, against almost impossible odds, it highlighted again the marine spirit and the navy-marine system of close air support from airfields afloat that could swiftly maneuver to the point of need.

When the decision was made to tighten up the allied front, calling for withdrawal from Wonsan and Hungnam, concentrated naval gunfire and close-in carrier air operations again proved priceless. Faced by day and night attack from these units that supported strong shore artillery fire, the Communist armies made no serious attack even against the evacuation rear guard.

Under this umbrella of protection, the allies evacuated from Hungnam 105,000 troops, 91,000 refugees, 17,500 vehicles, 350,000 measurement tons of cargo.

Significance of Naval Power

With the scientific-technological developments of this century, including aviation and precise long range gunnery, the power of the navy to overcome opposition ashore and to move the United States' total power to and from the beach had become almost irresistible.

But first of all it has to control the sea. This, of course, has been true throughout history. Dr. Field, in closing the pages covering Hungnam and other evacuations on both coasts, puts this truth into perspective over more than 2,000 years: ". . . freedom to come and go depends upon control of the sea. The Athenians at Syracuse, Cornwallis at Yorktown, the Axis forces in North Africa lacked this control. In those armies no one escaped captivity."

After the retreat to the south and then a thrust back again, the allies fought a long, weary siege on the ground in the general area of the 38th parallel with deep advance into North Korea prohibited. They fought "with one arm tied behind the back" since the United States—as today in Southeast Asia—continually made clear that she was not fighting to win. This, of course, encouraged the Communists, who respect only force and firmness and attempt peace only when it is to their advantage to do so.

After suffering severe losses, the enemy finally showed a willingness to come to terms. Armistice negotiations started in the summer of 1951, the United States eagerly anticipating settlement in a few weeks. Not so the Communists. Using the negotiations as a shield for building up force, for propaganda, and for extreme demands that would have meant subservient surrender, they dragged out the talks for two years—preview of Paris talks on Vietnam. The war, likewise, went on, each concession by the United States merely spurring Stalin's minions to hold out for the next one.

In these last years, as in the first, the navy continued busy twenty-four hours a day. Its role was as many-sided as it was indispensable. Its all-pervading influence reached into the lives of every man in little action or large. When navies clash in gigantic battle or hurl troops ashore under concentration of shipborne guns and planes, nations understand that sea power is working. It is not so easy to understand that this tremendous force makes its will felt silently, steadily, irresistibly even though no stirring battles take place.

In Korea the United States and the United Nations stopped aggression (and could have won a clean-cut victory) through the sound exercise of maritime strategy—happily possible for the weakened navy because the Communists lacked power afloat. Control of the sea is only one facet of national strength. However great its contributions, in itself it could not assure victory in the Korean War—or any war. Yet loss of control would have assured defeat. In this war, as throughout the history of our nation, sea power was the foundation for success and salvation against disaster.

7

Approaching Storm of the World?

Aᴠᴛᴇʀ the Korean armistice, which is still an uneasy truce, the belatedly strengthened 7th Fleet continued to function as a mainstay in checking Communist expansion. Crisis followed crisis along the troubled Asian coast. The ability of the fleet to change direction instantly, to concentrate strength swiftly at the point of crisis, and to stay with enduring force after arrival gave the United States singular advantages. Militarily, the Communists could not match them. But intrigue, subversion, and deception in nations near and far, including the United States, enabled them to prolong storm centers and to create new ones.

Many of the crises developed in the Formosa Straits region, where the 7th Fleet served as an insurmountable barrier to invasion of Taiwan. Others erupted in Southeast Asia. Matters took a turn for the worse when the major world powers agreed to divide Vietnam. In the nature of Communist manipulation, this assured even graver troubles in the future.

During this little nation's crucifixion, another unique advantage of sea power manifested itself—the ability to evacuate with ease a multitude of refugees and mountains of equipment. The "Passage to Freedom" began when the first frightened, starving refugees embarked in the USS *Menard* (APA 201) 16 August 1954. From then until July, 1955, in one of the remarkable humanitarian operations of history, the U.S. Navy transported some 40 percent of more than 800,000 refugees and would have helped more to escape except that the Communists prevented it.

These people are a mass indictment of communism. They gave up homes and possessions rather than endure its savage rule. The Berlin Wall serves as evidence that millions like them yearn for freedom behind the iron curtain of the Soviet and satellite frontiers.

Of the U.S. Navy's part in the Passage to Freedom President Ngo Dinh Diem of South Vietnam said: "In the name of all that you have helped, in the name of those who far away are hoping, in the name of all my compatriots whom you have brought south of the 17th parallel . . . with all my heart I thank you."

Since the first warship sailed into the far Pacific in 1800, scarcely a decade has gone by that the United States' warships in the Pacific have not had to respond to a crisis endangering freedom and the rights of men. From World War II on, however, the demands have been unceasing. In the month the Passage to Freedom began, President Dwight D. Eisenhower met Peking's boast that Formosa would be "liberated" like North Vietnam. He reiterated America's promise that the 7th Fleet would block invasion.

The Tachen Islands just off the China Coast and over 200 miles north of Taiwan seemed less important. After discussions Chiang Kai Shek accepted their loss and asked for help in their evacuation, which the 7th Fleet provided in February, 1955.

Directing the operations, Vice Admiral L. S. Sabin said, "We are going in with our muzzle covers on, but we are prepared to go into action" if opposed. This purpose and the power of the fleet are language aggressors understand. On 6 February, the United States had five powerful carriers in the area, with cruisers, destroyers, mine-sweepers, and submarines backing up the amphibians that embarked civilians and the garrison. Dug in only eight miles away, despite bluff and threats, Communist artillery did not open fire.

One cannot remind himself too often that gangsters respect power and the will to use it. And we cannot help but wonder if the United States would have suffered the losses and sorrows of Korea and its aftermath if there had been similar strength sailing in the western Pacific in June, 1950.

Without incident the navy evacuated in a few days all the island population, movable belongings, defense troops, and equipment. The *New York Times* termed it the "most forthright United States action against communism since the Korean War."

It would not be the last such action for the 7th Fleet or for the U. S. Navy elsewhere. Intrigue never rests. In July, 1956, the rumbling Middle East volcano threatened to explode into world war when Egypt's President Gamal Abdel Nasser seized the Suez Canal. Three months later Israel drove into the Sinai Peninsula while England and France half-heartedly invaded from the sea.

The 6th Fleet went swiftly to the scene and carried out Admiral Arleigh Burke's resolute order to "take no guff from anyone" while evacuating Americans and others. Under attack carrier air cover and the guns of heavy warships offshore, destroyers, and amphibious ships, air force transport planes went into Egypt, Israel, and Arab countries to bring out 2,177 Americans and other foreign nationals.

Something of the meaning of ready sea power decisively employed appears in the words of one of the evacuees speaking on board USS *Chilton* (APA 38).

> When we spied the first United States uniform on the dock, we felt wonderful, and when we were finally aboard *Chilton* we felt practically invulnerable. I guess we never realized how much the flag meant to us until we saw it on the stern of the landing craft, and we will never forget how it appeared that night on the *Chilton's* masthead with a spotlight on it.

The swift action of the 6th Fleet did more than bring civilians out of danger. Its appearance and readiness helped to deter the entry of "volunteers" from north of the Caucasus, and the fleet prevented the Soviets from exploiting the explosive situation to greater advantage. Of course it did not prevent continuing Communist subversion and promotion of turmoil. Americans must be reconciled to coping with unceasing problems until the ruling cliques in the U.S.S.R. and China alter their goals.

Jordan and Lebanon

A major Communist takeover attempt disrupted Jordan the following spring. A leftist revolution, street riots, and collapse of governing groups threatened King Hussein's rule. On 24 April 1957, President Eisenhower announced to the world that Jordan's independence was of vital concern to the United States. With this backing and the power afloat nearby, and supported by most of his people, King Hussein on 25 April charged Nasser with backing a conspiracy to oust him. As he spoke the 6th Fleet converged on the eastern Mediterranean, ready to give support if needed.

It could give plenty. Strengthened in those troubled times it could concentrate two carriers, one battleship, two cruisers, and twenty-four destroyers along with submarines, auxiliaries, and an amphibious group with ready marines embarked.

A writer in Britain observed, "Jordan has been saved for Western civilization by Bedouin knives and the 6th Fleet."

Failure at one point does not deter the Communists in their undeviating goal to win the world. Wherever unrest exists—and what nation doesn't have it?—subversion enters to fan the fires. If conditions are favorable and especially if terrorism can weaken the will to resist, disaster threatens. Only a year after Jordan the Communists engineered another crisis in the Middle East. This time it struck the lovely nation of Lebanon, where ancient Phoenicia's maritime power once flourished.

Political differences within the nation offered the opportunity sought by Communists. Threats of overt aggression seemed at the point of unseating the party in power—a favorite gambit, which Communists know how to exploit. The Lebanese government called for help. Turning again to the eastern Mediterranean, the tireless 6th Fleet dramatically appeared almost overnight off this ancient Levantine coast, where navies have shaped history for thousands of years. Some seventy warships, including three attack carriers, raced in.

On 15 July the force, representing America's power and intention, landed its marines at Beirut under massed guns and planes. Once more the Gray Diplomats confirmed a small nation's independence. Mobility and speed of reaction, inherent in fleets, were keys to this success. Another day might have been too late.

As the marines rushed ashore, backed by the rest of the 6th Fleet, the fuse was stamped out before it could trigger the bomb that might have exploded another conflict. U.S. Ambassador Robert McClintock, who handled astutely the diplomacy of this dynamite-filled crisis, stated the case succinctly:

> The American landing in Lebanon and the British air envelopment in Jordan were undoubtedly decisive in preventing the wiping out of the . . . governments by force. . . . The objectives which were achieved were not only in the interests of Lebanon and the United States, but also of the world.

To this might be added the words of Greek Foreign Minister Panayiotis Pipinellis, speaking for millions of troubled people at an earlier time of trial: "In the powerful Gray Diplomats of the 6th Fleet we see the guarantee of small people's independence."

Since the end of World War II, as the Soviets ever probed and fueled agitation, major crises threatening world peace had erupted on the average of once every two years in the eastern Mediterranean alone. By being on hand in international waters, which have no iron curtains, the U.S. Navy had checked each threat. Thus Soviet imperiaism, like Czarist imperialism before it, was blocked from breaking through the Balkans and the Middle East to the Mediterranean and the Indian Ocean. Would the next thirteen years tell the same story?

As the 6th Fleet quenched the Lebanon spark, on the other side of the globe the 7th Fleet trained out its batteries to meet the latest challenge there. In August, 1958, artillery from the Communist mainland opened sustained fire on the offshore Nationalist islands of Quemoy and Matsu. If the hail of shells could interrupt supply across the Formosa Straits, the islands could be seized as a step toward destroying the Nationalists.

Plagued by fear of escalating the conflict and not understanding that bullies play upon this kind of apprehension and the average decent citizen's yearning for peace, many Americans advocated that the islands be abandoned. The timid, irresolute, and disorganized thus become easy prey of ruthless, conniving men. Fortunately President Eisenhower held firm. The 7th Fleet convoyed supplies to the besieged garrison and patrolled within range of the foe's cannon while civilians were evacuated.

More ships arrived. The USS *Essex*, which had helped to settle the Lebanon crisis, now raced to the other side of the world, arriving ready for action on 13 September. Firm purpose thus projected across thousands of miles of ocean again won the day. The Communists relaxed pressure, lost the gamble, and lost face.

Naval Developments

These widespread demands for the fleet to maintain stability and world peace were instrumental in inducing the United States to limit naval cutbacks after the Korean armistice. The fleet stabilized about midway between the disastrous weakness of June, 1950, and the peak buildup in Korea. Although always critically pressed for ships to meet demands, naval leaders wisely continued to budget for research, development, and new construction that produced momentous advances in naval power and an increasing ascendancy of power afloat over that existing ashore.

During the darkest days of the defense cutback, when Louis A. Johnson served as Secretary of Defense, the professional navy had managed to keep research and development moving ahead in a broad spectrum of progress from the ocean depths to the heavens. The modern scientific navy cuts across almost the full range of the American economy. Operating above, under, and on the sea, it demands a scope of engineering, technical, and scientific skills incomprehensible even to most who serve in it. The skills include:

(a) Every aspect of oceanography, hydrography, and operation of ships undersea.

(b) Study and use of sound, light (including laser), magnetic infrared, radio, radar, and other waves in a myriad of devices. In many of these, such as radio and radar, the navy pioneered decades ago.

(c) Engineering of all kinds, including marine, mechanical, electrical, chemical, civil, electronic, aeronautical, and nuclear. In fact, the navy produced the world's first seagoing nuclear propulsion plant.

(d) Amphibious equipment and techniques—from underwater demolition teams, construction of docks, harbors, roads, and airfields to landing and support craft and helicopters.

(e) Explosives, armament, and countermeasures for underseas operations, such as torpedoes, mines, and submarine-guided missiles that will range the world; shipboard guns, torpedoes, and guided missiles to combat air, ship, shore, or submarine attack; and aircraft missiles of every type.

(f) Medicine and medical research of every variety.

(g) Construction of craft that will go miles deep; submarines that will cruise submerged for months; about a hundred types of surface ships; many kinds of aircraft that will land on ship or shore, for duties ranging from antisubmarine to close support of landing forces and attack on any type of target ashore or afloat; satellites reaching into space for communications, navigation, reconnaissance, surveillance, and weather forecasting.

The foregoing list is representative but not inclusive. No other organization in the nation has the complexity or diversity of engineering and technological demands of the navy. Hence it must devote tremendous effort to maintain progress through research and development afloat and ashore. Its various essential establishmnts for this purpose situated in the vicinty of Washington, D. C., alone, for example, comprise a group without parallel anywhere. These establishments —about a dozen in number and working on thousands of projects—have been vital to the navy's progress and the nation's safety. From them, and from numerous other naval activities, industrial plants and universities working on naval contracts have come some of the notable advances of our time—for both defense security and the advancement of the economy.

An outstanding example is radio, which in the early part of the century was controlled predominantly by the navy. Another is radar, with radio, the very keel of space flight, discovered and developed in the United States by the Naval Research Laboratory in Anacostia, Maryland. A later one is nuclear power ship propulsion, from which came the byproduct of nuclear power plants ashore.

The navy took the U. S. government's first halting steps in nuclear energy in 1939 and had made good headway on its own, looking toward nuclear power plants for submarines, when the Manhattan Project was initiated. Thereafter it contributed significantly to this outstanding organization, ship propulsion giving way to the atomic bomb. As one example, its armament experts—military and civilian —developed the ordnance components of the bomb.

With the successful harnessing of atomic energy for explosives, the navy pressed again for its use in ship power but could not get the allocation of effort or uranium pending buildup of the U.S. stockpile of A-bombs—the fatal "single weapon." In 1946 the Chief of Naval Operations (CNO), Admiral Chester W. Nimitz, received clearance to go ahead. Later, he wrote:

> The decision was based in considerable part on a major study completed by Dr. Philip Abelson of Naval Research Laboratory in early 1946. All the foregoing officers were enthusiastic about the prospects. [Vice Admirals Forrest Sherman, Vice CNO; Charles A. Lockwood, Naval Inspector General and World War II commander of submarines in the Pacific; Earle Mills, Chief of Bureau of Ships.] It struck me that if it worked, we would be far in front in the ceaseless race in armed strength to keep our country strong and free.
>
> The fantastic speed and unlimited radius of action offered by atomic power gave promise of at least making possible the submarine with indefinite endurance submerged. Its feasibility had been explored by the navy in the early forties, but the development had been set aside by the war and the single goal in atomic energy of the Manhattan Project. Now was the time to get underway. What remarkable results have followed.

Nuclear Powered Submarine and Guided Missiles

Captain Hyman Rickover was assigned to head the project. In less than a decade thereafter the navy worked with industry to produce a revolution comparable to that from sail to steam. On 17 January 1955, a new seagoing era was launched. There proudly flashed from USS *Nautilus* (SSN 571): "Underway on nuclear power."

The ability of naval operations was now vastly enhanced. In 1958 the *Nautilus* would travel over the top of the world under the polar icecap, and two years later nuclear-powered USS *Triton* would cruise submerged around the world on a 36,000-mile track.

The navy had an ancestor of guided missiles in a robot plane taken to France in World War I. It developed this concept further and in World War II added television control. From this achievement and its highly effective amphibious and aircraft rockets, the next step was guided missiles.

In the early 1950s the antiaircraft missile *Terrier,* with its complex launcher easily developed from the navy's experience with gun turrets, began serving afloat—the United States' first operating guided missile. In the air *Sparrow* and *Sidewinder* led the way in plane-launched guided missiles.

The submarine, of course, had long boasted a guided missile in the torpedo. Now the nuclear submarine would provide the platform for another of the most significant technical deveopments in United States history. Scarcely had *Nautilus's* underway message winged around the world before the navy began considering a seagoing ballistic missile.

With nuclear power the true submarine, with its oxygen, fresh water manufacturing equipment, and air purifier, cruised independent of the atmosphere. Of almost unlimited range and phenomenal speed, invisible under the sea and almost impossible to block, what a deterrent sentinel it could be if armed with a missile carrying a "Sunday punch" nuclear warhead.

Admiral Arleigh Burke, then CNO, assigned Rear Admiral W. F. Raborn to head the project. In less than four years, overcoming numerous apparent impossibilities, the Fleet Ballistic Missile Weapon system became operational, a development unprecedented in peacetime. Named USS *George Washington,* the first of the new revolutionary boats proudly launched her first Polaris missile on 20 July 1960. Far down range it hurtled over a thousand miles precisely on target. America had acquired a new and significant power arm and an important addition to its total defensive posture.

George Washington went on patrol that November, disappearing into the waves with her sixteen nuclear warhead missiles. One by one other submarines followed. The last of the assigned goal of forty-one joined the fleet in April, 1967. Meanwhile, the missile steadily improved so that it can now arch 2,500 miles through the heavens and land on target almost anywhere on earth. As Americans work or play, wake or sleep, these tireless sentinels—unlike shore targets—are immune to sneak attack. They stand guard over the world's oceans.

These undersea cruisers present virtually impossible problems to an aggressor. Hence they have a significant deterrent effect and so far may have given the United States the edge in preserving peace and security from global blackmail. Is this beacon passing with the aggressive Soviet buildup of her navy, whose overwhelming submarine fleet includes a growing number of Polaris type subs?

This sustained buildup may be the result of bitter lessons learned in maritime strategy that the hard-headed Kremlin leaders have espoused. We have already noted how Stalin's creation of a strong defensive navy—while the United States unwisely cut hers to the bone—encouraged the Korean aggression. America's comeback and success in Korea, the Formosa Straits, and the Eastern Mediterranean must have played a part in the next profound alterations in Soviet naval policy. Two momentous changes took place from 1950 to 1958.

The first was Stalin's decision to build a surface and submarine fleet that would give the U.S.S.R. a moderate outward reach. After Stalin's death, natural or arranged, this policy continued. Then in 1956, or the next year or two, a more significant change occurred. The Kremlin deliberations must have taken full account of how the United States had profited in the international trend through use of sea power and decided that two could play the same game.

Furthermore, with Soviet maritime power (naval and merchant) already closing on the United States, why not fish in troubled waters as well as those on the fringe of the Soviet empire? Nikita Khrushchev obviously now made the decision to expand the navy for overseas operations while continuing the expansion of the merchant marine and other segments of sea power.

With world superiority in submarines, he depended upon this awesome armada as the principal striking threat. The force had stabilized at the tremendous number of 350 to 400, constantly being updated by new construction that provides longer range and better design. Joined by the strong cruiser force, numbers of lesser warships and the multiplying merchant marine, Russian power seemed ready to reach farther out into the world, to other continents—even to the threshold of the United States.

Crisis in the Caribbean

Fidel Castro's takeover of Cuba in the mid 1950s, abetted by moral support of deluded Americans who portrayed him as a champion of liberty, gave the Kremlin an opening. Supporting Castro, if not engineering his intrigue, in 1959 Khrushchev saw another gamble frustrated by the U.S. Navy. As ominous signs indicated overseas invasion of Panama, the Organization of American States requested action. The U.S. 2nd Fleet, based at Norfolk and composed largely of ships that alternate in 6th Fleet duty, responded at once. Swiftly it established a sea watch north of this strategic country, where the Panama Canal ranks of first importance to Free World commerce.

World expansion of the Communist octopus troubled world peace sorely in 1960. Newly independent African nations offered fertile fields for intrigue. When violence erupted in the Congo in July, 1960, the Communists were there. Again the U.S. Navy helped to frustrate them. Warships, including the carrier *Wasp,* made their way quickly to Africa's west coast. Transporting troops, supplies, munitions, and fuel, the navy continuously supported the United Nations forces that helped to decide the prolonged struggle. By mid-1963 the Military Sea Transport Service had lifted some 40,000 United Nations troops and thousands of tons of cargo.

Also in 1960, the crisis spotlight turned again on the Caribbean. Castro now seemed on the point of directing invasion into Guatemala or Nicaragua to support Leftist manipulators. Responding to requests from the two governments, President Eisenhower sent warships. Steaming on station and ready twenty-four hours a day (yet in international waters and violating no sovereignty), the fleet sailed, a barrier to invasion. Soon the threat faded, and the ships shifted rudder to other duties.

This storm had scarcely calmed before another broke nearby. Early in 1961 violence raged through the Dominican Republic after the assassination of President Rafael Trujillo. Inciting and thriving on the turbulence, Leftists played an increasing role in the civil strife. By June the disturbance had mushroomed to the point that the lives of thousands of American citizens were threatened.

Again the president directed the ever-active fleet to the storm center. Amphibious ships landed marines in the capital, Santo Domingo, to protect the embassy and U. S. citizens. Some forty ships stood by to block infiltration from Cuba and to rescue civilians if necessary. With plenty of strength quickly on station, maritime power again helped to bring stability to a troubled area.

While this hurricane swept the West Indies, the Soviets fused another bomb over Berlin. The 6th Fleet was rapidly strengthened by some forty reserve ships and patrol and ASW squadrons manned by the 8,000 naval reserves called to duty almost overnight. The Communists stopped the action short of a shooting war, but at this time they built the infamous Berlin Wall. THEY NEVER HAVE PEACE Do THEY?

Never ceasing to probe, the Communist rash broke out next in Southeast Asia. In early 1961 pro-Communist Pathet-Lao bands renewed attacks on the Laotian government. As the attacks expanded, with increasing support from the north, President John Kennedy sent a 7th Fleet task force with 1,800 marines on 12 May to show the nation's feeling that directed subversion should not succeed in overthrowing a small nation. On 16 May the Task Force landed the marines in Laos, and other troops headed there at Thailand's invitation. Once again, through control of the sea, maritime strategy had projected just the right amount of force in time to extinguish a brush fire and then to withdraw quickly, as the marines did in early July.

The trial of trials for the United States, however, came that fall. Suddenly the nation was faced with the specter of Armageddon. In a dramatic televison appearance President Kennedy announced that missile sites secretly developed in Cuba directed disaster toward the Eastern Seaboard.

Photographs taken by reconnaissance planes gave convincing proof of their existence. President Kennedy sent a blunt demand that the launch pads be dismantled, ships en route with missiles recalled, and missiles ashore removed. Again warships gave strength to diplomacy. Responding to the president's quarantine proclamation on "that imprisoned island," ships moved quickly to their stations.

Well before the proclamation took effect on 24 October, ships on patrol in the Caribbean observing the influx of some thirty Soviet and Soviet-chartered ships a month steered to assigned positions off Cuba. Others evacuated dependents from the naval station at Guantanamo, Cuba. Others still raced to what was now the front line of activity. Soon more than 180 warships manned by 83,000 men plus 30,000 embarked marines with full battle equipment cruised ready on the 2,100 mile quarantine frontier encircling Cuba. Among them were eight carriers, with their long, devasting punch.

They were carrying out the spirit of President Kennedy's inaugural address: "Let every nation know that we will pay any price, bear any burden, support any friend, or oppose any foe to assure the survival and success of liberty."

The Kremlin had its answer. The United States had not gone soft. She had the will to stand up to the holocaust of nuclear conflict if that was the only method of preserving freedom. The U.S.S.R. backed down and withdrew missiles—or at least the visible ones.

The Charleston News and Courier summarized well this dramatic crossroads that opened for the United States because of ready strength afloat.

> Perhaps the key lesson of the Cuban crisis is that sea power remains the dominant force in world affairs . . . the deciding factor in the Cold War. This truth should not be overlooked by citizens whose security is being protected at sea.

One would think that the United States by this time had learned her lesson. Surely she at last knew the importance of control of the sea—that her future and the preservation of freedom depended on it. Swift in response, versatile, flexible, capable of concentrating a torrent of power or acting with muzzle covers on, the navy had entered masterfully into America's foreign relations near and far.

Having teetered on the brink of Armageddon, could the nation not perceive that sea power held the key to the struggle with the most immoral and vicious Communist imperialism? Could she not see the menace to civilization in the Soviets' growing maritime strength?

One of the poignant paradoxes of our era is that the United States cannot absorb this lesson, hammered home year after year since the 1940s. Somehow the majority of her citizens and her leaders—who should have more wisdom—cannot understand that in the nuclear age, as ever in the past, sea power remains a potent weapon of overseas diplomacy. It is the ready means of quenching brush fires before they rage uncontrolled. It can block the start of aggression. It is the only means of extending the nation's frontier overseas as the first line of defense in conflict.

President Kennedy said of the Cuban missile crisis:

> Events of October, 1962, indicated, as they have all through history, that control of the sea means security. Control of the seas can mean peace. Control of the seas can mean victory. The United States must control the seas if it is to protect our security.

Yet steadily and inexorably the United States lets this control slip away like the sands in the glass of doom. The sands are running low.

8

Vietnam: Nibbling and Nipping—
How Not to Win

Americans remembered the lessons of Cuba for a time, especially since new need for the versatile fleet erupted near and far. Crises came hard and fast the next year from Haiti to Zanzibar to Southeast Asia. Others followed as we moved into the 1970s, with two main storm breeding centers located in the Middle East and Southeast Asia. These areas flank India and dominate world shipping routes that converge on Singapore and the Suez. Control of either by the U.S.S.R. or her allies would advance the Soviet goal of world communism.

As time passed, the repeated lessons and the extended Vietnam war seemed to weaken rather than to strengthen the will of America's people and to dull the memory of what brought success from Constantinople to Cuba.

If the memory of success was dimmed in Washington, the memory of failure remained vivid in Moscow. To Khrushchev and his officials it was clear that maritime power decides overseas issues. We can date from this period the next stage in the swift expansion of Soviet strength at sea—one of the most significant developments of the post World War II generation.

Americans had every reason, therefore, to keep the lessons of Cuba fresh in their minds, with the knowledge that there was an almost certain chance of a future confrontation. Yet, instead of perceiving in the relentless probing of Communists the need for more vigilance, Americans became complacent as the Soviets lit short fuses under powder kegs. These efforts have strained the endurance of the United States' aging and dwindling fleets.

The enormous mass of Communist China and the U.S.S.R. combined in their aid to North Vietnam has placed a severe burden upon U.S. forces, fighting a war with one hand tied behind their backs. The burden lay particularly heavy on the 7th Fleet. It actually rested upon the whole navy, for fleets and world-wide reserves were drained to support this major war, which did not receive the necessary support from American citizens. Indeed, because of a high percentage of unbalanced news reporting, deluded politicians, and skilled Communist propaganda within and without the United States, citizens have been deceived about the real issues and real events in this stage of the world war for freedom.

The same factors helped to defeat France in the 1950s. Even so, had the United States provided the airplanes, river warships, and other timely military aid (and in far less quantity than employed later), the French might have won. Thus the failure of the United States to exert relatively small force at the right time, along with continuous refusal to believe Communist-stated aims, opened dikes to disaster.

By acquiring North Vietnam in 1954, the Soviets took a long step toward winning Southeast Asia. This first stage was not the end but merely a lever for the next grab. Previously they had had to depend on such guerrilla forces as they could stir up within the country. Meanwhile, arms support from China and the U.S.S.R. was limited by difficuties of land transport. They had half a nation they could regiment under a rule of iron—minus those people permitted to leave—whose homes, businesses, and personal property swelled the state coffers. They had agents and supporters in the South. And in the North they had Haiphong, a key port to which China and the Soviets could ship arms for a major build-up.

Infiltration from the North

In the first years after 1954, assisted by American economic and limited military aid, South Vietnam achieved formidable economic and social gains. In the North, with characteristic Communist tactics, Ho Chi Minh did not abide by agreements. With major outside aid he built a strong war machine. To destroy the stability of the rapidly developing South he greatly increased the number of Communist cells there. The new infiltrators were recruited from some one hundred thousand Communists and other dissidents who went North after the division of Vietnam, leaving behind secret cells operating under Hanoi's orders as a paramilitary political organization. After being trained in revolutionary guerrilla tactics, appropriate individuals among them were returned to their localities with arms and expertise in terror tactics. Masquerading as civil war and deluding most of the West, a campaign of cold-blooded takeover got underway.

Vaguely aware of the onrushing storm, the United States slowly expanded its small military aid mission (which included sixty from the navy and marines in 1960). But this help was a gentle spray compared to the tidal wave prepared by the Communists. South Vietnam did not have a chance unless substantial aid was rendered. Behind the front of dissidents ever present in any nation, the North poured in more infiltrators and agitators. They provided troops with arms and slowly mounted a campaign of terror, sabotage, and unrest in major cities as well as in rural areas. The Communist cells systematically tortured, mutilated, and killed loyal South Vietnam city dwellers, farmers, and local government officials.

Writing in the January–February, 1966, issue of MOWW Review (Military Order of World Wars), Lieutenant General S. T. Williams, USA (Ret.), said: "It is doubtful if there is a single village . . . that has not had two or more mayors beheaded by the Viet Cong since 1956. The more efficient and loyal a mayor and his village council were, the sooner they were killed and their heads stuck up on poles in the village street. . . . The wife was usually disemboweled and left at the foot of the stake."

The Communists murdered or abducted for a worse fate more than one hundred thousand government officials and other community leaders (over twelve thousand in 1962 alone). Hence the basic fabric of government getting underway was demoralized. Called Viet Cong to promote the illusion of civil war and controlled from Hanoi, the cells made the usual promises to the local citizenry such as liberation, land reform, and freedom from taxes.

As the Viet Cong forces developed and improved their organizational structure, they solidified their power. The small hamlet cells funneled through the village, district, and provincial chapters. These reported to regional headquarters with a central committee at the top. Thus a number of ruthless men supplied from Hanoi controlled an increasing percent of South Vietnam's population.

Conditions deteriorated steadily in this rice bowl of Southeast Asia as the Viet Cong and the North Vietnamese infiltrators expanded operations to gut the country.

The assassination of President Ngo Dinh Diem in late 1963 set off a succession of crises and coups. By January, 1964, conditions had so worsened that Secretary of Defense Robert S. McNamara proclaimed: "The situation in South Vietnam continues grave, but the survival of an independent government in South Vietnam is so important to the security of Southeast Asia and to the free world that I can conceive of no alternative other than to take all necessary measures within our capability to prevent a Communist victory."

Those are true and brave words indeed, but unfortunately they were not followed. The United States did take hesitant action but not "all necessary measures within our capability." Instead of leading from the strength of sea superiority and immediately, as in Cuba, setting up a blockade, the U.S. let the enemy call the shots.

Perhaps the government did take what it considered to be sufficient action, but as each buildup occurred, it proved to be too little too late. The cautious approach, chopping off the dragon's tail inch by inch, merely gave the Communists time to cap each move. The Soviet's expanding merchant marine, together with ships from other countries, disgorged a rising flood of war materials into Haiphong. The concentrated smashing strike and blockade of North Vietnam that would have broken the back of the military buildup was never initiated.

In the troubled years since, the United States has checked aggression so far (with the South Vietnamese pulling a strong oar) but at a heavy cost in lives, money, and bitter division within our nation, including massive alienation of the young. This might have been avoided if early strong action based on our navy capabilities had been initiated.

In any event, all that has been done was possible because the United States possessed the power to control the seas—and still does at a perilously reduced margin. Naturally, the first major support to South Vietnam, other than the aid mission, came from warships quickly sailing to key points of need. Though it had responsibilities ranging from the Indian Ocean to the Bering Sea, the 7th Fleet concentrated off Vietnam.

Washington initially restricted the fleet's duties to surveillance by ship and plane of the North and of Communist coastal activity in the South. With this came increased advisors, military aid, and buildup of airfields and port facilities. Ho Chi Minh continued expansion of his forces in the South, and in order to speed up the takeover, he sent in regular army troops for the "final mobile phase."

Tonkin Gulf

Perhaps emboldened by the mild action of the United States, Soviet-supplied PT boats from North Vietnam arrogantly attacked USS *Maddox* (DD-731) on 2 August 1964. The destroyer, patrolling the international waters of Tonkin Gulf, repelled the three boats (which fired torpedoes), sinking one of them. Two nights later *Maddox* again patrolled well offshore with a consort, *Turner Joy* (DD-951).

Again PT boats attacked and were repulsed in a wild night melée; two boats were probably sunk, and others were damaged.

The next day Washington permitted the 7th Fleet to retaliate.* At once planes from the two carriers on station, *Constellation* and *Ticonderoga*, attacked the PT boat bases, smashing most of the boats as well as gasoline storage and shore facilities.

Aggressors respect positive action. The North Vietnamese learned their lesson, but the United States did not. Repeatedly in this generation we have experienced the wisdom of Theodore Roosevelt's wise advice, "Speak softly and carry a big stick." Yet too often in Vietnam we have done otherwise.

The United States quickly resumed its mild program, consistently refusing to play its potent card of blockade. Had the foe been only North Vietnam, the tactic might have succeeded. But no one had any delusions that North Vietnam was anything but a pawn. Beyond North Vietnam lay China and the U.S.S.R.

Increase of the U.S. military mission slowly continued, rising from 16,000 in January, 1964, to some 23,000 from all services a year later. These included 1,100 from the navy, 600 of whom operated the Headquarters Support Activity—Saigon providing common logistic support for all U.S. military in Vietnam. The fleet cruising offshore was manned by more than 20,000 men.

Communists practice terrorism as standard operating procedure. On 10 February 1965 a particularly vicious act occurred (one of a series); its target—Americans. A bomb exploded in the U.S. enlisted men's barracks at Qui Nhon, a port between Saigon and Danang, killing twenty-three men and wounding twenty-two.

Landing at Danang

Mounting terrorism and threat to Danang Airport by North Vietnamese troops caused the United States to advance beyond simple retaliatory air strikes. The navy, with its ready amphibious forces, took the first important step. On 8 March 1965, the 7th Fleet landed 3,500 fleet marines at Danang. They were the first U.S. combat troops to enter Vietnam.

This ready force would have stamped out an ordinary brush fire, but the Communists had lit a thousand different ones, which threatened

---

*Washington controlled too much of the direction of the war. Admiral U.S.G. Sharp, Commander in Chief Pacific (following Admiral H. D. Felt), in his 1968 report observed, "The Vietnam War . . . has been the . . . most centrally controlled, most computerized and most statistically analyzed in history."

to merge into a holocaust. They had refined their Korean tactics. In hamlets, villages, and cities throughout the South burning infection consumed the vitals of the nation from within.

Soon after landing the marines with President Johnson's authorization, Commander 7th Fleet initiated an antiinfiltration patrol off South Vietnam that acquired the name "Market Time," supplementing the limited capacity of the Vietnamese. At the time neither had enough ships available to make it more than a very loose sieve.

On 15 March, likewise with Washington authority, the carriers launched the first nonretaliatory strike. Pilots from *Hancock* and *Ranger*, as usual attacking at close range on military targets, blew up an ammunition depot. A month later *Coral Sea* and *Ranger* planes made the first U.S. Navy strikes against the Viet Cong in South Vietnam. After another month, on 18 May, *Tucker* (DD-875) opened up the first U.S. naval gunfire support of the war.

Thus "all necessary measures" gradually got underway. However, in the long interval before these actions were taken, the enemy had been permitted to accumulate Soviet-Chinese resources to counter and surpass our piecemeal approach.

The United States gradually built up strength based ashore, having in South Vietnam by 31 December 1965, 184,000 men, including 38,000 marines and 8,700 navy and coast guard. By January, 1967, the total ashore had risen to 385,000, including 69,000 marines and 23,500 sailors engaged largely in coastal and riverine operations. Offshore the 7th Fleet sailed, manned by 36,000 more men.

As 1968 began, the number of U.S. servicemen in South Vietnam totaled 486,000, including 32,000 sailors and 78,000 marines. The untiring 7th Fleet offshore showed no increase during 1967, nor would it thereafter. The navy had scraped the bottom of the barrel for ships and men that could be drained from other world needs. Thus four years after McNamara's brave words the United States had forces on hand large enough to get the job done. Prompt and vigorous action in 1964, especially a blockade of the north, would have required only a portion of these forces. As Admiral Sharp said in November, 1969, "The policy of gradualism was the biggest mistake this country has ever made in a war. Had we been allowed to do what we were perfectly capable of doing, the war would have been over long ago."

Nevertheless, he goes on to say, the dawn of 1968 saw the beginning of the end. "We had that country licked." Yet in the next months, at the point of military victory, U.S. diplomacy changed course to abandon much of our hard-won advantage. I shall discuss this incredible action later. Meanwhile, what had the navy and marine files contributed to check and reverse the Communist tide?

Perhaps we can best give some idea of their decisive influence by examining separately some of their many complex functions. Carrier air, involved early, makes a good starting point.

Carrier Task Force Operations

Flying day and night in fair weather and foul off rolling, pitching decks, naval aviators played a giant role in the war. With their long reach inland and the ability to speed the mobile fields close to the target, the impact of the planes available was multiplied several times. Out of some five attack carriers available for the western Pacific, on the average three cruised constantly off Vietnam after mid-1965. Operating a total of under 250 planes, these three conducted about 40 percent of the air effort in the war zone. Supersonic reconnaissance planes from carriers and patrol squadrons photographed all of North Vietnam. In July, 1965, the A-6A Intruders (first effective all-weather tactical combat plane in any nation) joined the fray from the carrier decks.

Carriers on station would launch up to ten thousand combat or combat support sorties a month. When the situation became tight ashore, pilots often flew three sorties a day. They concentrated on enemy troops, arsenals, ammunition and fuel depots, bridges and trucks on lines of communication, radar, and gun and missile sites. Joined with the air force flying from a complex of fields in Southeast Asia, they hampered enemy activity to the point that the Communists were limited to only sporadic large-scale attacks. When these occurred, carrier planes helped to shatter them. Naval training in precise dive bombing and close support often stood the marines in good stead, as in 1968 during the seige of Khe San. A carrier steamed close into the Demilitarized Zone (DMZ). Along with the air force and the marine and army artillery the carrier's planes repeatedly smashed the enemy's troop and materiel concentration. The marines bled the North Vietnamese armies white in a seige that could not become another Dien Bien Phu because we maintained control of the sea and the air.

As a result of the fleet's system of inimitable underway replenishment at sea, the carrier task force could operate almost indefinitely. Day and night, service force ships steamed alongside, pumping fuel, transferring munitions, food, and medical supplies by highline and helicopter. Often high speed launch and recovery of planes on combat strikes proceeded simultaneously with replenishment from ships maneuvering alongside.

In June, 1965, MIGs made the mistake of attacking a navy flight and lost their first two planes. In the sky duels that followed over the years the navy won about 80 percent. Its Sparrow and Sidewinder missiles proved deadly. Besides F-4 Phantoms and other naval developments, these two missiles became standard also with the air force.

Antiaircraft guns and missiles inflicted the principal losses upon our carrier planes. Given years to introduce them and unhampered sea shipment into Haiphong, the Soviets provided massive antiaircraft defenses around important targets. Surface to Air Missiles (SAMs) streaked at the planes when they flew high; gunfire poured at them when they cruised low to avoid the missiles. In late 1966, after much pleading from the Pacific, Washington finally let gunfire ships operate north of the DMZ (for a few degrees). This not only hampered the foe's logistics, but it also reduced hazards to the planes and losses from the coastal radar, gun, and missile sites, which were then systematically blasted by the ships.

Then, in 1968, on the verge of victory, the United States unilaterally pulled her punches, ending both gunfire and bombing north of the DMZ. Swiftly enemy infiltration and the flow of materiel to North Vietnamese and Viet Cong forces increased as we relaxed our military pressure.

Surely no war has ever been fought with so many restrictions placed on the field commanders by one side while uninhibited destructive acts took place on the other. Blockade, the easiest and least costly means, would have throttled Ho's forces. This power having been surrendered, the next easiest was to strike the lines of communication at their source in Haiphong after the transfer of war supplies from Soviet and Chinese ships. The difficult way was to try to check the flow after it had fanned out to the south.

Buckling under the latest restrictions, the carriers continued to operate in 1969 and 1970. Their planes mounted thousands of attacks each month over the mountains, with necessarily reduced loads and reduced time on station because of flight distances involved. They continued to restrict Communist capabilities but obviously to a lesser degree.

Only love of country, understanding of the evils Communists perpetrate upon peoples who fall prey to them, and a keen sense of responsibility to future generations led these valiant men and their opposite numbers in the air force to their lonely flights against enemy installations.

Some Principal Naval and Marine Commanders in the Pacific Operationally Involved in the Vietnam War June 1964-January 1971.

CINCPAC

Adm Ulysses S. G. Sharp .... 30 Jun 64-31 Jul 68
Adm John McCain .... 31 Jul 68-

CINCPACFLT

Adm Thomas Moorer .... 26 Jun 64-30 Mar 65
Adm Roy L. Johnson .... 30 Mar 65-30 Nov 67
Adm John J. Hyland .... 30 Nov 67-30 Nov 70
Adm B. A. Clarey .... 30 Nov 70-

COMSEVENTHFLT

Vadm Roy L. Johnson .... 11 Jun 64-1 Mar 65
Vadm Paul P. Blackburn, Jr. .... 1 Mar 65-7 Oct 65
Radm Joseph W. Williams (acting) .... 7 Oct 65-13 Dec 65
Vadm John J. Hyland .... 13 Dec 65-6 Nov 67
Vadm William F. Bringle .... 6 Nov 67-10 Mar 70
Vadm Maurice F. Weisner .... 10 Mar 70-

CHNAVGP/COMNAVFORV

Capt William H. Hardcastle .... 31 Jan 64-10 May 65
Radm Norvell G. Ward .... 10 May 65-27 Apr 67
Radm Kenneth L. Veth .... 27 Apr 67-30 Sep 68
Vadm Elmo R. Zumwalt .... 30 Sep 68-14 May 70
Vadm Jerome H. King .... 14 May 70-

SERVPAC

Radm W. D. Irvin .... 2 Apr 63-20 Jul 65
Radm Edwin B. Hooper .... 21 Jul 65-17 Feb 68
Radm W. V. Combs, Jr. .... 17 Feb 68-Aug 69
Radm L. J. O'Brien .... Aug 69-

CG III MAF

BGEN Frederick J. Karch .... 8 Mar 65-6 May 65
MGEN William R. Collins .... 6 May 65-4 Jun 65
MGEN Louis W. Walt .... 4 Jun 65-9 Feb 66
MGEN Keith B. McCutcheon .... 9 Feb 66-28 Feb 66
LTGEN Louis W. Walt .... 28 Feb 66-31 May 67
LTGEN Robert E. Cushman, Jr. .... 11 May 67-25 Mar 69
LTGEN Herman Nickerson, Jr. .... 25 Mar 69-9 Mar 70
LTGEN Keith B. McCutcheon .... 9 Mar 70-

(Commander U.S. Military Assistance Command Vietnam [COMUSMACV] directing all forces in Vietnam were General William Westmoreland, 20 June 1964 to 3 July 1968, and his relief, General Creighton Abrams.)

The service of Lieutenant Commander Wilmer P. Cook, USN, highlights the shining achievements of hundreds of thousands of young men who have served valiantly in Vietnam, afloat, ashore, and in the air.

A 1956 graduate of the U.S. Naval Academy, young Cook soon won his wings at Pensacola. In 1966, flying from USS *Constellation* on his first Vietnam tour he received a Distinguished Flying Cross. After ordering the other flyers aloft, he singlehandedly entered "the envelope area" and destroyed a missile site.

After 120 missions he returned home for shore duty. Then because of the need for pilots he and others received orders to return to the war zone. He could have resigned.

When his wife asked him why he returned, he said, "I don't believe you would have any respect for me if I did not go back."

To his parents he said, "I'll always go where my country sends me and will always do whatever it asks. Perhaps what I am doing may keep my two sons from going to war."

On this cruise of approximately 300 missions the heroic pilot time after time chose the point of greatest danger to protect his fellow pilots. Just before Christmas, 1967, he was lost while leading an attack. His father's sad but proud account of his son's service ends with these words:

"While he loved his family, relatives, and friends very deeply, he put his country first. . . . In these troubled times . . . we can take some heart that from Washington's time until now, there have always been men to offer their lives for the preservation of freedom."

INDEED THEY HAVE, 500.000 OF THEM TO A COUNTRY OF 10.000.000.

"The Marines Have Landed"

Throughout America's history the spirit of man has shone like a beacon high above the mists of imperfect human nature. Every generation has produced not just the few who stand out but a host of gallant souls. It should encourage the United States that never before have more individual acts of heroism, dedication, faith, human kindness, and selfless sacrifice illumined her history than by Americans fighting in the Vietnam War.

This has been true of all elements of her forces. Accordingly, as you read about the sailors and marines to whom these pages are devoted, know that their valor and patriotism simply reflect those of most Americans there. For all but a handful of marines this began with the landing of the 3,500 at Danang in March, 1965. Later came the navy's Seabees, as usual building and fighting at the same time, to help make Danang one of the great ports of the Far East. Meanwhile, other landings followed to set up bases at Phu Bai, some forty-five miles to the north, and Chu Lai, sixty-five miles to the south.

The marines, anchored safely in the sea, characteristically hit hard and with success. They received powerful support far inland from naval gunfire, which the Communists could not withstand. Farther inland carrier aircraft often provided close support and constantly gave indirect aid in hitting troop concentrations, munition dumps, and transportation routes.

They had landed in the frontier I Corps area. A series of fire fights soon routed the Communists and reversed their sweep to victory. They also rooted out the Communist cells, the Viet Cong apparatus that had terrorized the inhabitants into submission. In ever broadening perimeters they forced the enemy back into the mountains and established an environment of safety and hope where decent government could function.

Terror and Pacification

The average American has no comprehension of the diabolical methods practiced by the Communists to intimidate and rule. Scarcely a day went by in the 1960s that the organized network of Communist cells did not assassinate, abduct, torture, and terrorize the local populace in various parts of South Vietnam. If they missed the head of the family, a common practice was to mutilate the wife or one of the children.

For example, in one village a marine was talking with the worried father and mother of seven children, trying to ease their fears. One of their little boys had been missing several days. This was shortly before the national elections, which the Communists were trying to disrupt. As they talked they heard a noise.

The little boy came running, crying, just freed by the Viet Cong. Both of his hands had been cut off. Around his neck there hung a sign, "If you dare to vote, this or worse will happen to all of you."

Similar reports came in constantly. Tens of thousands of South Vietnamese suffered wounds, brutal torture, or death. Where are the reporters and television announcers to damn this mass barbarity? No wonder so many Americans are deceived about the Vietnam conflict and do not comprehend the terror that could some day assail even the United States.

Wracked by such evils, South Vietnam could not help but encounter problems beyond its control. The perimeter pacification followed by the marines and other troops in South Vietnam has meant much to the people in providing them with an environment of law and order and freedom from daily terror. The method was effective. Before dawn the marines and South Vietnamese troops would throw a cordon around a village. They assembled all hands, screened them individually, removed them briefly to a compound for medical treatment and issuance of identity cards. Viet Cong trying to flee were caught by the cordon. Those hiding were rooted out. Wells were favorite hiding spots.

The Viet Cong would dig into the side of the well, below the water level, then tunnel up a short distance and hollow out a cave to hold two men. With an air conduit built into the well just above the water level they seemed to have a perfect hiding place. When the marines surrounded the village the Viet Cong dived into the well. Tear gas often worked to rout them out.

By 1968 the Communist hold in South Vietnam was rapidly weakening. The future forecast swifter decline as U.S. power at last began to be applied in strength and as the Communists lost the people. Accordingly, in January, 1968, during the truce they called for the Lunar New Year (TET), the Communists desperately tried to recoup.

In the middle of the truce they made nationwide attacks in cities and many smaller communities to destroy the sound civilian leadership that had revived in the pacified areas. (The section concerning naval operations in the Delta will more fully cover this deliberate campaign to shatter the reviving internal strength of South Vietnam.) The chaos that the North Vietnamese and their Viet Cong allies expected was calculated to discredit the government, cause widespread desertions from the army, and increase opposition to the war in the United States.

It is sufficient to mention at this point that the Communists surpassed even themselves in atrocities, including mass shooting of civilians and liquidation of groups as in the planned and systematic killings at Hue. Here they killed in three stages: first, murder of people on the "black list"; second and third, liquidations in an effort to leave no witnesses. In mid-1970 reports indicate that 2,810 bodies were found in or near Hue, with 1,940 people missing.

Pacification slowed during the heavy influx of North Vietnamese troops during 1967, and the TET offensive also set the program back. But by the summer of 1968, when they had suffered such heavy losses that the Communists could no longer sustain widespread large unit fighting, they must have been gratified indeed to see the United States pull her punches. Since then they have recovered losses and rebuilt decimated divisions.

However, pacification has continued so that at the end of 1970 perhaps 90 percent of the South Vietnamese could be considered to be living in relative security—certainly to the extent that an American citizen enjoys walking many streets of his capital and other large cities at night. Of the remaining 10 percent, part is contested with the foe. Viet Cong control exists predominantly on and near frontiers.

In 1971 terrorist activities are by no means ended. Rocket attacks, bombs set off in cities, assassinations—these have not been stopped, and perhaps never can be.* But the controlling internal apparatus has been largely smashed, and we can hope that it can never be revived.

Thus the Communists failed to win the war in South Vietnam. Tragically their campaign to triumph in the United States had more success. Massive propaganda, subversion, and misinformation, fed by the Communists and dispersed by the press, raised a tide of misguided dissent—much of it among the general populace, the activist segments of our youth, and numerous public opinion leaders. Many individuals were motivated by sincere convictions; others were merely following the popular tide.

It is not inconceivable that the Communists and their sympathizers can win the war in Vietnam right in the United States and from there, the larger goal of the world. And here they will win if the United States loses its determination to see the salvation of South Vietnam through to the end—if it refuses to follow President Kennedy's inaugural words: "Let every nation know that we shall pay any price, bear any burden, support any friend, or oppose any foe to assure the survival and success of liberty."

Amphibious Ready Groups

To support the military campaign and pacification programs the 7th Fleet formed two small amphibious ready groups. Each consisted of an LPH (helicopter carrier) with a marine battalion landing team and a helicopter squadron embarked, along with other amphibious ships and fire support ships as needed, until their last landing in September, 1969. They operated in conjunction with the marines and other troops ashore or in separate surprise assaults from the sea, speeding ashore by helicopter and boat.

The first landing was made at Danang in I Corps area to protect the key airfield there. Cruising day and night over the horizon, the amphibious ships would steam in to put the marines ashore in some seventy other landings from the DMZ to the Mekong Delta. These actions trapped the Viet Cong and North Vietnamese, destroyed bases in isolated areas, and quickly reinforced embattled allied troops.

Often the enemy "high tailed into the boondocks," abandoning

---

*According to the Secretary of the Interior, even the U.S. had 4,330 bombing incidents from 1 January 1969 to 15 April 1970 that caused loss of life or damage, and a third more attempted incidents.—*U.S. News & World Report,* 3 August 1970.

bases, munitions, and stores without a struggle in preference to meeting naval gunfire and the hard-hitting marines. In other cases they were trapped and overwhelmed. One of these encounters took place several miles south of the frontier near Quang Tri on 20 July 1967. Storming ashore, the landing force struck the exposed flank of an enemy battalion. Hastily abandoning supplies, the foe faded inland. But there they ran into a South Vietnamese force that stood fast and decimated the Communist battalion.

The battleship *New Jersey* joined the war in 1968; her giant sixteen-inch projectiles roaring to targets up to twenty miles away sorely hurt the enemy. Damaging hits wrecked the Communists' strongest concrete bunkers. On 10 October, seventy-five miles north of the DMZ, in a heavy downpour of the monsoon rains, *New Jersey* brought fortified munitions storage caves under fire. Air spotters from carriers later reported access roads cut and cave entrances closed.

In a later instance, as the battleship supported the marines battling the Communists in their heavily fortified "neutral" DMZ, a spotter exulted: "You may not believe this, but the first round destroyed two fortifications."

Though she operated primarily off the DMZ, where the need was great, on occasion, when situations required her special capabilities, she ranged the coast firing missions from as far as 270 miles south of the frontier to 145 above—the prescribed limit.

On the shores of Tripoli long ago and for generations since the marines have performed gallant acts in naval and national history. Yet none of these has been brighter than those in Vietnam. And no period has glowed with as many individual courageous exploits as those that occurred in the countless small-unit patrols as well as in the thousands of larger actions from 1965 to 1971. Sacrifice for others—both the natives and their own fellow marines—has been as common a virtue as valor. For example, time after time men have thrown themselves on live enemy grenades in order to give their lives for their comrades.

Some have so offered their lives and survived. On 27 October 1969, Staff Sergeant Victor J. Guerra was returning with his men from patrol. A grenade landed in front of them. Shouting a warning to the others, he threw himself on the grenade and remained on it until the marines had taken cover. Then rising to his knees, he grabbed the grenade and hurled it away. It exploded harmlessly.

In their almost innumerable operations the marines have suffered grievous losses, but they continue to face them courageously to serve the United States and the oppressed South Vietnamese people. Over forty thousand volunteered to extend tours in the war zone. Even wounded youths have asked to return.

Home from one of his visits to the fronts, General Wallace M. Greene, then Commandant USMC, stopped in Japan and visited wounded marines evacuated to the U.S. Naval Hospital at Yokusaka. One of them asked for "mast" (naval term for a session with the commanding officer) with the general.

"So I went over to this boy," General Greene related. "He was badly wounded in the stomach and in one leg . . . so badly hurt that he couldn't sit up in bed. . . . He couldn't speak very loudly, so I bent over. And he said to me: 'General, I know I'm going to be all right. It's going to take a few weeks, and I have just one thing to ask you, and this is that, when I'm able to walk, I want to return to my unit.' "

Naval Gunfire Support

Naval gunfire support, which began in May, 1965, quickly won the affection of every man it served—and the respect of the foe, who dreads nothing more than the precise fire of naval guns. The number of ships on the firing line increased until no more could be spared from the fleets thinly spread around the world. By 1967 the force could average one or two cruisers and about a dozen destroyer types and rocket ships on the line at any one time. Smaller ships in Market Time antiinfiltration patrol likewise participated with their lighter guns.

One of the fast moving warships with spotters overhead or on the ground might knock out a mortar concentration. Answering an urgent call, she might then speed twenty miles up the coast to save a trapped patrol, steam a similar distance to breech a fortified position holding up troop advance, and move to another area to place a Viet Cong troop under fire. All this might take place in one day. Then that same night star shells would be sent arching out over the jungle to expose infiltrators.

The targets might be close inshore, where rapid fire small guns added to larger weapons, or far inland. The eight-inch cruisers' main battery often reached up to fifteen miles inland to knock out fortifications and clear the way for troop advance or to check a Communist attack. At Hue during the 1968 TET offensive, cruiser gunfire was called in from the sea to obliterate defenses that had resisted other attacks.

Although they could take on many scattered missions daily, there were never enough ships for the troops ashore. As we have seen, *New Jersey's* arrival on the line in September, 1968, brought one mighty addition; but in April, 1969, she sailed home, and in the name of economy the powerhouse returned to moth balls.

During any one year the busy warships fired many thousands of missions, supporting troop and militia units along the long water-laced coast. A great number were not spotted, developing from sudden emergencies for small patrols or village pacification teams. Hence many salvos landed harmlessly in the boondocks. Nevertheless, the cumulative effect of these bombardments was devastating to Communist hopes. As the tempo relaxed in 1969–1970, long-established coastal cells of Viet Cong were largely rooted out, and infiltration through the rugged mountains was severely impeded.

One mission of the destroyer *John W. Thomason* shows why this was so. With an airborne army spotter the destroyer began to pump shells into a pass suspected of shielding a concentration of Viet Cong. The spotter directed the fire on the Viet Cong headquarters at the end of the trail, then into the foliage-covered camp, which was located in an inlet. After the first salvos "columns of water and shattered boats" shot into the air. "Three large secondary explosions were . . . followed by a tremendous fireball," and the camp was gone—forty-five buildings and twenty-five boats.

Operation Sea Dragon

"Sea Dragon" was an extension of naval gunfire support into North Vietnam. It began 25 October 1966, initially to strike at the coastal boat traffic—reluctant partial acceptance by Washington of the wisdom of using sea power against the hostile coast. Cincpac gained authority to extend operations only half a degree of latitude at first, then another timid thirty miles, then another somewhat larger extension. Two destroyers started the ball rolling. They were limited to a twelve-mile belt of water offshore for operations against coastal traffic and prohibited from firing on targets ashore unless fired upon!

On 27 February 1967, the ante was raised to the 20th parallel, three degrees above the border, still well short of Haiphong, where means of war poured in from the sea. One cruiser and four destroyers (one often Australian) now made up the average Sea Dragon force. In fair weather and foul, during daylight and dark, they cruised off the coast, restricting the flow of war materials southward and reducing the hazards to carrier pilots flying inland to attack military targets. Destruction of coastal radar and gun and missile sites saved many pilots and planes.

Route 1 in both Vietnams runs generally close to the coast. Paralleling it, heavy boat traffic carries munitions and other materials shipped from Haiphong, the port of entry. At Dong Hoi many craft go inland up the river to ship again by truck, bike, and backpack. Thus begins the Ho Chi Minh trail that winds through Laos in blatant violation of neutrality.

Sea Dragon ships performed with singular effectiveness, knocking out thousands of boats. In their allowed zone of operations they almost eliminated the sea and Highway 1 as usable routes. In August, 1967, they destroyed or damaged 261 logistic boats and bombarded more than 630 fixed or moving targets ashore. Thus they drove most of the logistic flow inland, beyond gun range. This required greater enemy manpower, and it slowed and reduced the flow of supplies and reinforcements to Communist troops in the south. And indirectly it saved American lives.

By late 1967 the Communists were really suffering. Their Viet Cong intrastructure was crumbling. Their concentrated military effort had failed. Hence in early 1968 they made two desperate gambles: the TET offensive and the mass effort to overrun the marines at Khe San near the DMZ-Laos frontier. Both failed.

If the United States had pressed her advantage, then the war might have been brought to a quick end. Instead, on 1 April 1968, she sharply reduced the area of North Vietnam that bombers could attack and ordered Sea Dragon to pull back to the 19th parallel. These restrictions had the desired effect of bringing the Viet Cong to the conference table. (The word "conference" is a misnomer. They have never intended to confer but merely to use the meetings for vituperation and as a sounding board for propaganda.)

Then on 1 November the United States cut back further without any quid pro quo, canceling Sea Dragon and all bombing north of the DMZ. This show of good will and readiness to end hostilities brought no concessions from the North Vietnamese. They naturally scorned America and interpreted the moves as proof of weakness. They simply hardened their line at the peace talks.

Fortunately gunfire support continued on South Vietnam's coast. The cumulative results brought more and more security so that Communist capabilities there steadily weakened during 1969 and 1970. The effect on fighting forces ashore is perhaps best summarized in a marine corporal's comment:

"I have seen the *New Jersey* fire, and I can tell you that the marines find it a great comfort to know that if we ever needed her, we could have her. I can say that I slept a little better knowing that she was around."

Market Time

Other naval operations offshore and inshore likewise helped to reverse the tide. The establishment of "Market Time" in March, 1965, to check infiltration by sea had great results. While steering shy of enforcing a blockade of the North that would have eased all problems, the United States took the second best step—tight patrol of South Vietnam.

For some time the South Vietnamese Navy had maintained a modest coastal surveillance, with U.S. Navy advisors participating. But they had too few ships, and the Communists continued to infiltrate munitions and men by sea. The cordon needed faster and better patrol craft. It needed patrol planes flying night and day on an outer detection barrier well at sea.

Patrol planes flew in. Radar picket ships arrived along with smaller warships, including coast guard cutters operating in war under the navy. Budget restrictions slowed the buildup until it became clear that the Communists were still running substantial support through the line. Then the navy got the money to do the job properly.

More vessels arrived, including numerous "Swift" boats, a new fifty-foot speedy class. These craft, capable of operating across the shallows inshore, eighty-two-foot coast guard cutters, and South Vietnamese Navy boats formed the inshore barrier. The offshore patrol included a few destroyer escorts, minesweepers, LSTs, gunboats, and large high endurance coast guard cutters. The navy's incomparable patrol planes flew seaward.

Before 1965 the Viet Cong received most supplies by sea. By the start of 1967, the Market Time force had grown large enough to maintain about 115 vessels on station, plus the South Vietnamese craft. With patrol planes ranging far offshore to track suspicious larger ships, the barrier line in depth cut infiltration to a trickle. Evidence of the effectiveness showed strikingly in 1968 when the enemy tried to recoup their large munitions losses during TET by running in four shiploads. Market Time ships destroyed three craft that got inshore and turned back the fourth, not being allowed to take it in international waters.

Thousands of junks and sampans daily navigate the watery maze of South Vietnam's long coast, as the normal means of transport and communications, as well as fishing. Thus the Market Time sailors found no dearth of jobs. During 1968 alone they boarded or inspected alongside more than 500,000 junks and sampans—and these were only the ones that seemed sufficiently suspicious out of the million sighted. They captured many infiltrators, quantities of munitions and supplies. Along with the South Vietnamese Navy they deserve much of the credit for turning the tide to victory.

In addition, swiftly bringing their guns to the point of decision when needed, the ships and craft effectively supported operations ashore. Time after time along the coast and in waterways they routed enemy attackers and saved a beleaguered outpost. They supplemented the naval gunfire support ships and aircraft regularly to operate with the forces ashore.

In 1969–1970, after training Vietnamese sailors on the job (and many at navy schools in the United States), the U.S. Navy transferred most of the vessels to them. The steadily developing South Vietnamese Navy operates them well.

Inland Sea Power Cuts a Broad Wake

Also in 1965 the navy began forming the first units of the Brown Water Navy, which would have a marked effect in breaking the enemy's iron grip in the 5,000-mile maze of rivers, inlets, canals, and swampy watercourses that intermesh like a sieve in the rich Mekong Delta.

The waterways serve as roads through the wet fields, dense jungles, mangrove and nipa palm swamps at the mouths of the Mekong and adjacent Rung Sat, or "Forest of Assassins."

This large, dark region, well deserves its name. Athwart the main ship channel to Saigon, it harbored pirates for centuries before the Viet Cong. The Communists roamed the area at will, concentrating on taking over the vast rice bowl of the Mekong—most coveted food producing region in Asia—for sustenance, for recruits, and for ease of receiving munitions by sea.

The navy's first value to the United States is that it keeps an enemy's main force overseas. It controls the oceans for her use, denies them to the foe, and makes his coasts the frontier of war rather than those of America. Nor does it stop there. Sea power projects the nation's total power like a resistless tide inland beyond the coast. It reaches inshore with guns, with carrier planes—if need be with missiles such as Polaris—and wherever water will float a boat, as in the case of Game Warden.

In the spring of 1966, the navy established Task Force 116, the River Patrol Force entitled Operation Game Warden. This expanded the Market Time operations into the watery inland region. The South Vietnamese Navy, with American advisors, the police, and customs force, had tried to check the Viet Cong use of the river roads. But their limited resources could only nudge the problem.

Now the U.S. Navy brought proper craft manned by enterprising sailors to help carry out the herculean task. Shore bases were set up, and mobile bases were installed on LSTs.

Taking a thirty-one-foot fiberglass yacht hull, the navy quickly fitted warship "insides and topsides" and had the boats operating on the Mekong within a few months. Bugs worked out in operations led to a Mark II boat that proved outstanding. Speedy, with water jet propulsion that drives them at twenty-five knots and more, they can turn in their own length. Of shallow draft they can swim in knee-deep puddles. They are formidable in combat with twin .50 caliber machine guns forward, a 7.67mm machine gun and 40mm grenade launcher amidships, a .50 caliber aft, and for unusual missions, special weapons like a 90mm recoilless rifle. Flotation gear keeps the boats afloat even if riddled by bullets. Holes in the hull can often be patched with "a brush and a bucket of goop."

At both shore and mobile bases heavily armed helicopters—"Seawolves"—joined the team to add long vision, speed and striking power. "Seals" also joined — Sea-Air-Land Intelligence and Reconnaissance teams. These navy counter-guerrillas passed rigid training as parachuters, frogmen, and jungle infiltrators. Skilled clandestine operators, they penetrated hidden Viet Cong bases by water, air, and land and defeated the foe at his own game.

Together the teams blocked known enemy routes, supported and expanded the operations of the South Vietnamese, carried out constant inspection of boat traffic similar to those of Market Time offshore. The flood of native boats even surpasses that along the coast. They are the autos, trucks, trains, and mules of this land where the waterways are the highways. In an average good weather month the Game Wardens inspected well over 100,000 junks and sampans out of perhaps a quarter million sighted. Old Vietnam hands say a junk is a boat in which a caribao can stand athwartship; when he has to stand fore and aft, it's a sampan.

In 1968 Task Force 116 grew to a point where it consisted of some 250 river patrol boats (PBR), and some began to be turned over to the Vietnamese. That year Game Warden and Market Time sailors inspected more than a million boats out of two to three times that many sighted.

By disrupting Viet Cong movements, throwing him constantly off balance, and interrupting his supplies (flowing in through Cambodia), the River Patrol Force made large gains. These especially benefited the civilian population. They had endured Viet Cong tyranny virtually unchallenged for years in this watery region that demanded "control of the sea" by a large force to insure peace.

With these increasing responsibilities the navy established a new flag command, Commander Naval Forces Vietnam, to coordinate and direct naval activities based in Vietnam. Rear Admiral N. G. Ward laid a sure foundation, on which Rear Admiral K. I. Veth built splendidly. The job grew to such an extent that it became a three-star billet, held by Vice Admiral E. R. Zumwalt, who in July, 1970, catapulted from the Mekong to the Potomac as Chief of Naval Operations.

ComNavForV had manifold duties. Under his administration came: (a) naval advisors who helped build, train, and equip the South Vietnamese Navy. (b) Seabees constructing for the military and the civilian economy.* (c) Navy Medical Corps ashore. There, from the battle front to Danang and offshore in hospital ships they cared for sailors and marines. Along with most Americans in Vietnam, they gave themselves freely to help the populace—providing medicine and hospital facilities, helping in hospitals, sending teams regularly into hamlets that had never known medical care. (d) Naval Support Activities Saigon and Danang, which handled navy and marine logistics that at Danang in the critical frontier I Corps furnished common support to all forces in the zone. By 1948 these totalled more than 200,000. (e) Naval shore-based air operations such as patrol planes in Market Time and ASW surveillance. (f) Market Time, Game Warden, Mobile Riverine Force, and Sea Lords.

Admiral Nimitz said correctly of Iwo Jima, "Uncommon valor was a common virtue." This has been true also of countless Americans in the Vietnam War, but none more so than in the several riverine navies. Heroes sailed out daily. Valiant, dedicated, ingenious, and skilled, they represented Americans at their best. Their exploits may be illustrated in the battle for which James E. Williams BM 1/c USN, deserved and received the Medal of Honor.

Stocky and rugged, modest but self-reliant, Bosun Mate Williams inspired confidence. Boat captain of PBR 105, with another boat in company, Williams was suddenly taken under fire by two sampans. If they thought to kill the sailors or lead them into a fatal ambush, they miscalculated.

Instantly returning the fire, the PBRs wiped out the crew of one sampan. The other fled into an inlet. Pursuing, the PBRs ran into a hail of small arms fire close aboard from concealed troops. Then they met head-on two junks and eight sampans. The ambush was complete. They were trapped, but only temporarily. In the savage battle that ensued, Petty Officer Williams, with disregard for his own safety, exposed himself to the withering hail of enemy fire to direct counterfire and inspire the actions of his patrol.

---

*Commander Service Force Pacific Fleet, Rear Admiral E. B. Hooper, during the hectic buildup years played a significant role in the success of these units. He provided men, money, boats, equipment, and exercised command responsibilities, except operational control. Other type commanders, such as Commander Aircraft Pacific Fleet and Commander Amphibious Forces Pacific Fleet, had similar duties covering units under their cognizance.

Calling for Seawolves, Williams maneuvered to clear the ambush but in doing so caught sight of an even larger concentration of boats. Without waiting for the armed helicopters Williams boldly attacked before the enemy could disperse. Fearlessly, he led the patrol through intense fire to destroy or damage fifty enemy sampans and seven junks.

When the Seawolves were in sight, Williams in the tradition of the sea gave terse instructions: "I want y'all to go in there and hold field day on them guys."

Night was falling, but Williams refused to quit. Braving the increased hazards, he turned on the boat's searchlights and closed the beach to complete the rout of the enemy. The citation he so well deserved ends with these words: "His extraordinary heroism and exemplary fighting spirit in the face of grave risks inspired the efforts of his men to defeat a larger enemy force, and are in keeping with the finest traditions of the United States Naval Service."

Mobile Riverine Force

The PBRs, light and speedy, had as their primary mission interdiction of Viet Cong movement by inland waters—about five thousand miles of it. To attack the VC base camps required armor, concentrated punch, and staying power. The South Vietnamese Navy had inherited suitable craft from the French* and organized them into river assault groups, but they were too few in number and were old and in poor repair.

Thus, in 1966, as Game Warden got underway, planning proceeded for a U.S. Navy River Assault Force, which became the MRF. In early autumn Amphibious Force Pacific Fleet established River Assault Flotilla 1. Realistic training began in upper San Francisco Bay's waterlogged lowlands, which resemble the Delta. The crews then quickly moved on to Vietnam, the first arriving in early 1967.

The U.S. Army's 9th Division furnished the basic combat troops, though in the fighting years ahead the MRF often operated with South Vietnamese army, marines, and militia groups. For maximum flexibility the navy established mobile bases that shifted to different locations, as necessary, to give the assault boats a short run to any objective. The five-ship base provided logistic and repair support including berthing, messing, and working space for 1,600 sailors and 1,900 soldiers.

To get going fast the navy modified existing landing craft for most of the force. In fact, to start operations promptly, some were taken off the skids of amphibious ships in the area, "armored" with steel plate

---

*Many of them supplied to the French by the U.S. Navy.

and sent into action with assault craft borrowed from Vietnam. Principal types developed in the States were:

(1) Monitors—Conversion from the Landing Craft, Medium (LCM-6) by addition of a conventional bow, armor, a turret forward and superstructure aft with pilot house and guns. Like the battleship on blue water, it could hit the hardest and take the most punishment. It normally mounted a 105mm. howitzer, 81mm. mortar, or 40mm. machine gun in the turret, along with 20mm., .50, and .30 caliber machine guns bristling from every available site.

(2) Armored Troop Carriers (ATC)—LCM hull well armored to protect against the heavy fire often met at close quarters. For firepower they mounted an assortment of 20mm. and smaller machine guns. Rugged and reliable, each boat carried a platoon of forty men with battle equipment. By the addition of a helicopter landing pad some were converted into very useful minicarriers.

(3) Command and Communication boats—modifications of monitor, they give the battalion and river squadron commanders an Army-Navy Command Post on the forward wave of battle, similar to command ships offshore.

(4) Assault Support Patrol Boat (ASPR)—the one new design, this multipurpose boat is well-armored, heavily armed, and relatively fast—fifteen knots versus eight or less for the conversions. It patrols, minesweeps, and escorts with equal facility.

The initial operation, with improvised and borrowed craft, struck hard beginning in February, 1967. The Force razed VC camps, capturing or destroying large numbers of boats and quantities of weapons, munitions, mines, and other supplies. It was so successful that by April operations could shift to the Delta. By June enough boats and trained crews had arrived to set a tempo of six to eight offensive strikes a month.

This self-contained sister of the ocean amphibians routed the Viet Cong near and far. For example, on 4 to 6 December 1967, in long reach up the Mekong toward the Cambodian border, the MRF and 5th Battalion Vietnamese Marines struck a devastating blow in a long infested area.

Sailing up a narrow canal, the force came under automatic weapon, recoilless rifle, and rocket fire from both banks. Boat after boat was hit and some severely damaged, but they drove on to the selected landing point.

Supported by the boats' fire, the marines gallantly assaulted and captured the foe's fortified camp. The allies lost fifty-one men killed, including eleven Americans, at a cost of many times that for the enemy.

More important, the Communists lost a powerful stronghold whence they had ruled the area for years. With it went 161 bunkers destroyed and stocks of munitions, weapons, supplies. The setback materially reduced the effectiveness of the Viet Cong in their attempts to infiltrate the Saigon area for the nation's next crisis in January.

By that time American strength in all areas neared its maximum afloat and ashore. Also with the steady rooting out of the Viet Cong infrastructure, South Vietnam's recovery and strength accelerated. Hence the Viet Cong's decision to launch the vicious TET offensive.

Preparations began after the end of the southwest monsoon in October. Hanoi moved main forces into heavily populated regions of the south, built new secret bases in Cambodia accumulating quantities of arms supplies and troops. Week after week they stockpiled munitions and weapons near Saigon province and district capitals. They hid other stocks in the cities themselves and as TET approached infiltrated disguised troops into the cities. Among other methods, they used funeral processions to smuggle weapons and ammunition into Saigon.

The Communists' other strategy having failed, they opted for destroying leadership in the cities in the hope of creating chaos, discrediting the government, and turning the tide of war in their favor. TET seemed an ideal time—a period of relaxation, festivity, happiness, success. The middle of the seven-day truce, they declared, should insure maximum relaxation.

Attacks in the upper provinces began on the night of January 29th. Then toward midnight of January 30th and during the small hours of the 31st, brutal attacks exploded throughout the rest of the nation, including the Delta. The Viet Cong struck in forty-two key cities and more than one hundred others—in many bringing with them political cadres and organization blueprints to set up a "liberation government." They committed unspeakable atrocities against government officials, women, children, groups of refugees.

MRF and Game Warden crews not already on patrol manned their boats on the run and went into action with guns blazing, aiding regional troops and local police. At Chau Doc, near the Cambodian border, which the Viet Cong almost overran, Game Warden PBRs, Seals, and Seawolves operating nearby saved the day. With them spearheading a fierce counter attack, the two hostile battalions were quickly shattered and routed.

With the inherent advantage of mobility afloat, the Brown Water Navy sped from point to point wherever most needed. Of special importance was the provincial capital of My Tho, southwest of Saigon.

Combined with South Vietnamese troops, the powerful MRF expeditiously cleared that city.

Within two days the TET offensive was broken in the Delta. The Communists had lost thousands of men, large caches of arms and supplies, and tons of ammunition. Even more important, they lost the people. The two riverine fleets had starred in the turn of the tide in the Delta (and also in I Corps area to the north) that would have long range effect of deep importance. General Westmoreland said they "saved the Delta."*

Sea Lords (South East Asia Land Ocean River Delta Strategy)
By autumn, 1968, expanded to full complement, the riverine navies had the upper hand of the VC on the principal waterways flowing to the sea. Market Time strength and success had likewise increased so that ships could be spared more readily for inshore expeditions. Com-NavV, therefore, commenced joint operations with the three forces from the Gulf of Siam through the interconnecting waterways that roughly parallel the Cambodian border, nearly to Saigon. Called Sea Lords, it was a campaign to interdict infiltration of munitions and supplies from Cambodia, where much came in by sea as well as land.

Reducing the forces on the lower rivers, in late 1968 about half of Game Warden's PBRs, along with Seals and Seawolves, shifted toward the border, as did all the MRF.

Swifts from Market Time took over on the seaward portion of the Delta Rivers. Combining the speed and striking power of the various riverine forces, including South Vietnam's, three major campaigns got underway along the interlinking waterways.

Sea Lords struck into areas the Viet Cong had dominated for years and drove them from their secure haunts. This greatly furthered the interdiction campaign that disrupted infiltration lines from Cambodia and reduced the Communists' offensive power in the Delta. Through 1969–1970 government authority was established in ever larger areas.

Besides patroling, inspecting, and fighting, those in the Brown Water Navies served as ambassadors of good will. They helped to rebuild villages and to transport medical teams to the villagers at regular intervals. Their boats often became ambulances.

Following some earlier transfers, in mid-1969 the United States began the wholesale turnover of the riverine forces, including Market Time to the South Vietnamese Navy—first training the crews on board in operations and repair detachments at the bases. The MRF dissolved 25 August 1969, after transfer of much of the force. The remainder

---

*Overall U.S. Commander in South Vietnam, June, 1964, to July, 1968, when he was relieved by General Creighton Abrams, USA.

of the boats, along with those in Game Warden that had not been transferred, continued in Sea Lords. By mid-1971 the United States had turned over to the competent South Vietnamese Navy some 825 naval craft of all types. Expanding in men and skills, it now operated more than 1,200 boats, including nearly three hundred junks.

This was not abandoning responsibility by the U.S. Navy. It was handing on a going organization at its operational peak. The South Vietnamese Navy has taken the helm with zest. It has had time to get ready as the south shapes into a nation out of the crucible of perhaps the cruelest campaign of murder, brutality, and ruthless terrorism ever recorded by history.

Logistics—Material and Spiritual

Body, soul, and mind are equally important to man. If the soul must have the body for its earthly home, the body must have the soul if it is to live rather than just to exist. Servicemen in the Vietnam War know this, though it seems often forgotten at home.

Americans require more logistic support per man in the field than any other people. They expect reasonable conveniences and comforts and receive them as far as is feasible. The forces are highly motorized. They have superb medical facilities. Their ship services and canteens bulge with personal gear, souvenirs, and "gedunk." Great attention is given to sports, entertainment, and recreation. Consequently, added to the great fighting needs of fuel and munitions, the logistic problems are tremendous, amounting to at least a ton per month per American ashore.

About 97 percent of these supplies arrive in Vietnam by sea, primarily in flag or chartered ships of the Military Sealift Command (MSC)—until 1 August 1970, called MSTS.* Even a brief interruption of control would mean disaster, though most Americans accept it as a fact of life and have no understanding of how difficult it was to achieve, how dangerously slim it has become, and how easily it can be lost.

Even for air operations, nearly all the army and navy's requirements and nine-tenths of the air force's came in by ships of MSC. These included the needs of the eight major jet bases and about one hundred widely dispersed lesser airfields built in South Vietnam by 1969. Many of the ships that brought these and other needs were chartered from foreign flags because of the United States' inadequate merchant marine.

In 1968 army and navy logistics commands in Vietnam handled

---

*The buildup to handle the escalating demands was dynamically directed by successive commanders of this force, Vice Admirals G. R. Donaho and L. P. Ramage.

close to 15 million tons of munitions and supplies for U.S., Vietnamese, and other allied forces. They handled 50 million barrels of petroleum products. The tempo diminished little in 1969. In addition the navy's highly efficient service force supported the fleet offshore in day and night replenishment, including nearly a million and a half barrels of petroleum products a month for ships and carrier planes.

To take care of the flood of cargo ashore, the United States built over a dozen large and small ports. The Seabees and civilian constructors working for the navy transformed Danang from a lighterage anchorage to a splendid port, having piers with six deepwater berths plus ramps and space for many shallow draft ships. This gave cargo capacity of about 4 million tons a year, plus petroleum.

Service force ships and craft transported material from port of entry to the point of need up and down the coast and along inland waterways. Without this coastal supply the course of the war would have been far different. General Westmoreland said of it in relation to the heavy fighting in I Corps in 1968, "We were utterly dependent upon the sea logistical line."

Nor did eight-hour days exist for engineers such as the Seabees. They played a notable role not only in building ports but also in other military construction of airfields, roads, bridges, bases, hospitals, and missile sites. For one missile site on jungle-covered Monkey Mountain near Danang, not having flat ground, they soon created it by cutting off the peak and making their own plateau. In addition the Seabees helped the civilians to restore ravaged villages and build hospitals, schools, sanitary systems, homes, and wells. Part of this they did as teams sent through remote regions of the republic to train and help the populace. Much they did in any off time they had, as volunteer acts of kindness and mercy.

Most found deep satisfaction in what they were doing. One Seabee incident portrays the attitude of a high proportion of Americans in Vietnam. At Danang an amazing number of men requested six months or more extension in the country. To prevent a feeling of drudgery, the extendee was assigned to a different job or location. One nineteen-year-old youth with a difficult and dangerous job demanded to keep it, operating his rough terrain forklift at an ammunition handling ramp. When his chit was turned down, he went to see the executive officer, who asked him why he insisted on staying with it.

"Commander," he replied, "I enjoy my work, and I want to come back to it. It's hard work, and somebody's got to do it, and I like it. So why can't I come back to it? I sing when I'm on top of that forklift. I sing all day. I like it. The guys like it. It helps the work. They call me 'Jukebox Jerry.' "

He stayed.

The medics minister to both body and soul. Their work surpasses the finest in the past—not only in service to their own American shipmates but to the tortured Vietnamese as well. They serve in combat ships offshore, in hospital ships, in the Brown Water Navy bases, in naval facilities ashore, and with the marines and navy units in combat. Each marine platoon has a hospital corpsman, each battalion, a medical officer with several corpsmen. So it goes up the line with care on the spot from the center of danger to Division Headquarters, the hospital, and hospital ship.

The navy has dispensaries at their bases. A 700-bed hospital was built at Danang, and in February, 1966, the navy stationed the first hospital ship off I Corps, the USS *Sanctuary*. As early as 1966 General Wallace Greene pointed up something of the meaning of this dedicated group. "The medical treatment our men are receiving now is really outstanding. We're losing less than 2 percent of our wounded . . . For example, we are getting people that are struck on the front line back to the States, undergoing final treatment, in five days. . . ."

At Chu Lai General Greene decorated a badly wounded boy just in from the front. "Two days later, when I was at Clark Field in the Philippines, I went into an evacuation plane that was about to take off for Andrews Air Force Base near Washington, D.C., and the first man I saw was this boy."

The courageous, sacrificial spirit of these medical men dedicated to giving themselves to help others stands out in the account of one young navy corpsman. Reaching Vietnam, HC2 Eugene S. Hancock, USN, joined the 7th Marines. On a mission to rout out the foe, his outfit came under heavy fire. Several advance marines fell wounded. Hancock, with others, sped to their aid. Having taken care of them, Hancock saw another wounded marine in an area swept by machine gunfire. Despite the obvious peril of venturing into the spot, Hancock did not hesitate. Racing to the man, he applied tourniquets to both legs to stop the bleeding and supervised his evacuation. He himself remained in the hail of fire, for he saw another wounded shipmate he might save. As he crawled to him, a stream of bullets ended his short, valiant service dedicated to his fellow men.

All sane men oppose war, as I believe most Americans do. Few could be mad enough to go out deliberately to get shot and be killed. But when tyranny rolls in a giant tide over the fragile dike of freedom and the United States stands up to it before it is too late, then any true American must do his part.

How can one understand, then, the Supreme Court's ivory tower decision in 1970 that moral as well as religious conviction can exempt a citizen from military service? Do the convictions of those who oppose war keep them from going to the field of danger to give medical care to their friends who see the need to defend freedom?

Most Americans in Vietnam understand their responsibility. None has put it in clearer focus than another naval corpsman, Samuel G. Orlando, a second generation Italian from Michigan. Serving with a Marine Corps unit, he wrote to a friend a few days before he was killed on the field of battle tending a wounded marine:

> I do not like this war in Vietnam, but I have a job to do, and I must do it to the best of my ability.
>
> We are here at the request of the people . . . to help them maintain their freedom from the Communists. . . . We are also here to protect our own interests. . . . This is not only a threat to us but to the whole Free World. And Vietnam is just a stepping stone to other countries. . . . I long for the ones I love and home.
>
> But I have a job to do, and if I die, I know with all my heart it won't be in vain.

Compassion, sacrifice, unselfish aid, love of fellow men—hundreds of thousands of servicemen have exhibited these noble traits in Vietnam over the years. They help the war-ravaged people in every way to build and to move ahead in the industrial age. This service strengthened each man's soul which, in the sum, becomes the soul of America.

For example, when marines routed Viet Cong from a small hamlet, a squad of marines and two of local militia formed a team to protect and to help the people rebuild it. Freed from tyranny, the villagers elected a mayor and council. They started improving their hamlet. Sailors in the area, along with the marines, provided materials for construction, trained the villagers, and helped with their own hands. Navy doctors and corpsmen became the medical department for the community— they gave more than one and a quarter million treatments in I Corps alone in 1968. From their own supplies and pay servicemen provided food, clothing, soap, and scores of other things to the villagers.

Most of all, they gave friendship and compassion—compasssion because they see with their own eyes the tremendous needs of these simple people who have suffered privation, terror, and brutality at the hands of a godless aggressor.

More than fifty thousand marines and sailors volunteered extension of service in Vietnam. Many returned for a third tour. BM2 Sam Swenson, a navy petty officer, leaving for his third tour, gives some of the reasons motivating the men:

Nobody is making me go—I volunteered. . . . My wife understands. Even though I'll be leaving her and my two little girls, twelve months and twenty-eight months, she knows I have to go.

It's hard to put my feeling of responsibility into words. . . . If there is a job to be done, you don't wait for somebody to tell you all the details. You just go ahead and do it. . . . People talk about losing your freedom in the navy. You don't lose your freedom—you learn to respect it and accept the responsibility that goes with it. . . . That's what the navy teaches you. Stick in there and fight and overcome the problem. That's what we have to do in Vietnam.

Being free is a funny thing. We've had our freedom for so long that we are misusing it. . . . I think every generation should have to fight for freedom. It unifies them and they begin to appreciate what having freedom is. My father fought for his generation, and I'm willing to fight for mine. Then when my girls get to be sixteen and ask me where I was during the fighting, I won't say: "Well, I was in Canada dodging the draft."

Why should I risk my freedom for somebody else? It's the same thing as helping the guy in a car wreck or robbery. So many people don't want to get involved now, but if they don't they'll be fighting the robber or the Viet Cong on their own doorstep. . . .

I am a member of a fighting team that doesn't go out to conquer, but it goes out to stand up for our beliefs. And the cornerstone of our belief is freedom—not just for us but everybody. It's only when we mature and accept this responsibility for others that we are really free.

Misinformed division at home has hurt the United States gravely. Yet in balance, the nation has gained more for her future leadership in the growth of heart and soul of so many who have served the Vietnamese in their struggle against darkness. In the words of navy chaplains we can begin to see what is happening. Over 700 of the 1,000 in the corps served one or more tours in the war. As Rear Admiral James W. Kelly, then Chief of Chaplains, said in January, 1970, after his latest trip to the war zone, "Their purpose is not to support policy but to support men and women, many of whom have left their private dreams to answer their country's call to duty."

They see the depths of men's souls, and they find what they see inspiring. Witness the words of two of them:

I felt that in Vietnam more than anywhere else in my ministry I did not have to search for evidence of God's presence. I found God every time I saw a marine reach over and pick up a little Vietnamese child or help an old man or woman across a narrow bridge or give them a drink of water from his canteen. . . . Many of the troops found God without actually knowing what was happening in their lives. Much of this came from fear when they had no one else to lean on except God.

I have never felt closer to the reality of God . . . than while I served with the marines in Vietnam. I found Him in the ministry to men in a situation where often the issue was life or death and all other values faded. I myself, living in the midst of such circumstances, found the peace that comes from putting oneself in God's hands.

No one found Him more completely than Lieutenant Vincent R. Capodanno, USNR, padre of 3rd Battalion, 5th Marines. During his twentieth month with the corps in Vietnam, in a battle with a much larger force of the enemy, he heard that the advance platoon was being overrun. He left the company command center and ran through crossfire to reach the platoon. There he found wounded and dying marines.

Sometimes running, sometimes crawling, he zigzagged across the battlefield while bullets filled the air around him. He gave medical aid, comfort, strength to those in need, administered last rites to those called. His strength seemed endless; his courage inspired every man.

Then a mortar round knocked him down, blew off part of his right hand, and wounded him severely in his arms and legs. Nevertheless, Chaplain Capodanno refused aid, would not retire from the front of danger, and continued to serve all about him with boundless dedication. Finally, he saw a marine trying to help a badly wounded navy hospital corpsman to cover. Just then Communist machine gunners advanced to point blank range. The valiant chaplain did not falter but dashed to the wounded man to help. The Communists gunned him down inches from the wounded youth.

Negotiations?

Negotiating from weakness is an easy way to lose. The first pullback of ship and air bombardment of military targets in North Vietnam did bring the Communists to the conference table. That's what they wanted anyhow. This gave them a world sounding board, which they used constantly for propaganda and vituperation. This makes news.

Unhappily, many foreign correspondents and air wave announcers obligingly repeat the distortions and untruths to the misguidance and confusion of the average free world citizen, who does not comprehend that this is normal Communist practice. Consequently, misinformed opposition to U.S. policy mounted at home and abroad.

The pullback also gave the Communists an opportunity to rebuild their war losses. Reconnaissance revealed vast accumulation of munitions, petroleum products, trucks, and supplies in the Haiphong-Hanoi area. So after seven months of this, in late 1969, the United States made another major concession—halting attacks in the remaining part of North Vietnam. This was probably more to please the vociferous minority in the United States—prompted and often unwittingly led by Communists—than in hopes of similar concession by the Communists. At any rate, it got only a continuation of propaganda, accusations, and lies fed by reporters to the world as news. The big lie repeated often enough for many people becomes the truth.

A nauseating example of this occurred in July, 1970, upon the return of a congressional committee from South Vietnam. A member of the staff criticized the imprisonment of political prisoners—some no doubt Communists—in concrete cells. The U.S. press highlighted this with headlines and pictures. Within hours the North Vietnamese in Paris blew it up into a major propaganda exposure that resounded throughout the world.

As newspapers and commentators repeated the story—a combination of truth and lies—how many of them commented about the inhumane treatment of U.S. prisoners in North Vietnam? There are no news releases on these. No one in the press, no foreign visitor or diplomat is allowed to visit American prisoners in North Vietnamese prison camps. The Communists know there would be a thousand tales more shocking and all true.*

Throughout the war the North Vietnamese violated the neutrality of Laos and Cambodia. These became sanctuaries for movement of war materials by land (and by sea also in Cambodia, end-running Market Time), for building up large reserve stocks, and for secure bases from which to mount attacks. This opens all parts of the long, narrow nation to invasion. Saigon is only thirty miles from the Parrot Beak of Cambodia. Oddly, this blatant disregard of international treaties and national rights raised no similar hue and cry in U.S. or foreign news media.

As the pseudonegotiators ground along, the United States continued to withdraw, training the South Vietnamese at top speed and turning over to them the means of defense on hand. For the navy this consisted of accelerated transfer of the river and Market Time vessels. On-the-job training increased, bases were built, training schools established. Many of these craft would serve well during the allies' strong and wise move in the spring of 1970.

---

*In December, 1970, Secretary of the Navy John H. Chafee gave an account of one of the many harrowing stories of North Vietnamese cruelty toward American war prisoners that have come to his attention:

"I had a young navy lieutenant in my office not long ago—one of the very few prisoners who have returned to describe life in the enemy compounds—and this kind of information is, of course, the most valid information we have. He told me how he was beaten, his wounds untreated, held in solitary confinement until he began talking to the rats, forced to sit on a narrow stool without moving for four days until his legs bloated and he lost consciousness and fell off.

"In the twenty-two months he was a prisoner, he lost almost seventy pounds on the two meals of pumpkin soup, pig fat, bread, and water he received each day. He told me about other prisoners who had had their fingernails pulled out; who had been hung from the ceilings of their cells; who had been dragged along the ground with broken legs; who had not been allowed to sleep or eat for long periods."

Meanwhile, freed from attack in the north, the Reds had markedly increased their stockpiles of munitions and supplies in Laos and Cambodia. Thus in 1969–1970, as the U.S. reduced military force in Vietnam, extreme danger mounted across the frontier from Saigon.

At the end of April, 1970, President Richard Nixon, as Commander-in-Chief, launched forces in conjunction with the South Vienamese into Cambodia in a calculated spoiling operation. Although it might, perhaps, have been better handled with Congress, this was a wise decision of great consequence.

Striking swiftly, with the support of the Brown Water Navy up the Mekong River into the heart of Cambodia, Allied troops overran bases and captured huge stocks of munitions and stores. With the monsoon rains approaching, and with the sea coast of Cambodia now denied them, the losses set the Communists back six months, perhaps a year in their time schedule. Thus the South Vietnamese Republic gained time to grow stronger to compensate for U.S. withdrawal, and the swift block unquestionably saved thousands of Allied lives.

U.S. troops and sailors with their boats withdrew across the border by June 30, as the president had promised. For the rest of the year the foe conducted only guerrilla operations, striking into South Vietnam from Laos and making small force attacks on Cambodian cities. United States aircraft assisted in checking them.

As 1971 and its successors unfold, what will be the end in Southeast Asia? The United States government has not fought the war to win. Yet the valor of the men in the forefront of danger, their comprehension from seeing with their own eyes the Communist horrors that lacerate the Vietnamese, and their dedication to the salvation of this brutalized people may bring victory.

Long under the thumb of others, the country has no heritage of self-government. In fact, the Vietnamese people have no background of loyalty to government much beyond the family, clan, and hamlet. In the crucible of subversion, invasion, and war they began to forge a nation. The pacification program rooted out most of the agents of the north, trained in ruthless Communist rule by terror. Gradually an environment took shape for a happier kind of government.

The transfer of resources, such as riverine and Market Time craft, and the training in operation and maintenance of equipment and key bases provide the military means for defense. Although a slower transfer would have been better, the South Vietnamese have taken hold with zeal and effectiveness, as shown in the Cambodia operation.

With these aids, the republic might soon stand up alone without fear of North Vietnam—if that nation were the only foe. But to stand up to it as a puppet manipulated for aggression by the giants of communism requires more strength than a small people can possibly muster.

In the middle of the Vietnam War Australia's Prime Minister Harold Holt spoke with heartfelt understanding of the United States' service to "individual liberty, human dignity, and national self respect throughout the world. . . . There has been nothing in history to approach the totality of American generosity and enlightenment . . . and dedication to the cause of freedom everywhere."

She cannot possibly stop now in a great course still unfinished. To serve her treaty obligations to this persecuted people, to serve justice and humanity, to serve the cause of men everywhere seeking freedom as well as the hope of keeping it for herself, the United States must stay with her commitment. She has a charge to keep. If she abandons it, she abandons her soul and her future.

This magnificent spirit shines like a star in the words of a gallant young naval officer who gave his life for all Americans.

Lieutenant William M. Roark graduated from the U.S. Naval Academy in 1960, married his childhood sweetheart, became a naval aviator and the father of two fine boys. He served ably from a carrier in the Vietnam war, had a brief time in the States, then returned to action in the USS *Coral Sea.*

Near the end of this second tour, not long before he flew off not to return from action, he wrote to his wife at home:

> I don't want my sons to fight a war I should have fought. I wish more Americans felt that way. I'm not a warmonger. It will be me who gets shot at. But it's blind and foolish not to have the courage of your convictions.
>
> I will not live under a totalitarian society, and I don't want you to either. I believe in God and will resist any force that attempts to remove God from society, no matter what the name.
>
> This is what we all must do if we believe in what the Founding Fathers stood for.

The events in this chapter are taken from a multitude of unclassified sources. These include, in part, reports from Vietnam and Pacific Fleet commands; correspondence with commanders of various forces during the events recounted; Navy Department studies, surveys, statements, speeches, medal citations, etc.; conversations with those returning from the Pacific; numerous published accounts both in naval publications (in Washington and the Pacific) and in civilian ones like *American Ordnance, Navy Times, Navy,* and *United States Naval Institute Proceedings,* as well as general news weeklies. A comprehensive, reliable account covering events through June, 1968, appears in *The Report on the War in Vietnam,* Washington, GPO, 1969 (with separate reports by Admiral Sharp and General Westmoreland).

A good short survey of the Brown Water Navy appears in Naval History Division's *Riverine Warfare,* Washington, GPO, 1969. Most issues of the U.S. Naval Institute's annual *Naval Review* contain depth studies on some aspect of the Vietnam operations. A view showing how newsmen may be led astray by careless use of Communist propaganda appears in Phil G. Goulding's *Confirm or Deny,* N.Y., Harper & Row, 1970.

9

Rushing Toward Shipwreck

THE foregoing pages can only touch on the large meaning of U.S. sea power to the Vietnam War. It affected all that happened ashore. Even the most remote operation inland had its seagoing influence and overtone. Thus the United States in building up the South Vietnamese Navy, training crews, and turning over to them vessels, bases and equipment, has passed on a great heritage.

Yet as she does this, as she once again finds overwhelming evidence of the irreplaceable need for superiority at sea if she is to survive . . . as the U.S.S.R. surges forward to be master of the seas, where does the United States steer?

She has slashed her strength at sea, in larger combat ships as well as the smaller ones. In gradually withdrawing from Vietnam, she has acted as if the need for a powerful navy had diminished, though developments in all quarters of the globe cry precisely the opposite. At no time in the post World War II age of crises has the urgency for U.S. maritime superiority been greater. At no time has her margin shrunk so low. At no time has the resulting danger facing her been so great.

Every thinking American must have witnessed with dismay the quantum reduction of the navy from 934 ships at the start of fiscal 1969 to about 700 as fiscal 1972 begins. The United States did not have the margin to cut that she possessed in 1964 at the start of the Vietnam buildup. The Joint Committee on Atomic Energy with clear foresight states, "The navy and the nation are at a turning point in their history." But our nation is not turning. In stormy seas with breakers on every hand she is racing toward disaster.

Half a generation ago, after the Korean War, the U.S. stabilized its navy at a level more suitable for worldwide duties than in the disastrously reduced fleet of the late 1940s. This fleet would have remained adequate except for developments that make a stronger one imperative. These are of such magnitude that it seems a fantasy that in 1971 the United States has cut its active warships sharply below the number afloat in 1956.

One development is the lengthy Vietnam struggle. Although it had no fleet to combat, the U.S. Navy was obliged to engage otherwise in a full-scale war against the shore. With its capability of projecting strength inland it exerted effort in many ways comparable to the demands of a major war. It developed the largest riverine navy of modern history. With this and complementing coastal operations, it fought a significant "small ship" conflict.

The coastal and river craft produced on a crash basis eminently filled the need even though it took some three years to get the required number of vessels on station. But had the enemy possessed a navy of modern small warships, such as the Soviet PTs armed with surface-to-surface missiles and supported by land-based aircraft, the ball game would have changed.

The navy's carriers steamed offshore conducting round the clock bombing in interdiction, destruction of enemy fortifications and arsenals, and direct support of troops. The annual rate of sorties and munitions expended per carrier greatly surpassed that of World War II. The marines' prolonged operations ashore exceeded anything in their long and gallant history. The amphibious landings by the 7th Fleet Amphibious Force, though modest in size and generally unopposed, averaged over one a month from 1965 on. The gunfire support and other surface ships worked unceasingly. As an example, in fiscal 1969 the navy's warships offshore fired close to 500,000 rounds of three-inch to eight-inch projectiles and rockets.

The Need for Replacements

A navy can't fight this kind of war without wear, strain, and cost. Guns, ship power plants, machinery, equipment in constant use all need overhaul and parts replacement. Ammunition stocks decline. Planes are lost in combat operations or simply wear out. These and many other factors placed a strain on the navy operating within a circumscribed size and budget. Other parts of the fleet and shore establishment were drained to support the Vietnam struggle.

The transfer in 1969–1970 of most of the small ship navy and shore facilities, along with the gradual withdrawal of the marines, helped to reduce the strain. Yet there cannot be much rest for the navy as a whole until worldwide Communist subversion and aggression stop.

Heavy commitment for the 7th Fleet, 6th Fleet, and forces elsewhere promises to be a way of life for some time to come. A modestly trimmed navy might serve adequately for normal peacekeeping duties and fielding flareups that subside in a few weeks. But when the squall develops into a typhoon that rages for years, then for its own safety the nation must have on hand more ships, planes, munitions, and men in uniform than she had when the fleet began Vietnam operations in 1965. Instead, she has scaled down all of these items below the lowest point of the last twenty years.

Another development that carries with it an intrinsic warning to the United States to maintain its strength has far more ominous implications. This is the change in the relative size of the U.S. Navy and Russia's—and, for that matter, in most other components of maritime power. Every part affects the navy's capabilities and its operations in war.

It can be argued correctly that most of the approximately three hundred ships retired in the past two years were old, and that more went into mothballs or to replace still older ones with reserve units than were scrapped. But retired ships don't come out fast. It takes months for destroyers. The battleship *New Jersey* required over a year and a half before she reached station off Vietnam. True, the passing of the three hundred reduces the average age of the remainder so that it draws closer to the more modern Soviet Navy. But when will replacements come for them?

The navy has knocked constantly on appropriation doors for new ships for many years. Progress has been made, but appropriations have invariably fallen short of providing the number of ships needed.*

---

*The experts without practical knowledge in the Systems Analysis section of the Secretary of Defense's office have been one of the roadblocks. They have usually cut the navy's request for the final budget to go to Congress and have repeatedly delayed important naval construction for which Congress had appropriated. The hearings of April, 1969, and March 19–20, 1970, of the Joint Congressional Committee on Atomic Energy stated: "The systems analysts have a long record of causing delays or cancellations of naval nuclear propulsion projects that Congress considered vital to our national defense . . . the systems analysts staunchly opposed nuclear propulsion for the carrier *John F. Kennedy* [She was ultimately completed with conventional engines in an age of nuclear power]; opposed the nuclear frigate authorized by Congress in fiscal year 1966, which the Department of Defense refused to build; opposed the nuclear frigate authorized by Congress in fiscal year 1967 [and Defense held up release of funds for eighteen months]; opposed the nuclear frigate authorized by Congress in fiscal year 1968 [and Defense held up these funds 22 months]; opposed continuation of the nuclear attack submarine building program beyond a force level of 69; opposed the electric drive submarine authorized by Congress in fiscal year 1968

Hence new construction has plodded along at a rate much below that necessary to replace ships on a twenty-year life expectancy. In fiscal 1971 enough new ships commissioned to meet this necessary rate (about four a month on the average) but not enough to make up for delays of other years. Unfortunately, the scant appropriations in the past have created a bulge of older ships, even after the decommissioning and retirement of the three hundred ships mentioned.

The Chief Council of the House Armed Services Committee places the danger in clear focus: "While our aging fleet is going from bad to worse to the scrapyard, the Soviet Navy is coming into its own." The navy budget of $2.7 billion a year for shipbuilding over the next five years will not even replace the ships lost because of age. To replace these and part of the three hundred by the end of 1975 would require doubling the present rate of construction.

Such a crash program would be costly. It would be difficult on a peacetime basis, if it could be accomplished at all. Ships on the ways today are taking four to six years from contract to commissioning. The first three of the fine new destroyers of the "Spruance" class, which will take the place of some of those scrapped, were contracted for in mid-1970 after long delays, mostly forced on the navy. The United States cannot possibly have many of these by 1976. As Admiral Moorer said in 1970 before quitting his navy office on the Pentagon's 4th deck to go below into the hold as Chairman of the Joint Chiefs of Staff—if he had a "wheelbarrow of money" he couldn't get a ship from concept to launch, commission, and readiness for fleet duty in much under five years.

Realizing the danger, President Nixon made a start toward cor-

---

[and Defense held up into fiscal 1969]; opposed the high speed submarine which Congress authorized. . . .

"President Nixon stated his dissatisfaction with this record and his strong support for nuclear powered . . . warships in his campaign pledge on October 2, 1968, to restore the goal of a Navy second to none. . . .

"It is clear that the Soviets have made their nuclear submarine construction program a matter of high national priority. In contrast, the Department of Defense in the last several years has delayed new submarine programs and has approved fewer submarines than recommended by the Joint Chiefs of Staff.

"The rapidly increasing Soviet naval threat . . . makes it essential that the United States get submarines of the new high-speed class into the fleet as soon as possible."

To this, Admiral Rickover added in the hearings of March, 1970, that for years he and his staff have had to divert countless hours from technical work to point out errors in official documents of Dr. Herrington of the analysts opposing nuclear warships programs. "Therefore you can imagine my feelings when I learned that he has been assigned by the Department of Defense to assist the Defense Program Review Committee which has been established to advise the National Security Council. In my view this is like a farmer selecting a goat to watch the cabbage patch," Rickover stated.

recting the situation in his 1972 budget message to Congress early in 1971. He requested $3.3 billion for new warship construction—nearly $1 billion more than that of the previous year. If Congress approves this will help, but the pace should be accelerated even more rapidly if the United States is to avoid falling farther behind.

Fewer ships also mean fewer trained men on hand. These do not come easily in the complex, fast moving highly technical navy of today. To meet the budget the navy cut its 770,000 men of 1968 by about 150,000 by July, 1971. This reduced number of trained men gravely weakens the nation's quick-response capability to a major crisis in the years ahead. As we shall see, this also weakens ability to handle U.S. worldwide commitments.

The decline in naval strength that the Defense Department, White House, and Congress have allowed endangers the United States as nothing has since the mad flinging away of sea power in 1945–1950 that helped bring on the Korean War and the string of disasters since. Indeed, it may be greater folly with even more significant consequences.

In the preceding chapters we observed how the United States used its superior sea power as the mobile arm of a determined policy to stand between the world and Soviet aggression. Without the fleet and the will to use it to project national power, including economic and military aid, the free fringe of Western Europe as well as the remaining sea-washed free nations of all Eurasia would likely be under Communist rule today.

Today the U. S. S. R. has the largest submarine fleet in the world, unprecedented in peacetime size and quality. It has remained in the 350 to 400 range for a number of years, but new boats have steadily replaced older ones. Since eliminating the problems that cropped up in their first nuclear submarines, the Soviets have concentrated on building them while continuing to bring out new design diesel boats so as to keep the force large, modern, and versatile. They have paid special attention to attack "killer" types, and, as we shall see, in recent years have put massive effort into ballistic missile boats. During the interval the United States has also built fine new attack submarines, improved detection and attack capabilities greatly on surface ASW ships and planes, has made large progress in long range detection and other important ASW advances. But with all those combined advances can they match the increased capabilities of the Soviets?

U.S. Antisubmarine Capacity vs. Russian Undersea Power

In World War II the real "secret weapon" that won the battle of the Atlantic against the German submarine was not radar, nor hedgehog forward-throwing depth charges, nor improved sonar, nor even tactics, important though these elements were. *The secret weapon was enough ASW ships and planes—thousands of them.* Human error as well as mechanical and electronic defects will inevitably lower the anticipated effectiveness of weapons in war. Ships and planes are lost or damaged. They must be repaired. Men must be replaced—in an emergency often with green hands. A sufficient margin in numbers must be on hand. *The United States does not have that margin.*

Accordingly, she is rapidly sinking toward second place as a maritime power. And once the U.S.S.R. has pushed ahead, freedom will be threatened. Some of the fateful and frightening changes show in this table:

TABLE 1

U.S. Antisubmarine Capacity versus the Soviet Submarine Force

	U.S. ASW FORCES			SOVIET SS FLEET			
	Destroyer Types	Smaller Surface	ASW Carrier	Nuclear FBM	Other	Non-Nuclear FBM	Other
30 June 1955(1) (After Korea)	313 (DL/DD/ DE)	ASW 15	8 (CVS/ CVHE)	0	0	0	c.400
30 June 1968(2) (near peak of Vietnam ops.)	318	33	9	13-15	40-50	30-40	255-275
30 June 1971(3) (Estimate)	220±	0	4	29-34	65-70	30±	230-250

Sources by lines:

1. U.S.: SecNav Report on Status of Forces.
   U.S.S.R.: CNO unclassified estimate.

2. U.S.: Hearings of Special Congressional Committee on Sea Power (Oct., 1948—Jan., 1969), status reports, etc.
   U.S.S.R.: Estimate from *Jane's, Weyers,* other published sources.

3. U.S.: CNO/SECNAV speeches, Navy Dept. releases including current status reports, projections from present trends.
   U.S.S.R.: Hearings, Joint Committee on Atomic Energy, 91st Congress, Mar., 1970; Hearings, Armed Services Committee, 1970; SECDEF/SECNAV/Chairman Joint Chiefs of Staff/CNO speeches; projections from current trends.

Another view of the Soviet underwater menace comes from this second table, covering all types of combat submarines. It, too, is dismal.

TABLE 2
Submarine Force Levels

	SSBN	SSB	SSGN	SSN	SSG	SS	Totals
U.S.	41	0	0	53	0	50	144
U.S.S.R.	29-34	30±	35-40	30-35	30±	200-220	355-375

N—Nuclear Propelled   B—Ballistic Missile   G—Other guided missile
Estimates as of 30 June 1971.
Both the U.S. Polaris and U.S.S.R. "Yankee" SSBN carry 16 ballistic missiles. The latest Soviet "Sawfly" missiles are believed to compare with the 2,500-mile range Polaris A-3. The United States is now converting boats to take the new Poseidon missile, a project that will continue to run for a number of years. Poseidon, with its greater hitting power, accuracy, and versatility probably surpasses any Soviet submarine missile. But even if that is true, the Soviet-demonstrated capacity in missiles makes clear that our superiority will not long continue.

The United States' nuclear submarines can dive much deeper than those of World War II. Not only can they run at far higher speeds submerged, but they can maintain speeds of over twenty-five knots almost indefinitely with their nuclear reactors, as opposed to a few hours at half this speed in later World War II types. They can operate on station submerged also almost indefinitely. They don't need to come up for air, nor for navigation, nor to recharge batteries. Instead, they can run submerged as long as man can stand it; and the present atomic charge needs replacing only after ten years.

These facts should interest Americans deeply, because of the protection they demonstrate—and, on the other side of the coin, the menace from the giant Soviet submarine force. Today Soviet submarines with capabilities not unlike the above, carrying warheads of massive destruction, cruise off the United States hidden in the depths of the sea.

U.S.S.R. submarine-building shipyards can produce twenty nuclear boats a year, and in a crash program, many more if they worked three shifts instead of one. The U.S.S.R. has put enormous resources into expanding, modernizing, and building shipyards—the very keel of a successful shipbuilding program, which the U. S. has neglected. In 1966, the Soviets had only two new yards constructing nuclear submarines. Now they have four and perhaps five—the largest and most modern in the world for this purpose. One Soviet submarine yard, in fact, contains several times the area and facilities of all U.S. submarine building yards combined.* At least two yards build Polaris type

---

*The industrial base in the United States for building nuclear submarines and other large modern warships has gravely eroded. Unhappily this erosion is far more

boats. Most of the yards lie in Europe, but Komsomolsk in Asia builds for the Pacific fleet.

The U.S. Navy has consistently sought more ASW capability but has only a small portion of what is urgently needed. In the decade after Korea, up to the small buildup during the Vietnam War, the navy managed to hold close to the level set after the Korean fighting ended. When new ships joined the fleet, aged ones retired. But the new ships joined at about half the rate required; hence the overall age of all ships rose steadily.

Upkeep costs also slowly pyramided. Manufacturers stopped building spare parts for much of the machinery on older ships. Modernization and installation of improved ASW and other equipment became increasingly costly and difficult to obtain. On some ships it proved impossible because they could not absorb the added weight. As a result, the older craft generally became less and less effective for the job at hand and, to meet the administration's economy defense budget, the navy retired the failing old warriors wholesale.

It was assumed appropriations would come through to launch the needed replacements. But the Secretary of Defense cut the navy's construction funds request in the 1971 budget, as had been habitually the case in the past. The House of Representatives added funds, but the Senate cut back again. Construction of the modernized fleet the nation must have will be too little and too late.

One must inevitably conclude today that the first sea power of the world, charged with safeguarding the course of freedom in our time, is not living up to its responsibilities.

The Increasing Threat

In World War II surface ships, aircraft (lighter than air as well as fixed wing), and convoys provided the principal means of defeating the submarine. In September, 1939, Britain had over 200 destroyers and other escort types, no ASW Escort Carriers with planes, and 249 Coastal Air Command patrol planes, though few were available for ASW for a long time. At this time Germany had 49 operating submarines and 8 training. Thus England had roughly 4 surface ships with good ASW capability for every submarine. Note Table 1 for the paltry U.S. ratio. More planes are available today, and

---

pervasive than in shipbuilding alone. A shakeout of very large proportions in the aerospace industry has run for some time. According to a knowledgeable Vice Admiral, if it continues, in a few years only two or three aerospace companies will have the capability of designing and building naval aircraft, including helicopters. Americans seem to accept this erosion in fundamental capabilities with apathy. They fail to realize its serious, long-range implications upon the United States' ability to survive.

other conditions are different, but not that much so. In 1939, as also today, one should know that because of their manifold duties few destroyers can ever be used exclusively for ASW; escort types are another matter, though like most naval ships they can and do perform varied duties.

Hitler was slow to realize how important his submarines could be, so he gave little priority to constructing new ones. Hence, fifteen months after the outbreak of war, through losses and damage, he had only 22 operating submarines (with others under repair and working up). Yet those few U-boats raised awesome havoc with allied shipping. Indeed, with them and at last an intensive building program that got underway to give Germany more than 400 commissioned submarines in 1943, she came within a hair's breadth of winning the war. This was so even though the Nazis had given England and the United States the long lead and though they both frantically built planes and ASW ships that finally gave them the upper hand in 1943.

To make the comparison precise we should include the Italian and Japanese submarines, but the former would not affect the ratio much, and the United States was providing aid to Britain, including the transfer of fifty old destroyers, before the Pacific war erupted to involve us completely. Naval construction is long and costly. Nothing a nation can do will quickly rectify a serious deficiency in naval and merchant ships.

In World War II the United States had more than two years to prepare, to learn from the British and the hard lessons of war. Nevertheless, she experienced many dark and desperate days.

There will be no such leeway this time. The confrontation looming over the horizon will be blackmail of the most dangerous sort. Or it will be a catastrophe that will make Pearl Harbor look like a picnic.

A single submarine in the vast ocean offers a most elusive and difficult target. Therefore, to expect any success one must have several ships and planes for each sub. Convoys require fewer per submarine since it must come to the target to attack. But in a showdown confrontation with the Soviets, what time will there be for convoys in the initial critical hours? Hundreds of submarines scattered over millions of square miles of ocean will have to be found and met at the outset.

Since 1945 the United States has made much progress in understanding long-range noise transmission in certain water layers of the oceans. With their spy network aiding their emphasis on oceanography, no doubt the Soviets have made similar advances. The United States Navy has set up stations for investigating the vagaries of underwater sound transmissions, and for long-range submarine detection. Geography is against the Soviets, but unquestionably they have also made a beginning and will do more with the acquisitions of necessary sites, as in Cuba. Although long-range underwater detection has much improved over World War II, other factors have also changed. In the 1940s distant detection of submarines based on their radio transmissions (and on radar for shorter ranges) became very effective. Now that atomic submarines don't have to surface, this advantage fades. Therefore, on balance, it is doubtful that this element of antisubmarine warfare has greatly improved.

At any rate, the need for ships and planes to fight or (of first importance) to check Soviet blackmail is grave and critical. We get another view of how the United States has failed to prepare below:

TABLE 3

Opposing Forces—Submarine versus ASW

Opposing SS Forces	U.S. & British Commonwealth Ships and Planes Available for ASW
1945 April: *Germany*—429[1] (of which 166 operational) June: *Japan*—31	*British Comm.*—41 CVE,[2] 874 DD/Escort types, 131 SS,[3] 1,500-2,000 planes. *U.S.*—71 CVE,[2] 738 DD/DE, 240 SS,[3] 1,207 PC types, 3,000 plus planes.
1971 July: *U.S.S.R.*—355-375 (of which 94-100 nuclear powered)	*British Comm.*—3 ASW CV, 132 DD types, and under 200 planes. *U.S.*—4 CVS, 220± DD types, 144± SS (of which 94 have nuclear power), under 500 planes.

Sources: *Jane's, Morison, Roskill, Watts, Weyers,* SECDEF/SECNAV/CH., JOINT CHIEFS/CNO speeches, Congressional Testimony.

1. Roskill. Germany's submarines on hand reached a maximum of 444 a year earlier, and the most she ever had operational was 240 in April, 1943. After mid-1943 she never again had half her submarines operational.

2. Only part of these were ever assigned exclusively to ASW—U.S. CVEs, for example, escorted amphibious attack forces and supported amphibious landings (partly ASW) to greater extent than they functioned in convoy escort or hunter-killer ASW forces. DDs, the workhorses of the fleet, performed a thousand tasks besides ASW. But all could concentrate on ASW. There were never enough ships and planes for all demands in the first years of the war—and not enough destroyers almost to the end.

3. In World War II submarines were not designed with ASW as a principal function and few ever operated in purely this mission. However, hidden in the depths they could be deadly. U.S. and British submarines sank over forty opposing submarines in the war—while losing a number themselves to submarines. Today's specially designed nuclear attack boats will be dangerous hunters indeed, and *the United States must stay ahead—present building programs do not guarantee this.*

4. Other U.S. allies have moderate ASW forces, but how many can be relied upon in the unknown developments of tomorrow? Only a few gave support to the Vietnam

The U.S. currently has the lead in nuclear ballistic missile submarines of the Polaris type, but she will lose it by 1974, perhaps 1973, *and nothing she can do will prevent it.* She gained it in one of the outstanding achievements of all technology. Concentrating talent, leadership and money, Admiral Arleigh Burke, then CNO, assigned the job to Rear Admiral W. F. Raborn, a dynamic naval aviator.

Within four years, on 30 December 1959, scarcely the time ordinarily needed to build a ship, the incredibly complex and powerful Fleet Ballistic Missile submarine USS *George Washington* commissioned. Its fantastic offensive and defensive capabilities make the Polaris submarine a weapons system without parallel in history for power, accuracy, concealment, range, and effectiveness. In the next seven years forty others followed. USS *Will Rogers* (SSBN659), of the latest *Lafayette* class, commissioned on April Fool's Day, 1967, completed the Defense Department limit of forty-one.

Boat and blow developed simultaneously. The long-ranging missile, which then had no counterpart, got its name from Polaris, guiding star of mariners for aeons. Avoiding the liquid fuels then used exclusively for long-range missiles (because of extreme hazard on board ship), the navy stayed with solid propellants. The resulting small two-stage rocket hurled its nuclear warhead 1,200 miles with accuracy that one found hard to believe until it was actually witnessed.

"Once one has seen a Polaris firing," said President Kennedy, "the efficacy of this weapons system is not debatable."

A Polaris (FBM) submarine has two crews—Blue and Gold. These alternate on approximately sixty-day patrols, with crews shifting overseas more often than not as at Holy Loch, Scotland, and Rota, Spain. As she takes departure from port, the submarine dives. At that moment or, in fact, before she sails, the boat is ready to hit assigned military targets with missiles that now range to 2,500 nautical miles. She proceeds to her station submerged, operates there in the depths, and returns to surface for the first time two months later as she enters port.

Always on station and always ready, Polaris submariners cruise immune to sneak attack and are nearly invulnerable. Do those who op-

---

War. Governments can change. Forces can be suddenly overwhelmed or immobilized, as was France in 1940. The Soviets also have satellites and allies with navies, a number heavily endowed with guided missile craft. Even the smallest can have respectable capabilities, as demonstrated in the sinking of Israel's destroyer *Elath* by an Egyptian (formerly Soviet) guided missile boat. In any event, the United States, with world needs and obligations, must certainly have the force to exceed any other single power, or she will not survive as a great nation.

pose the military really understand the sacrifices of men such as these submariners, whose lives are devoted to serving them?

Polaris-Poseidon Submarines

Each of the several major breakthroughs that entered into the evolution of the FBM submarine would ordinarily have taken years. The fact that all the diverse elements were synchronized simultaneously seems almost miraculous. "SINS" navigation was one of these elements. This Ships Inertial Navigation System positions the submarine accurately beneath the surface at all times. In the missile itself a compact self-contained inertial guidance takes over as it bursts out of the sea and steers it unerringly to its target. The concentrated propellant (that soon was incorporated into Minuteman missiles ashore) amazed observers with its range and precision of impact.

This unprecedented weapons system development was, most of all, a technological advance that gave sea power quantum new advantage over that ashore. The increasing capability of sea forces—as opposed to those on land—represents a long trend. It began to speed up last century with the development of steam propulsion (and later other major steps like the submarine and aircraft). Now atomic power and the Polaris missile brought a new dimension to strength at sea. Even blockade and amphibious assault shrank in importance compared with the fantastic capabilities of the new weapons systems. Sea power could now strike suddenly and overwhelmingly at the heart of far-spreading empires.

It would appear that a development of such complexity and magnitude would stand superior for many years, thus providing the United States with a distinct edge in its labors to preserve peace. Yet through espionage* and a massive diversion of national effort toward the expansion of this area—as well as other areas—of maritime power, the U.S.S.R. soon had a similar submarine. Today, in 1971, Soviet submarine and other naval construction and capability steadily increase. The "Yankee" type (copy of the U.S. Polaris) has first priority in new or much expanded building yards. Today the Soviet Navy has operat-

---

*Part of the U.S.S.R. success with the FBM submarine rose from its swift achievement of nuclear power in the wake of the United States. Under Admiral Rickover the United States developed and had a strong lead in nuclear propulsion that should have lasted a long time. But Moscow "turned on the heat." She produced the power plant for the nuclear icebreaker *Lenin* within four years. The Soviet spy network contributed to this success. When the Swedish spy Wennerstrom asked if he should penetrate NATO, his Soviet masters told him, "Lay off . . . NATO. We have that completely covered. You stick to the United States."—(JCAE Hearings, 1970, p. 8).

ing or has launched about twenty of this type, and it builds at a furious pace while our nation has long since discontinued the Polaris construction program. In this era of lightning change, America's safety demands that new construction proceed without interruption.

On 27 March 1944, Admiral Ernest J. King, CinC U.S. Fleet and CNO, reported to Secretary of the Navy Frank Knox on the progress of the war up to that month and peacetime events leading up to it, including errors such as those today.

"Our failure to build progressively," he stated, "was a mistake which it is to be hoped will never be repeated."

The navy did progressively improve each new group of Polaris subs as they were built. It continues to do so. Boats have been modified to take the new longer range missiles. The 1,200-mile A-1 was succeeded by the 1,500-mile A-2, and it, in turn, by the 2,500-mile A-3, making the boats a true global deterrent.

In 1970, a Jovelike successor began to enter the fleet. Twice as powerful and even more accurate than Polaris, each has several separately targeted warheads (MIRVs—Maneuverable Independently-targeted Reentry Vehicles). This new submarine missile is almost as certain a deterrent as a nation could have. Poseidon, like its namesake god of the sea in ancient Greek mythology, is both "Earthshaker" and "Preserver," or "Calmer," of the sea.

However, the Soviets build the same, knowing that in a short interval this latest fantastic addition to strategic warfare will make it possible for either power to knock out the hardened short missile sites of the other. One can be certain that the Russian Sawfly missile (larger than Poseidon) has or soon will have similar MIRV capabilities, as do the Soviet intercontinental missiles in the U.S.S.R.

Shore-based retaliatory systems such as Minuteman have far less chance against submarine-launched missiles than against those coming from overseas. Since submarines can launch relatively close to shore, their missiles have a very short flight time. This puts shore-based retaliatory systems in special jeopardy because of the possibility that they can be destroyed before they can launch their missiles.

The Kremlin has come to the conclusion that sea-based power has vast advantages over power ashore. And to insure that they gain the edge, the Communist leaders rush to construct not only Polaris type submarines but also nuclear attack submarines whose mission will assuredly be to concentrate on the U.S. Navy's Polaris-Poseidon boats.

To stay in the race the U.S. has plans for a later champion that could stand off thousands of miles farther than Polaris, deep in the southern oceans, and still hit any part of the Soviet Union. The ULMS (Undersea Long-range Missile System) would be a very large submarine to carry super long-range missiles. This would remove all deterrence missiles from land and shift them to the sea so that a submarine attack would not destroy the Minuteman part of U.S. retaliatory power. The ULMS would astronomically increase the millions of square miles of ocean against which the Soviets would have to guard in event they initiated war without warning. Preliminary work on this new missile system has gone forward, but even with full funding the ULMS could not be ready before 1976–1980.

Not only do the Soviets hurriedly build Polaris type submarines, but, as Table 1 shows, until they reach superiority they can rely on a fleet of some thirty diesel-powered ballistic missile submarines. These have fewer missiles (most with three launching tubes instead of sixteen)* and lack the nuclear submarine's ability to cruise at high speed submerged indefinitely. Nevertheless, the missiles carry knockout punches like those in nuclear boats.

To the Soviet Navy's large and growing ballistic missile capability one must add the dangerous low altitude, or "cruise," *Shaddock* guided missile. It is carried in numbers by both nuclear and diesel boats and can deliver either a conventional or nuclear homing warhead. *Shaddock* is carried in three types of Soviet submarines. Boats of two of these types must surface to launch, but they can do so, fire and submerge again in a very short time. The third type, nuclear-powered, can fire hidden beneath the depths so that a surface ship's first warning might be a missile streaking toward it from out of the blue.

These cruise missiles are fast, can reach out to several hundred miles, and have variable flight profiles, including low altitude terminal flight. They carry very sophisticated electronics with excellent countermeasure resistance. The Soviets have put major effort into cruise missiles.

Besides the large concentration in submarines, they have this hard-to-combat missile in many surface ships and aircraft, as will be covered in the next chapter. In 1970, Admiral Moorer advised Congress that "the security of our sea lines of communication in both oceans is jeopardized not only by the torpedo and cruise-missile equipped submarines but increasingly by surface units and long-range aircraft with standoff antiship missiles."

With as many as 125 or more missile-firing submarines available in these various types the Soviets could (and in fact often do) position them wherever U.S. fleets sail or bases exist overseas—as well as off the United States proper. They represent a threat for blackmail or surprise that mounts each year.

The Russian Navy had troubles with its first nuclear submarines, but

---

*The first Russian Navy FBMs mount three to five tubes instead of sixteen in the Yankee type.

they were ironed out. A respectable force of atomic submarines sailed under the red star by 1965. Since then the number of Soviet craft has steadily multiplied. Besides twenty-nine or more nuclear FBMs (after the first fifteen all mount sixteen missiles), the Soviet Navy enters fiscal 1972 with at least sixty-five others under nuclear power. The Russians' growth potential is better than twenty new boats a year. On the average, Soviet shipyards in 1970 launched more than one Polaris type or other nuclear sub each month. On the other hand, the United States launched fewer than one-fourth as many in 1970. Whatever action she subsequently takes it will be difficult to increase this quantity appreciably for several years. Only a small number of submarines are now on the ways. Ship, power plant, and intricate equipment all take a long time to construct and install.

Just as the best defense against an airplane is another plane that can reach out to attack it, so is a submarine one of the most effective means of fighting submarines. A Polaris submarine can destroy bases, along with boats and missiles not on patrol—which would be one of the calamities of a surprise attack against the United States. Any submarine can stalk to kill another submarine at sea, and with nuclear warhead torpedoes the duel becomes grim indeed. Submarines designed especially as hunters are naturally most effective. Each of the powerful opponents has some.

In the 1960s, after much research and experimentation, including a new design hull, the U.S. Navy built a new class of nuclear attack submarines with the primary mission of ASW. Somewhat shorter than World War II submarines, with a true fish nose and a hull designed for underwater speed they are highly maneuverable in all directions. Engineered to run more quietly than any other submarine ever built and to operate at far greater depths, they excel in concealment, stealth, speed, and surprise. With latest sonar and weapons for attack, they constitute a formidable defense against the large Soviet submarine force. But there are not enough of them and their improved successors.

As the listing earlier in the chapter shows, the Russian Navy may have as many as thirty to thirty-five hunter type subs, and they are adding new boats to the fleet at a rate double that of the United States. To these must be added thirty-five other nuclear boats mounting cruise missiles that would also be very useful in ASW operations.

In the remaining categories of submarines the United States might hoist the "no contest" signal. Long ago the Navy Department concentrated on nuclear power for fighting submarines. Today, some fifty diesel boats remain, including a few experimental and special ones.

Laid down for the most part during World War II, they become antiques compared with the fantastic nuclear submarines. The navy gradually retires them, but lacks the funds to replace even a reasonable fraction of them.

Against these, the Kremlin can match 200 to 220 diesel boats in addition to the 60 to 65 carrying ballistic or guided missiles. Nearly all of these have been commissioned in the last fifteen years or less.* These cannot compete with nuclear submarines in ASW warfare since they lack the latter's underwater speed and endurance. For attacking surface shipping, however, there are numerous situations in which the diesel boat might match or even be preferred over nuclears.

In confined waters such as the Mediterranean, the extreme quietness of diesel submarines running on battery power makes them useful for waiting in straits and passages among islands. Here destroyer sonar would have difficulty detecting them until too late. Furthermore, diesel boats are comparatively cheaper to construct, operate, and maintain. As the Russian Navy matches and passes the U.S. Navy in nuclear powered submarines, the added strength of more than 260 diesel boats gives the U.S.S.R. an enormous advantage.

This writer believes that the U.S. submarines, boat for boat, are technically superior to Soviet nuclear boats of similar type — even though the Russian Navy's latest ballistic missile submarine, dubbed "Yankee" class, is almost a carbon copy of the United States' Polaris submarine. Despite this conviction, it would be a weak reed to lean upon even if the two fleets remained the same in size. With Russia's skyrocketing building program and ever-improved types, it seems clear that the Soviet submarine fleet in early potential effectiveness, as in numbers, outmatches that of the United States.

Therefore, considering only submarines, her main sea offensive arm, the U.S.S.R. has capacity unparalleled in history to: (a) devastate the United States by means of nuclear missile attack; and (b) cut the sea communications between the United States and her forces overseas, her allies, and her essential raw material import sources. For example, without the petroleum of the Middle East or the petroleum and bauxite of the West Indies and South America (sources of most of the aluminum that goes into our airplanes) the United States would be in dire straits.

For years the United States had a strong lead in ballistic and other nuclear submarines as well as surface and air ASW forces. Lulled

---

*Older ones retire annually, replaced usually by nuclear boats in the Kremlin's determined drive to rule the seas—and by them the world.

by Secretary McNamara's endless cost effective studies, which drowned common sense in theory, did the government thereby become complacent?

Certainly this was not the whole cause. Communist infiltration and progaganda have played their roles. Some influential newspapers and television pundits have also been responsible for deluding the nation with slanted or unbalanced reporting. Not least must we hold culpable the proponents of peace at any price, who block action in Congress, or by the administration even as they watch the Soviets overhauling America at full throttle.

Much of the blame, however, lies in the gargantuan, overorganized, overcentralized, overpopulated Department of Defense.

"The longest delays in our new submarines are caused by the endless reviews and studies by the Department of Defense," states Admiral Rickover.

Almost any other senior officer in the service departments could say the same of his field of responsibility. Layer upon layer of people have ideas but not knowledge, experience, or the ability to assume responsibility for the results. The ballooning defense staff that has multiplied out of all reason has thrust its influence into an increasing number of technical and operational matters it should leave to the services.

A service has enough layers of its own bureaucracy without smothering it with more. Each is composed of as experienced, intelligent, and informed men, uniformed and civilian, as are likely to be assembled. By any sensible concept it ought to be responsible for its own programs and allocation of funds within the national budget as authorized and appropriated by the Congress. If these selected, trained, and knowledgeable men don't have the competence to make the proper decisions within their spheres, who can have it?

When President Richard Nixon campaigned for election in 1968, he promised to reverse the accelerating relative decline in U.S. maritime strength. However good those intentions may have been, the ship of state has made ponderous progress in changing to a safe course. Five years ago the United States sailed comfortably ahead of the U.S.S.R. in nuclear power and the uncheckable Polaris deterrent. Now having lost way while the Soviets accelerated, she will be hard put to stay in the race. It won't be easy. Arms limitation agreements then might have preserved a favorable balance, insuring safety of the seas (though one would have to enter such an agreement with eyes wide open considering the Soviet's unchanging record of violation). Every American should realize that the results would be far different today with the U.S.S.R.'s new nuclear strength at sea (as well as in ICBMs ashore) and the United States' constricted navy. Men speak glibly, and without full awareness, of stopping the arms race. As the House Armed Services Committee stated in reporting out the 1970 procurement authorization bill:

"There has been no arms race—the Soviets have been running forward at full speed all by themselves."

Information in this chapter has come primarily from Department of Defense and Navy Department releases, statements, status of forces reports, published interviews, and speeches; Congressional Hearings and speeches by Members of Congress; various articles and news items in *American Ordnance, Armed Forces Journal, NATO's Fifteen Nations, International Defense Review, Navy, Navy Times, Naval Institute Proceedings,* and the standard references of *Brassey's* and *Jane's*. Samuel Eliot Morison's and Stephen Roskill's fine World War II histories provided information for statistics of that period, as did Fleet Admiral Ernest V. King's reports. *The Soviet Navy,* by M. G. Saunders, ed., (New York, Praeger, 1958) and *Soviet Sea Power,* by the Center for Strategic and International Studies, provided much information of value for this and subsequent chapters.

10

Naval Air and Missiles

THE Soviet power buildup to reach beyond the seas accelerated in the 1960s. The purpose is plain in Marshal Sokolovskii's words, printed in *Red Star* in 1964: ". . . equipping our navy with atomic submarines carrying missiles, and with aircraft carrying long range and nuclear weapons permits a shift from carrying out wartime missions along the coast in cooperation with the ground troops to independent and decisive operations on the broad reaches of the oceans."

It would be serious enough if the drive of the U.S.S.R. for control of "the broad reaches of the oceans" had stopped with submarines. But it extended far beyond. From a concept of defense of the coast the Kremlin has progressively expanded horizons to run the gamut of sea power. Frustrated from the Dardanelles to the Formosa Straits and from Korea to Cuba by U.S. power, projected to the farthest shore behind fast attack carriers and amphibious task forces, Russia's leaders became acutely aware of the need for a balanced fleet. With it they would also require the supporting elements of total maritime power if they really hoped to convert the world to communism.

Russia and Carrier Aviation

Since the early 1950s the U.S.S.R. has made dramatic progress in nearly every facet of maritime power. Only in carrier aviation does she significantly lag. Why?

No one outside the U.S.S.R. really knows the answer, but the following reasons have been advanced by observers. Any one or more of them may have influenced the Soviet decision at different times, depending upon the leader in power:

1. The Kremlin has not considered aircraft carriers essentially useful or effective as an arm of naval offensive power.
2. The attack carrier is desirable as the heart of a balanced navy but is more vulnerable than other types of ships or land-based air strength.
3. The cost effectiveness of aircraft carriers has seemed less than other means of serving the Kremlin's ambitions.
4. Natural geography, conquests, and other territory have blessed the U.S.S.R. with vast land areas but provided restricted sea exits. (Further expansion could eliminate this reason.)
5. Desire, need, or the simple strategic decision to build up other parts of the navy first—and no doubt the wish that other elements alone can bring supremacy at sea.

We might examine each of these possible reasons. *Have the leaders in the Kremlin considered the attack carrier not a particularly useful instrument of sea power?* If so, they have shut their eyes to historical experience, which demonstrates overwhelmingly the opposite. That the leaders do understand the importance of these powerful ships is obvious in their violent attacks on the carrier—they condemn what hurts.

Year after year, indeed almost day after day, throughout the past generation the far ranging, versatile carrier task forces have spearheaded U.S. success in war and in an uneasy peace.

In World War II, in Korea, and in Vietnam, where the missions occurred over water, the fast carrier task force launched the first tactical air assault against the foe. This was made possible by the fact that these moving airfields, self-contained with all they needed on board, could speed to the scene of action *and stay the*re. They cleared the seas of opposing surface ships. They struck hard and repeated blows against shore installations. They served so well and the need for them was so great that in World War II the United States built as many as possible, celebrating VJ Day with twenty-eight attack carriers in commission. Escort carriers for convoy and Hunter Killer ASW, as well as other purposes, were in similarly great demand (as I have noted, in 1945 the U.S. had seventy-one of them).

The atomic bomb delusion almost did away with the carrier, contributing to the unpreparedness that helped to precipitate the Korean War. Attack carriers had dropped to seven on the disastrous road to elimination. The crying need for them caused America to more than triple the number by 1956. All but two came out of mothballs, for it takes years to build a giant complex carrier.

Worldwide international problems forced the nation to maintain the carrier force; hence fifteen served when the situation in Southeast Asia began to boil. Even for Vietnam, a different kind of war from any of the others, the United States had to transfer temporarily an ASW carrier to attack status in order to have the necessary sixteen for operations. There ought to be and may well be more in the future. Existing world unrest and increasing Soviet maritime power, as Admiral Moorer noted on 19 August 1969, might well cause the sixteen to give way "to a national need for a greater number."

Earlier pages in this book have summarized the indispensable services of carriers in helping to ease international tension around the world and to hamper the Soviet takeover of small nations by subversion. The carriers made possible a maritime strategy that has played as important a role in peace as in war. Some of their greatest victories for America came during peace years. Moscow's leaders well know this. So it is no lack of understanding of the carrier's value that keeps them from building this incomparable force in sea power. They would like nothing more than to see the United States abandon this one significant superiority, as men without foresight in our nation have recommended time after time since the 1920s.

In the past twenty-five years the carrier has been under attack in the Defense Department almost constantly for one reason or another. The Navy Department has gone to general quarters countless times to prepare "a new study" to justify to the Secretary of Defense or the Congress what should be self-evident from all proof. In the air age the navy must have wings over the sea. Yet tens of thousands of man hours, often on short fuse and burning the midnight oil, have been devoted to a never-ending repetition of studies to rejustify what is today the nation's one clear superiority in maritime power.

Most recently the defense department reduced active CVAs to thirteen, while the Senate eliminated initial funds for a third Nimitz carrier at a time when only nine of the attack carriers are younger than sixteen years old; the remainder are twenty-four years and older. The navy cannot possibly replace more than one of them by 1975. Today could be 1947–1950 all over again, but this time the United States has no recently built carriers in mothballs. The cupboard is bare.

Fortunately—though at least in one case at the cost of the CNO's job—the navy has served the nation well by battling to preserve the carrier. This is a force the Soviets cannot match. The United States' superiority in carrier air power compensates in part for weakness in other areas of maritime strength. They have contributed the weight of their mobile massed power with telling effect from Piraeus to Inchon and from Lebanon to Cuba to Vietnam.

Is it because CVAs are vulnerable that the Kremlin does not build them? Carriers, of course, are vulnerable. For that matter any weapon system is vulnerable in war. But in more than thirty years of distinguished service, covering three wars and dozens of crises, none has been sunk by aircraft based ashore—on which the U.S.S.R. must rely. Actually, after the loss of four carriers in the first desperate years of 1942, when the underdog U.S. Navy fought against heavy odds in the Pacific, *no active heavy attack carrier has been sunk by any cause.* *

On the other hand, carriers have inflicted inestimable damage on America's adversaries. They have destroyed in the air or at enemy shore bases thousands of planes; they brought victory in the Pacific in World War II and contributed immensely to a degree of world stability in the postwar years.

These contributions, of course, were in non-nuclear war, which all sane men will do anything possible to avoid. Even in a nuclear holocaust, in which everything on land or sea is vulnerable, properly screened carriers, because of their great speed and maneuverability, have a good chance of escaping destruction. Hence the attack carrier joins the submarine in being one of the nation's most reliable deterrents.

Any ship can be sunk, just as any land base can be smashed. But the modern carrier is the toughest ship afloat—tough in armor and water-tight integrity, tough in self-defense because of its planes and missiles, and rugged in ASW (accompanying ships provide ASW and added AA defense besides that of the carrier itself). She is a difficult missile target. With her high speed she can steam at least twelve miles during the flight of an ICBM.

Even after she is sighted and her position precisely flashed to the Kremlin, it would take time to get the message to the missile launcher. Within an hour the carrier can be anywhere in a 2,800 square mile circle and in two hours, one of 11,000 square miles. Since a ballistic

---

**Lexington, Yorktown, Wasp, Hornet*—all of these could have been saved if their crews had had more experience in damage control and handling fires caused by hits or if the U.S. Pacific Fleet at that time had been strong enough to maintain local control of the sea around them. Even these pre-World War II carriers were so tough that U.S. torpedoes had to help sink three of the four as a precaution against their falling into enemy hands. In the following three years heavy attack carriers were hit on some forty different occasions, mostly by Kamikazes. All survived. Most resumed air operations in an hour or two. Only a handful required more than a few weeks for permanent repairs. This rugged survivability has been markedly increased in the nuclear carriers *Enterprise* and *Nimitz*.

missile must be fired at a known point, fixed or predicted, the chance of hitting a carrier at sea is microscopic.

Ballistic missiles are not likely to be fired at carriers or other ships at sea. Guided missiles, however, are a menace to ships. The Soviets have both short- and long-range air-to-surface, submarine-to-surface, and surface-to-surface missiles. Some of the long range types extend for hundreds of miles with in-flight guidance. For the last segment of its journey the missile has a homing head (such as radar, TV, or infrared), but the missile must be guided approximately on target into fairly close range before the homing system can "lock on."

Thus the missile launcher, whether ship, plane, submarine, or shore site, must "see" the target by radar or by other means. To extend the line of sight the launcher may have a mid-flight airplane, ship, or submarine assistant that has the target on its detection equipment and transmits the necessary information to the missile guidance system.

For a nation without carriers stand-off or "cruise"-guided missiles provide a partial substitute for sea-based aircraft. They can be highly effective against ships at sea without air cover. A force protected by airplanes, which carriers alone can easily provide in the broad oceans, is a different matter. For a surface or air-fired missile the foe's mid-flight airplane or surface ship would have little chance of surviving against a properly composed carrier task force. The launching aircraft or ship would not have a much better chance. A hundred miles or more on the perimeter of the task force early warning planes fly with giant pancake radar domes rotating. These detect enemy ships and aircraft much farther away and direct air patrols to destroy them.

Closer in surface ships and helicopters operate in the antisubmarine and guided missile screen. The ships' batteries of guns and guided missiles can shoot down planes and perhaps missiles. A cruise missile is not much different in size or performance from a small high-speed plane—though the very short interval from launch to flight gives less time to pick one up and take it under fire. This applies particularly to a missile fired by a submerged submarine.

Thus if a missile should get through the successive barriers—including the inner air patrol—it still will have to survive the point defense of the carrier and the close-in screening ships, which will markedly increase in the future. Furthermore, ships in the force are equipped with electronic devices to mislead and confuse the homing heads.

The carrier aircraft that the launching ship or plane would have to face include some of the world's finest. The twin engine all-weather McDonnell-Douglas F-4 Phantom II, first flown in 1958, has long been the world's outstanding intercepter. Both the U.S. Air Force and various U.S. allies have adopted it as the best plane available. (The navy also flies the very useful LTV single engine F-8 Crusader.) The F-14 replacement fighter intercepter, too long delayed by the ill-advised TFX F-111, will soon move into production. Mounting the new Phoenix missile system and other technological advances, it marks another important step forward in the United States' defense of the seas.

Two splendid day attack aircraft have long been workhorses in the navy: the McDonnell-Douglas A-4 Skyhawk and, following it, the LTV A-7 Corsair. The Corsair delivers up to seven-and-a-half tons of munitions in a strike and can carry seven different types of missiles, such as the Shrike, which homes on radar emissions, and the Walleye glide bomb, with television self-guidance. The all-weather shipmate of these two planes, which have given remarkable service, is the Grumman A-6. The navy is proud of the Grumman as the world's only airplane that can operate in any weather and in the darkest night with pinpoint accuracy. It carries a powerful wallop and has flown over 3,600 miles without being refueled.

The antisubmarine carrier plane Grumman S-2 Tracker came out as the world's best of its kind in the 1950s. It has performed well but has long since passed the time of its replacement because of developments of search, detection, and attack and the growth in the Soviet submarine menace—particularly from nuclear power and ballistic and cruise missiles. Because of budget and other problems, the S-3A, designed to replace the S-2, has come along too slowly. It will have advanced infrared sensors, television type display of sea targets, improved radar, and magnetic detection equipment (which indicates disturbances in the earth's magnetic field from metallic objects such as submarines). The S-3A should meet the nation's needs for the next decade.

The fleet has suitable helicopters for amphibious assault and for operation from ASW carriers. However, it needs many more for ASW operations from destroyer types. Over the years the navy has participated with other nations in the testing and development of helicopters and equipment to handle and house them on rapidly pitching and rolling decks of small ships.

For example, Canada has successfully solved most of the problems encountered in this type of operation. This progress will speed up the U.S. Navy's own program, which bears the acronym LAMPS (Light Airborne Multi-Purpose System helicopter). Designed to use "off the shelf" equipment as much as possible, it begins to join the fleet in late 1971. It will extend the ship's radar horizon; it will also greatly improve defense against the submarine and, consequently, against the most serious cruise missile threat.

The aircraft carrier has better protection against the submarine than does any other surface ship. While the submarine has the unique advantage of invisibility to eye or radar, sonar and other means can detect it at a reasonable range. With dunking sonar in helicopters, the range is measurably extended. Against a well screened carrier, even a nuclear submarine would have difficulty reaching position for a torpedo shot—though it would experience less trouble achieving the range necessary to launch a cruise missile.

Against a nuclear carrier such as *Enterprise* or *Nimitz,* now building, the sub's problems would increase. With their continuous high speed, decreased need to slow for refueling (required only for aircraft fuel), armor, and improved antitorpedo hull design, these nuclear carriers are the least vulnerable of any surface ship.

A grave problem affecting all the foregoing and, indeed, all the navies and the nation's overseas commitments, is of course a scarcity of ships. The drastic cutbacks that have slashed the navy by one-fourth since the Vietnam withdrawal began—even as the Soviets build at full speed—have placed the United States in a very precarious position.

Have the Soviets avoided big carriers because of cost? For a nation that probably put more billions of rubles into space flight than the total cost of the U.S. carrier fleet, this suggestion seems improbable. Is it, then, the "cost effectiveness" of carriers compared to land-based planes? This idea, too, is unlikely. The cost of a complex of shore air bases and a carrier task force is about the same in capital investment and annual operation—though for overseas one would have to add to land base costs those of harbor terminals and internal land transport.

In times of crisis, of course, the cost factor must necessarily give way to considerations of assured availability and promptness on the scene of action. In both these areas the carrier will usually excel. Unless the shore base exists within operating range of the hot spot, it can't be readied for many months. In Vietnam, for example, the minimum activation time was nine months and, in some cases, as much as two to three years. The carrier arrives in days and, depending on locations involved, sometimes in a mere matter of hours.

Though bases in other nations overseas may be in place today, there is no guarantee that they will be available tomorrow. Even those located on the territory of a close ally are vulnerable to a change in political environment. The United States has only a few bases so situated for ships, such as at Yokusaka, Japan, and Rota, Spain. Loss of these would be a handicap, forcing longer turn around voyages, but would not seriously affect naval operations, least of all carriers.

Highly developed at sea replenishment and efficient service force tenders keep the navy mobile. If necessary ships can operate for months at sea without entering port. The army and air force naturally face a more critical problem. Forces overseas require land bases. They must have secure ports for ships to unload and ceaseless flow of supplies and fuel that enable them to function.

Bases and ports outside her own territory available to the United States have decreased by two-thirds since Korea. When France left NATO, a vast infrastructure and investment in bases and support that had seemed politically secure was suddenly lost. When the regime changed in Libya, the new rulers threw the United States out of large and costly Wheelus Air Force Base, climaxing a series of ejections elsewhere in North Africa. Hence the United States now has no air bases in that large continent so strategically important to the Mediterranean, the Middle East, and the Indian and Atlantic Oceans.

In fact, the United States has no air base or other bases to protect the long sea route from the Persian Gulf (where most of the world's petroleum lies) or from Africa, with its rich raw materials of increasing need to the United States. To exist it is imperatve that she control the sea, and to control it she must have mobile airfields, self-sufficient and ready to operate wherever necessary.

The United States must have carriers to help avert world calamity, as in the mission that saved Lebanon in 1958. Planes might have flown to that troubled area from Turkey, but the distance would be difficult for any sort of effective continuing close support. It would have been almost impossible for planes to arrive soon enough from fields now available in Italy and West Germany. The effective radius of tactical air is considered to be about six hundred miles (from ashore or afloat), but the usefulness of planes naturally increases if the distance can be cut to a half or a third. This was demonstrated by carriers off Lebanon, Korea, North Vietnam, and numerous other places in the past two decades.

A glance at the globe shows the large number of air bases that would be needed to cover all possible trouble spots in the world.

One can increase the range or time on station by air refueling. This, of course, entails considerable additional effort and cost. In one year of the Vietnam War, Air Force tankers ably flew about a hundred thousand hours in support of shore-based tactical air operations against the foe. The total cost of the missions was $130,000,000.

A marvelous weapon system such as the aircraft carrier doesn't come cheap, but neither does a fixed base ashore with supporting complex. One carrier replaces several overseas airbases, and it doesn't disappear with a change in political climate. When the need arises for tactical air operations, a carrier can steam to the crisis spot swiftly. When the emergency has been resolved, it can hoist anchor and disappear over the horizon in an hour. It can deploy or disengage at will on the ocean, which has no frontiers, iron curtains, or political problems. When it sails, the U.S. still has her investment and her deployed strength ready for the next go. Undoubtedly, the United States has spent more on building base complexes overseas (now defunct as a result of compulsion or volition) than she has spent on carriers since World War II. Fortunately for her safety she still has the carriers.

In the next decade the United States will certainly lose more of her remaining air bases overseas, built at great cost and effort. Over a quarter of the giant jet complexes are located in Vietnam and Thailand (plus numerous satellites and smaller fields; in Vietnam these numbered in excess of one hundred besides the eight main jet bases). Others are situated in countries in which hostile political movements seek to eject U.S. military presence. Congressman Chet Holifield observed that "we see more and more in the news media that our overseas base structure is coming under attack from all sides. . . . The Turks are challenging our presence in Turkey, the Japanese want Okinawa back, even in the Philippines our presence at Clark Field is a political issue."

Air power is vital to military operations. If possible, both air bases and carriers must be available overseas, provided that the land bases have strong defenses, sure access to sea logistics that can supply most of the needs, and a reasonable chance of surviving changes of government.

Because none of the previously advanced reasons for the failure of the Soviets to build a strong fleet of carriers is valid, we must consider *the element of geography,* which some experts believe to be a factor in Kremlin decisions.

Other powers (dwarfs compared to the U.S.S.R.) control choke points on the routes of egress from the Black and Baltic Seas and, to a lesser degree, the straits opening to the Pacific from the Sea of Japan. This geographical fact did not deter Czarist Russia from maintaining fleets of predecessor capital ships, the graceful ship of the line, and the awesome battleship. However, these were used before the day of the airplane, with its long reach, guided missiles, or nuclear explosives. The twilight days of the Czars coincided with the beginning of the submarine's phenomenal growth as a decisive force in navies.

Against these changes one must consider that in time of peace, Soviet warships and merchantmen freely use the international straits. Thus the straits are not true barriers. Furthermore, the smaller nations bordering the choke points lie "under the guns" of Russia.

The Kremlin's desire to walk before running is certainly another possible reason for delaying construction of CVAs. Stalin had worked up to the point of initiating construction of battleships and planning carriers when World War II raged into Russia. Resulting devastation and the opportunities to extend communism into the nations along Russia's frontiers after the war made it necessary to concentrate, first of all, upon power at home. The submarine, the airplane, the long-range nuclear missile, and a massed army combined to form a barrier of defense and a deterrent against attack. These also provided the Politbureau with a blackmail threat to the West while covering successful takeover attempts as in Poland, Czechoslovakia, and Hungary. They failed in similar ventures in Turkey, Greece, Korea, and so far in Vietnam, where in each instance U.S. sea power could aid.

Land-based planes are very effective within their range of operations; hence the Soviets could have reached down into the first three of these countries. But in that time the U.S.S.R. had not recovered from war and could not begin to match the United States in atomic explosives. Today the situation is different.

Thus in the first postwar years Soviet leaders pragmatically concentrated on attaining military strength most quickly feasible. At the same time their empire digested the direct territorial gains and the satellites behind the iron curtain that had no choice otherwise—as demonstrated by several abortive revolts that the Kremlin has ruthlessly stamped out.

Meanwhile, the Politbureau continued the unceasing boring from within to weaken and overthrow non-Communist governments near and far. The U.S.S.R.'s successes and failures in the struggle for the world and the reasons for failure must have determined the successive decisions to expand maritime strength.

Distant victories in the seizing of power by Communists or near-Communists, as in Egypt, North Vietnam, and Cuba, brought overseas allies. The U.S.S.R. needed merchant ships to reach them with military and economic aid. More ships would also make possible direct economic and political influence in other nations. As overseas commerce and "friends" increased, the Soviets also required warships on the scene for prestige, power, and political pressure.

The First Step toward Soviet Carriers

Failure left its lessons. Bitter experience often teaches better than success. If the Kremlin leaders thought they would gain the maritime power needed through missiles and long-range submarines, they came up with a "round turn" in the Cuban missile crisis of 1962. This failure, plus the daily frustration of their world ambition by the 6th and

7th Fleets built around the versatile attack carriers must have precipitated the decision to aim for a more balanced fleet. That the Cuban setback influenced this view seems likely since the 1963 edition of the *Red Star* speaks of the "new missions assigned" to the navy, especially "combat with the enemy's navy."

With this next stage in development, the Soviet Navy had reached the point at which the construction of carriers could no longer be delayed. It seems reasonable that the Kremlin would start with an ASW/Amphibious carrier. After all, these are not minor warships. At 19,000 tons, *Moskva* and *Leningrad* are larger than USS *Ranger* (CV-4), the United States' first carrier built as such, and not markedly less in displacement than *Enterprise* (CV-6), famous warrior of World War II.

Because of the construction cycle, the decision to build *Moskva* had to have been made in 1962 or earlier. True fleet carriers with jet planes might have followed except for the United States' notable achievement in the rapid commissioning of Polaris submarines and the Minuteman ICBM ashore developed from the Polaris missile.

Ballistic Missiles

The Kremlin then turned the nation's highest energies toward surpassing the United States' Polaris submarine fleet as well as speeding up other nuclear submarine construction. The preceding chapter outlined the alarming progress of the Soviets in both these fields, the momentum they have achieved, and the certainty that they will pull ahead of the United States both in nuclear attack submarines and in the awesome "Yankee" boats patterned after the Polaris.

It is certain the Soviets will pull ahead because of the long lead time required to build the atomic power plants as well as the hull and the specialized equipment of the intricate ballistic missile boats. Soviet submarines cannot yet deliver more ballistic missiles than those of the United States, but they are swiftly approaching that goal.

The Kremlin concentrated also on surging ahead in shore-launched ICBMs. Estimates in 1971 give them up to 1,400 ICBM launchers versus 1,054 in the United States. Not only does the number of launchers continue to increase but the size and power of the missiles is becoming notably greater.

Perhaps a quarter of the Soviet Union's inventory in mid-1971 consists of the huge SS-9. It can carry a single warhead with explosive power up to twenty-five times that of Minuteman or several separately targeted warheads in one missile—similar to the U.S. MIRV—the multiple independently targeted reentry vehicle that can strike out against a number of individual targets. While turning out large numbers of this huge weapon of destruction, the Soviets are working on even more sophisticated missiles. In 1970 they shot some of these with multiple warheads into the northern Pacific.

Soviet Superiority in Antiship Missiles

In surface attack missiles other than ballistic ones the Soviet Navy has left the United States in its wake. Early in the 1950s Khrushchev apparently decided that if missile-armed ships and planes were added to subs, U.S. naval superiority might be matched. One does not have to be concerned about recoil with a guided missile. Hence a destroyer, or even a small patrol craft that would have trouble handling a three-inch gun, can launch a missile with the punch of a sixteen-inch battle-ship gun. Guided missiles should also register a higher percentage of hits than a gun unless they are shot down or diverted by electronic jamming equipment. However, a small guided missile vessel such as the Soviet *Komars* (100 tons) carries only two missiles, and the *Osa* class (200 tons) mounts four similar ones—a fraction of one percent of a battleship's outfit of projectiles. Like any other ship a battleship could also carry guided missiles. But the small vessels can be produced quickly in order to deliver the big punch soon. Then larger ships can follow.

The Soviet Navy has 125 to 150 missile boats of these two classes. They back up almost 40 guided missile cruisers and destroyers, of which about half mount surface-to-surface missile launchers or both AA and surface-to-surface.

In addition, the navy has 65 or more guided missile submarines. Their "cruise" missiles—similar to those discussed earlier in this chapter—have characteristics and performance levels comparable to super-sonic aircraft; with mid-flight observation and correction they can fly hundreds of miles. Fitted with conventional or atomic warheads, they present a problem to most surface ships but not so much to carriers or ships in a carrier task force, the planes of which can destroy them and their mid-flight monitors at a distance (provided the force gets early warning, as it should from its air patrols). Not overly vulnerable either are modern warships unaccompanied by planes but mounting the latest AA/antimissile and electronic jamming systems. Most vulner-able would be the host of merchant and other logistics ships that plow constantly through the "furrowed sea," supplying the economy of na-tions and the needs of military forces in war or peace.

The larger surface ships carry medium- or long-range missiles that reach out 100 to 300 miles with midflight guidance. NATO has coined the name *Styx* on the short-range missile mounted on the numerous fast patrol boats. It ranges up to 18 miles and gives the patrol boat a mighty punch, as was demonstrated in the sinking of the Israeli destroyer *Elath,* hit at a range of 13 or 14 miles.

The finest of the surface-to-surface missile ships is the new *Kresta* class of light cruisers. Built at a Leningrad shipyard, the first one appeared in the late 1960s. The Soviet Navy has five or more of these 6,000-ton gas turbine powered, fast and versatile cruisers that have no counterpart in the U.S. Navy. They mount surface-to-air missiles (SAM) probably comparable to those in the U.S. Navy. In addition their armament includes long-range surface-to-surface missiles, four 57mm. rapid-firing guns, torpedoes, multibarrel ASW launchers, and a helicopter. They speed through the water at thirty-four knots. The cruisers combine the qualities of the earlier *Kynda* cruisers and the *Kashin* class destroyer, said by some to be the fastest destroyer in the world, with speeds reaching thirty-seven to thirty-eight knots.

The U.S. Navy probably had superior AA gunnery and missiles before Vietnam, but Soviet experience and development on that battle proving ground may have closed the gap. The Hanoi-Haiphong area had the heaviest and most effective concentration of guided missiles and gun AA defense of any shore area in history. The experience gained there has, of course, been absorbed by the navy.

Antiaircraft

The USN AA missiles, which took the lead early over any others, were *Tartar, Terrier,* and *Talos,* in ascending order of range. *Talos,* carried by cruisers, ranges well over sixty-five miles. A radar beam rider, it has a semiactive homing head. It is fitted in seven cruisers, all but one of which are conversions of old World War II designs. It may well be the best long-range AA system in the world, as was the navy's five-inch thirty-eight-gun system in its heyday.

Terrier, a mid-range homing antiaircraft missile, is in over thirty USN destroyers or larger ships. Models have steadily improved in performance and range since they were introduced into the fleet some two decades ago as the nation's first effective AA missiles. Early versions had a range of about ten miles. Current operational ones double that, and future models will extend still further.

Tartar, the smaller short-range AA missile, appears on about forty ships of the navy, mostly destroyers. It has an effective range of nearly ten miles. The *Standard* missile, developed in two versions, will replace *Terrier* and *Tartar;* each version will have a greater range than that of the present missiles.

With AA missiles on more than seventy-five ships the USN surpasses the Soviet Navy in this category by a margin of two to one. This superiority is crucially important. Large numbers of Soviet aircraft carry air-to-surface guided missiles. The naval air arm, equipped with planes designed predominantly for the Soviet Air Force, flies between 750 and 850 aircraft. These include 300 *Badgers* (TU-16) with a range approaching 5,000 miles; 50 *Bears* (TU-95 turbo props) with a range of about 7,800 miles; some *Blinders* (TU-22, supersonic); at least 100 helicopters, 200 transports, and 50 amphibians. Most of the heavy planes came from Soviet long-range aviation after 1958, when complete *Badger* regiments, planes, and crews transferred to the navy. Other planes and crews will undoubtedly transfer if needed.

The naval air arm is adept at patrolling and ASW. A large portion of the planes can carry air-to-surface missiles. Some *Badgers* with radar jamming gear installed accompany missile flights. The AS-2 missile has a range of about 100 miles. The newer *Kitchen* missile, carried by the fast *Blinder* medium bomber, flies 150 miles. Like ship surface-to-surface missiles, these would be most effective against vessels unaccompanied by planes and least effective against a carrier task force.

The best protection against any missile is to destroy the missile-bearing ship or plane before launch. The carrier task force has the best existing means of accomplishing this. Developments underway will greatly increase this capability of the task force as well as defense by individual ships against guided missiles.

The United States and NATO allies are producing the *Sea Sparrow* antimissile system. This will provide important progress in coping with the cruise missile. It will be followed in a few years by the *Aegis* (Shield) and *Phoenix* missile systems. The latter is now being installed in the navy's new F-14 intercepter, and it has already proved highly successful in tests. It should become an effective counter to the Soviet air- and surface ship-launched cruise missiles. *Aegis* will counter the far more dangerous submarine-launched cruise missile as well as those from ships and planes. While adding capability against cruise missiles, each new system also brings significant advance in antiaircraft and antiship effectiveness.

Guns still play an important role in naval operations, as the Vietnam War has demonstrated. For AA defense the missile has become more important than the gun, but the latter can be a good backstop. U.S. Navy ships mount the World War II champion five-inch, thirty-eight caliber gun, its powerful, much heavier successor the five-inch, fifty-four caliber, and the rapid firing three-inch, fifty. The latter has taken the place of forty-mm. and twenty-mm. machine guns of World War II in ships large enough to accommodate it. Among other advances strengthening ship fire power, Ordnance System Command has put into production rocket-assisted projectiles that increase the range of guns and a new lightweight five-inch, fifty-four caliber gun. This remarkable weapon weighs only one third as much as the original heavyweight it replaces, and it operates with a six-man gun crew instead of sixteen. It automatically loads, sets fuses, and fires all types of five-inch, fifty-four caliber ammunition, including the rocket-assisted projectile. The gun crew need not enter the mount. The gun is loaded, controlled, and fired from remote positions.*

Perhaps the Kremlin hopes that by gaining superiority in ICBM, Polaris type missile submarines, nuclear attack submarines, and air- and ship-borne offensive missiles, the United States' aircraft superiority will be overcome.

If this should not work out, helicopter carriers provide a start on another option. Their appearance coincided with Soviet work on STOL (Short Take Off and Landing) and VTOL (Vertical) planes. They now fly at least three STOL fighters with maximum speed ranging from mach 2 in the slowest to mach 2.8 in the Flagon B (NATO designated name). Development models of VTOL planes are also flying. The *Freehand* subsonic plane represents an important step toward a supersonic successor. Thus it would be possible for the Soviet Navy to begin attack carrier operations with the present helicopter carrier or a modified design that would be available much sooner than large types.

In any event, except for unforeseen developments, it seems inevitable that as Soviet spheres of influence develop overseas, the U.S.S.R. will go to attack carriers within this decade. It would be unwise to conclude that they will let this formidable weakness continue. They have examined the usefulness, and they have copied and tried to match the U.S. Navy's superiority in other fields, such as atomic energy and the Polaris submarine. By utmost concentration of talents, work force, and resources the Soviets have moved forward at a pace that has amazed knowledgeable observers. They forge ahead with such momentum that they now have the lead in nuclear subs. It seems inevitable that they will surpass the United States' Polaris fleet, which is frozen at forty-one boats. The Kremlin follows Clausewitz's maxim, "Strategy is always to be very strong, first generally, then at the decisive point."

With their other problems under control, the Politbureau may now be readying for the assault on the carrier lead—the one American trump card that has remained while other U.S. advantages have wilted

---

*Several models of smaller, very rapid firing guns are now available, mostly of foreign manufacture. These and other developments may well return the gun to prominence in AA defense, against plane or missile.

away. In August, 1969, Admiral Thomas Moorer made several statements that America should heed:

> The aircraft carrier is an extremely effective system . . . to serve either a strategic or a tactical need. . . .
> With its air wing, it is a positive means by which we can control the sea or air, if required, in most vital areas. We saw this at Suez, Lebanon, Cuba, Vietnam, and off North Korea.
> It is a logical substitute for the fast diminishing number of U.S. Air Bases located at critical points worldwide. U.S. overseas air installations have dropped from nearly 150 in 1954 to around 45 in 1968.
> Except for Polaris, there is probably no item of U.S. sea power the Soviets would prefer us to cut back more than our aircraft carriers.
> . . . I believe our aircraft carriers are the key to our present superiority. With too few, or none, the Soviets would probably be the leading naval power.

Besides sources listed with Chapter IX, I have found useful *Jane's All the World Aircraft, Naval Aviation News,* and Navy Department studies on attack aircraft carriers.

11

Amphibious and Other Power

Along with carrier aviation, ASW operations, and Polaris submarines, no other part of the complex navy has been as important to the United States and world peace as amphibious capability. This depends upon suitable amphibious ships and craft to transport the ever ready, hard hitting fleet marine force, which the navy projects on the far shore. Amphibious capability depends also, in one way or another, upon most of the other surface ships of the navy as well as on submarines and airplanes. An amphibious assault becomes an extensive overall naval effort—first to reach the objective, next to land the marines, and finally to withstand any force.

Without aircraft, fire support ships, the unceasing flow of resupply ships, or the protecting fleet at sea, no amphibious operation against a foe with a strong fleet or air force can succeed. If the landing is on a shoestring with any key element of the fleet in short supply (or if control of the sea is uncertain, as at Guadalcanal in World War II), the role of the cutting edge ashore becomes difficult and perilous indeed.

Considering the present status of the two navies, we can say without question that the U.S. far surpasses the U.S.S.R. in distant overseas amphibious power. This would not necessarily be true for short-range landing operations within supporting range of Soviet tactical aviation.

The United States must have superiority in deep water amphibious ability. Overseas events have highlighted this truth time after time during the past twenty-five years. The amphibians rank only after the carriers in helping to ease tension, to calm unrest, and to promote peace. When war comes, they and the rest of the fleet will be irreplace-able—and judging from all past experience I think it will come again.

During the 1930s the United States developed amphibious tactics and doctrine, but budget strictures impeded development of amphibi-ous craft. The demands of World War II forced the nation into a crash program of building amphibians unlike anything in her history. These provided the lift and the ship-to-shore movement for the series of sledgehammer assaults that drove irresistibly on to the shores of North Africa and Europe and up and across the Pacific.

The wholesale disposal of the navy after VJ Day included most of the amphibs. Many were sold or transferred to other nations, includ-ing Japan, to serve the occupation forces. After the Korean War the United States maintained a modest amphibious capability in each ocean. Amphibious commands on both coasts (with the USMC) con-stantly trained and maintained a productive program of development of amphibious craft, equipment, and techniques.

In the past decade, as the aging World War II veterans vanished from the active and reserve fleets, splendid replacements—though in smaller numbers—have joined. These are larger, faster, more complex, and more versatile craft, which greatly increase the speed of response and effectiveness of ship-to-shore movement of an assault force.

Some are modern versions of old craft with the same function. This applies to the workhorse LST, unheard of before World War II but needed everywhere in the far-flung campaigns of that conflict and in subsequent wars. Launched by the mile and cut off in convenient lengths, LSTs still could not satisfy the demand until after the defeat of Germany. Normandy landings had to be delayed a month from the set target date of 1 May 1944, in order for additional amphibious vessels to be rolled off American production lines. The planned co-ordinated assault in southern France had to be omitted and did not take place until six weeks later, when part of the Normandy fire sup-port and amphibious ships were able to participate. During the heated discussions leading up to these decisions Churchill said with dismay, "The destinies of two great empires . . . seem to be tied up in some goddamned things called LSTs."

One gains some idea of the magnitude of the amphibious shipping problem when one recollects that besides a vast amount of other ship construction, the United States built nearly 80,000 small landing craft and more than 4,000 large beaching vessels, including 1,041 LSTs in World War II. The World War II LST displaced at full load about 4,000 tons; it transported about 150 troops and lumbered along with a fair wind at ten to eleven knots.

Today's LST is the fourth generation of the World War II class. USS *Boulder* (LST 1190), now relieving the slow old warriors, is typical of these new ships. It displaces over 8,000 tons, transports amphibious craft, tanks, and other combat vehicles, along with up to five hundred men to the hostile shore at over twenty knots. Like its predecessor, it is designed to be beached (defying the law of the seaman never to run aground), but unlike the old LST it has an extendable ramp. The ramp is supported by two huge projecting derrick extensions rising on each side of the bow like arms reaching for the shore. As the ship runs aground, the ramp shoots forward hydraulically, stretching 112 feet forward. Vehicles and men start speeding ashore at once—dry shod if the incline is steep, through the last shallows if the beach slopes more— or onto a pontoon causeway. Meanwhile, amphibious tractors in the tank deck chug through the stern gates.

The Multipurpose LPH

Other developments include a completely new type: the LPH, an amphibious assault ship that transports and lands the assault combat team with helicopters. The LPH combines certain functions of two large predecessor ships. Into it are incorporated duties of the assault transport (LPA) with its combat-loaded assault troops and some of those of the assault cargo ship (LKA) with combat-loaded supporting equipment, munitions, and supplies. In the future, as V/STOL combat planes go into service, the LPH may also take on some of the functions of those skilled escort carriers (CVEs) of World War II and Korea that provided such splendid close air support.

This is the world's first ship designed specifically to operate helicopters. An LPH such as *Guam*, for example, at some 18,000 tons full load, displaces not much more than the larger assault transports of World War II such as *Clay* (APA 39).* The new ship transports about two thousand troops swiftly to the objective at speeds over twenty knots, as opposed to about fifteen for the World War II craft. As she arrives off the landing area, there is no delay in boating the assault troops, in assembling at the line of departure, or in breasting the waves in a long run to the beach.

Instead the troops board their helicopters, quickly rendezvous, and wing through the skies at speeds fifteen to twenty times that of the boats. V/STOL planes will undoubtedly soon provide close support, though CVA planes must also be on hand for air protection and for suppression of enemy fire. Antisubmarine planes and helicopters will also be needed. The LPH significantly increases ease and speed of

---

*Letter designation now LPA.

assault and decreases dependence upon the condition of beaches and the state of the sea.

The navy will have seven of these fine LPHs and twenty of the new LSTs, now active or commissioning by about mid-1972. Since the peak of the Korean crisis, the navy has also built or is completing 13 LSDs (Dock Landing Ships) and fifteen LPDs (Amphibious Transport Dock).

The New LSD and LPD

The newer LSD follows its useful World War II predecessor but is tailored to meet the needs of swift vertical envelopment. It is larger—the five newest craft displacing up to 14,000 tons at full load—it makes over twenty knots against fifteen for the World War II version, and it has a helicopter platform that will accommodate the transport helicopter. Its stern gates open to allow amtracs transported in the "dock" to proceed fully loaded directly to the beach. The newest ones can move about five hundred troops to the objective with their amphibians and all other combat equipment. Like its predecessor it can drydock and repair landing craft off the hostile shore.

LPDs incorporate the functions of LPAs and LKAs. To the characteristics of these two large assault ships it adds those of the LSD with some of the helicopter capabilities of the LPH. *Cleveland* (LPD-7) is representative of the seven latest ones. It has a full load displacement of close to 17,000 tons and can attain a speed of over twenty knots, as can the other modern amphibians. It transports about one thousand combat-loaded assault troops with equipment and amtracs and boats in its dock. A helicopter flight deck covers the dock for about the last third of the ship's length. The LPD can launch simultaneously amtracs for the frontal assault and helicopers for vertical envelopment to the rear of the beach.

The 40,000-Ton LHA

A handful of other amphibious warfare ships have joined the fleet since 1945. Under contract for commissioning in 1973 are five large LHAs (Amphibious Assault Ships—General Purpose). These will be the navy's biggest ships after the carriers and AOEs.

Expected to displace as much as 40,000 tons, these ships are comparable in size to our World War II *Essex* class carriers. The LHA is an alternative, in varying degrees, to the LKA, LPD, LPH, and LSD. It will have the capability of maintaining the tactical integrity of the embarked marines by carrying a balanced load of troops, combat vehicles, and combat cargo for a battalion landing team and the flexibility of landing this team ashore by any combination of transportation using embarked helicopters and landing craft. In addition, it will have a sophisticated automated command and control system for the embarked commanders, a unique cargo handling system, a modern 300-bed hospital, and a highly automated engineering plant and damage control system.

Thus, as the world turns into the crises of the complex 1970s, the United States in mid-1971 has some thirty-five large, fast modern ships designed for quick amphibious reaction and the same number of post-war LSTs. This is a far cry from the more than four hundred LPAs, LKAs, LSDs, and about nine hundred LSTs with which the U.S. ended World War II.

The United States could not possibly mount a giant assault against defended beaches such as Okinawa without years of buildup, and her seriously reduced merchant marine would aggravate the situation. However, the nation does, for the first time in her peacetime history, have modern and fast amphibious forces.

Big Gun and Close Air Support Wane

Amphibious ships and craft themselves make up only part of the required team. Most of the fleet must participate in landings against important opposition. Therefore, we might summarize the status of those elements not covered previously.

The big gun is critical in overcoming fortifications of strength. The slashes in budget after 1945, reducing the fleet to a skeleton of victory years, included the wholesale retirement of battleships and cruisers and the ultimate scrapping of most of them. The frightening crisis of Korea interrupted the trend but did not terminate it. Nor has Vietnam. Of the twenty-three battleships that ended World War II, most have been scrapped and now no doubt exist in automobiles, television sets, radios, and other comforts so prized by Americans. States have memorialized four of them. The four latest, now a generation old, lie mothballed and could not be made ready for action for more than a year—though *New Jersey's* service off Vietnam demonstrated that for shore fire support the battleships' value remains undiminished and irreplaceable.

Much the same has happened to cruisers that deliver a punch second only to that of the battleship. Of the ninety-one that ended World War II or were completed afterward, today nine remain in commission; only one of these retains eight-inch guns. The others have been converted to missile ships. As such, with Talos and Tartar missiles, they are invaluable to the fleet but do not provide the heavy gunfire support needed. Other eight-inch cruisers lie in the mothball fleet. In a crisis the marines would have to do the best they could without the precise, penetrating, heavy caliber gun support that smashes hard defense and reduces American casualties. A new rocket-assisted projectile extending the reach of the five-inch gun helps to compensate for the long-range advantage of the heavy gun but not for its hitting power.

Opponents have provided many witnesses to the effectiveness of big gunfire from offshore. Both Germans and Japanese testified to their dread of it. In reporting on the Saipan operation Admiral Harry W. Hill wrote: ". . .naval gunfire is the most feared and most effective of all weapons . . . Without exception, prisoners of war have stated that naval gunfire prevented their movement by day or night and was the most deciding factor in accomplishing their defeat."

With the fading of the big gun punch, part of the skilled close air support provided by the escort carriers in World War II and Korea has gone also. The escort carriers may have a partial future replacement in the LPH. Helicopters have valuable capabilities for close support, but they lack speed and heavy firepower and are more vulnerable to strong AA defense. If their duties in protecting the assault landing area and sea lanes permit, CVA and CVS can participate effectively. But because this is not their primary function, the planes—unless they belong to trained marine squadrons—will not obtain the same results achieved by the CVE squadrons experienced in working with the troops. V/STOL planes operating from LHAs and LPHs may, in time, fill the gap.

Auxiliaries and Smaller Amphibians

The navy has over one hundred types of ships. Most of these serve in overseas operations. They include tankers, ammunition ships, reefers, repair tenders of several sorts, net ships, minecraft, gunboats, and various other kinds besides amphibians, submarines, and the powerful surface combat ships of several destroyers and larger types. During the last decade the navy department has made significant improvements in both combat and auxiliary ships. One example will suffice.

In World War II the U.S. Navy developed underway replenishment to such a science that task forces were able to keep the sea for months at a time. Critical types were tankers, ammunition ships, and, to a lesser degree, others such as reefers—refrigerated provision ships.

Now a single large, fast, versatile ship has come along to carry out the duties of the first two and many duties of the reefers and supply ships. The AOE (Fast Combat Support Ship), for instance, *Detroit* (AOE 4), delivers fuel, ammunition, provisions, and supplies while steaming at high speed. These transfer to the receiving ships on each side by fuel line, high line, and helicopter (which can lift many tons), thus trimming replenishment time to a minimum. Nearly 800 feet long with a beam of 107 feet, displacing over 52,000 tons and speeding at better than 25 knots, the AOE marks a notable advance in the capability of the fleet to keep the sea serving the needs of the nation.

Like other World War II construction, the multitude of smaller amphibious ships—LCI, LCT, control craft, and others—has been retired and/or scrapped. The United States has some 75 postwar LCUs (Landing Craft, Utility), replacements for and somewhat larger than LCTs, of which the United States built over 1,400 in World War II.

The new LCPL (Landing Craft, Personnel, Large), built in small numbers since Korea, guides and controls assault waves of amphibious craft and polices traffic off the beach. It has higher speed than its predecessors, with radar and good communications so that it can replace the APD, which was used as a control vessel for larger assaults in World War II.

A limited number of small ships has joined the fleet, such as the fast aluminum-fiber glass-balsa wood gunboat. New developments include also surface effect craft and small hydrofoil vessels under evaluation that could be forerunners of suitable ASW and inshore amphibious types.

Thus the U.S. Navy possesses an excellent nucleus for a quick reacting and effective amphibious force—well tailored to cope with peace crises such as those of the past quarter century. It can lift the assault echelon of an expeditionary force of marine division and air wing in one ocean at twenty knots—a speed scarcely dreamed of in World War II. With the addition of older ships and the accepting of slower speed, it approached this capability for the other ocean; but after the severe defense cutbacks of 1969–1970 it can no longer do so. The nation could handle a limited crisis but could not meet sudden large demands which, as the leading nation of the maritime free world, it must be prepared to encounter. The dwindling merchant fleet and almost complete disappearance of active passenger liners under the American flag compound the problem.

Soviet Amphibious Capabilities Steadily Grow

These deficiencies reduce but do not negate the fact that the United States still retains far better capability than the Soviets for sizable long-range overseas operations. However, the U.S.S.R.'s rapidly expanding merchant marine, new helicopter carriers, and other late naval types make more than a dent in this lead. Should their *Moskvas* begin to come off the ways in significant numbers, the situation would change. And well it might before long because of Moscow's perception of the importance of amphibious operations as well as carriers and submarines in the international poker game.

A different picture emerges for shorter range amphibious operations. In these the Soviet Navy, with support from the army and air force, could become quite effective for subversion, enforced persuasion, or conquest, especially of weak nations.

Throughout their maritime history the Russians have demonstrated skill, bravery, and ingenuity in limited amphibious operations within or near the growing empire's frontiers. Preparing for the future, in recent years they have begun to build large specialized amphibious ships, including the "Alligator," an improved version of the U.S. World War II LST, and more LSMs (smaller tank landing ships), many of which were built in Poland. The Soviet fleet has perhaps 100 of these and older types, a similar number of smaller ones of 200 to 800 tons, and any number of commercial coastal and riverine craft that could be employed, as in World War II, for short amphibious hops.

The Soviets have powerful river flotillas on the Danube, the Amur, and possibly elsewhere. Representative of these, the Danube force consists of approximately a hundred craft with two battalions of "Black Beret" naval commandos and tanks. Built mostly in the last decade, the flotilla boasts 120-ton armored gunboats and similar size landing craft, fast artillery boats, minesweepers, and hydrofoils. It also has various amphibians and other craft developed for assault, river crossing, and artillery support for the troops.

With more than two hundred cruiser and destroyer types and many more frigates and patrol craft, the Soviet Navy could provide strong shore bombardment and fire support at sea and in the deeper rivers. Naval and air force planes flying from Soviet fields provide reasonable air support for limited range operations, backing up the helicopter carriers.

The revival of the naval infantry in 1964 (after Cuba), with the *Moskvas* and Alligators, reveals the outward direction of Soviet thinking. The naval infantry has reached only a portion of the USMC's strength—probably less than a division—but it could serve to calm insurgency in one of the "democratic peoples' governments" such as Syria. If needed, the army could provide backup troops transported by merchant ships—all marked for military use.

It seems clear that the Soviets could launch powerful operations against any amphibious objective in the Baltic or Black Seas (including conquering their entrances), where they have achieved significant success in the past. If their penetration into the Middle East grows— as in Syria, Egypt, and Yemen—they could leap frog a long way. This could be accomplished simply by using satellite powers buttressed and reinforced by a constant flow of Soviet planes, tanks, missiles, artillery, and other arms, as in Korea, Vietnam and, most lately, the frustrated Syrian invasion of Jordan in late September, 1970. Would the United States be willing to take up arms a third time, after Korea and Vietnam, to try to halt a "limited" step in the ever outward surge of Soviet ambition, increasingly facilitated by her maritime power?

Soviet amphibious capability could extend even farther afield. The navy and commercial service have sufficient tankers and tenders available for distant expeditions. In the past few years naval task forces have operated in the Indian Ocean, constantly in the Mediterranean, the Atlantic, and even the Caribbean, depending upon at-sea replenishment and repair.

For illustration, in 1969 and in the spring and autumn of 1970, task forces cruised the Caribbean and visited various ports, other than Havana. They have included missile ships, conventional and nuclear submarines, support ships, and an amphibious ship in 1970's fall maneuvers. Even a few ships could weight the scales in favor of Communist success in a fomented revolution in which small force promptly and efficiently exerted would suffice.

A more serious development was the administration's announcement in late September, 1970, of indications of Soviet preparations to build a submarine base at Cienfuegos, Cuba. These actions demonstrate that Moscow intends to establish a permanent naval presence in the Caribbean. Accelerating Soviet maritime power and the dwindling strength of the United States at sea have encouraged increased boldness in overt actions to promote the spread of communism overseas.

Intelligence-Gathering Ships

Intelligence- or Information-Gathering Ships will be noted in this chapter, though their functions relate to the whole national security problem and only in certain instances to amphibious operations. These ships and planes outfitted with special electronic gear gather information on radar, communications, ship and plane movements, gun and missile sites, and any other vital data concerning a nation's navy, air and missile operations, and coastal areas.

This is a legitimate function, not a nefarious one, as some news reporters and other Americans tried to make of *Pueblo's* operations. To this observer it seemed as if much of this confused, if not vicious, thinking was prompted by Communists to excuse North Korea's disregard of international law.

Unfortunately the captain of the *Pueblo* surrendered his ship rather than sinking her. In due course, thereafter, the United States withdrew the handful of small, slow, and unarmed vessels of *Pueblo's* ilk, depending upon aircraft, satellites, and warships for the accumulation of valuable information.

The U.S.S.R., relying upon the United States' regard for international law, has similar means of gathering data. In addition, she continues to operate a number of specialized intelligence ships. *Jane's Fighting Ships* lists nineteen by name, and, considering the number sighted at sea carrying detection equipment, there are probably others. Admiral Moorer states, "These are mostly trawler hulls equipped with modern electronic surveillance gear and used for intelligence collection against U.S. and NATO forces, particularly naval forces. They station these ships off Polaris bases. They attempt to monitor fleet exercises and tests, and they observe our space activities."

These ships appear in all waters in which it would be profitable, often operating as fishing trawlers. They attach themselves to U.S. naval forces at home and overseas, often interfering with maneuvers. The 6th Fleet can usually depend upon having its trawler or warship shadows around. So can ships in exercise areas such as those off New England, Virginia, North Carolina, Florida, California, and any place where Polaris submarines can be observed. The trawlers and other ships keep close tabs on East and West Coast missile ranges.

In July, 1970, USS *James Madison* (SSBN 627) prepared to make the first submarine undersea launch of the Poseidon missile. The patrolling Soviet oceanographic survey/tracking ship *Khariton Laptev* stayed so close that the launch had to be deferred. When the successful launch took place some days later, the Soviet ship nearly collided with *James Madison's* surface escort as the Soviet ship tried to recover fragments of the launching collar. The Soviet ship struck out.

Riverine and Mine Warfare

Riverine and mine warfare have close affinity to amphibious warfare, so I will consider them in this chapter. In both these areas the Soviet Navy probably leads. As for riverine war, if this were being written in the mid-1960s we could say that there is no contest, so great was the Soviet lead then.

After taking over Russia, the Communists carried on the Czarist Navy record of effective river and coastal war, particularly in combined operations. The U.S.S.R. ended World War II with numerous small vessels for these operations. As noted earlier in discussion of river flotillas, she has maintained this capability with new and better craft.

The 150 guided missile patrol craft in the Soviet fleets add significant strength and enormous punch in restricted waters as well as elsewhere. The host of small craft that navigate the U.S.S.R.'s mighty rivers as a normal means of transporting people and cargo provide a reserve of small transport and cargo ships far beyond the needs for combat on river or limited range campaigns on coastal seas.

The United States, with different requirements than the U.S.S.R., had limited capabilities for riverine operations before Vietnam except where the depth of inland waters permitted operations by the smaller ocean going ships. Necessity in the watery maze of Vietnam forced the development of respectable riverine and inshore task forces.

Besides existing small ships of the navy and coast guard, several new types developed, such as the Swift, River Patrol Boat, and River Assault Boat, which the Soviets may or may not have. But if they do not, they can easily duplicate them. Should the United States need them in the future, she also would have to build them since the true river craft—and many of the inshore ones—have properly been turned over to Vietnam. Operating there under a new flag, they are too valuable to be withdrawn for use elsewhere.

The U.S. Navy will try to maintain its riverine capability. But under the present severe budget restrictions and grave demands in other duties, it will be, at best, on a very minor, austere scale. Thus, the Soviet Navy, with its strong and active river flotillas, will continue to stay in the vanguard.

In mine warfare the Soviets also appear to be well out in front. Mines have claimed the interest of both the United States and Russia for more than a century. The first important use in U.S. history was by the Confederate Army in the Civil War, when they sank a number of Union warships.

In World War I the U.S. Navy carried out the largest mine-laying operation in history up to that time in the great North Sea mine barrage against German submarines. Lean budgets between the wars resulted in the navy's possessing very limited capability in mine warfare when the storm burst in 1939.

Knowledge gained from the German and British experience and subsequent concentrated efforts corrected the deficiency in time. This war brought forth sophisticated magnetic, acoustic, and pressure mines as deadly shipmates of the contact and electrically detonated types.

Development in delay devices made it possible for mines in the same field to lie quiescent for moments or months before arming, thus increasing the difficulty of sweeping and passage without danger. Surface ships, submarines, and aircraft laid these mines. The United States' largest operation of this kind was performed by army air corps B29s flying navy mines out of the Marianas to the Sea of Japan. There they helped to secure the noose of the navy's blockade that was strangling Japan long before Hiroshima.

After VJ Day, the large cuts in the fleet seriously diminished the navy's capabilities for mine warfare as well as for its many other responsibilities. The deficiencies hurt in Korea, and they could have been fatal. Had the Soviets moved mines a little faster down Korea's west coast (or had General MacArthur not insisted on moving swiftly, regardless of incomplete readiness), Inchon might have been a different matter instead of one of history's most brilliant amphibious campaigns.*

A few weeks afterward at Wonsan, on the east coast, the Communists sank four vessels and held up the landing for days by adding magnetic influence mines to the contact ones. A Soviet naval detachment accompanying the mines held a short school for the North Koreans, planned the minefields, and supervised their placement. They showed what could be done by makeshift methods without existing minecraft or experienced men. Sampans towed barges loaded with mines. Coolies loaded the barges and rode them into the harbor. At the proper point on the chart, designated by the Soviets, they simply rolled them off the stern, planting a field of 2,000 mines in a short time.

Korea underlined the critical problems the future might bring. Accordingly, since that time the United States has continued to maintain reasonable mine warfare capability. Mine forces function in both the Pacific and Atlantic Fleets.** The navy has designed and produced several types of improved minecraft, including small nonmagnetic vessels for sweeping some of the advanced firing mechanisms in modern mines. Like the Soviets, the United States has continued to develop mines and sophisticated firing devices in naval ordnance laboratories such as that at White Oaks, Maryland.

Explosive Ordnance Disposal (EOD) experts are taught in the navy at schools and in practical application to dispose of bombs and other dangerous explosives. EOD units keep constantly on the go

---

*Because of an eight to ten knot current the waters would have been difficult to mine, but means probably could have been found.

**In July 1971 the navy consolidated these into a single command.

to meet fleet needs. At their bases these units are trained to disarm all types of ammunition, including nuclear devices. Mines, like projectiles, rockets, guided missiles, and bombs, can be nuclear. Riding the fleets on the frontiers of danger, these skilled men often have to disarm the most deadly munitions.

Following in the Czarist Navy's wake, the Soviet Navy has maintained a record of effective mine warfare. In World War II, as already noted, the Soviets employed mines ably in the Baltic. For defense they continue to consider this weapon a guardian of great importance for home waters. In the area of offense they have made extensive preparations for mining by plane, surface ship, and submarine. Mines could be a serious matter off the large U.S. Navy complex in the Norfolk-Hampton Roads area or off most other port approaches in which a few nuclear mines could cause incalculable problems.

From the allies and from German scientists lured to the U.S.S.R. after Germany's fall the Soviets obtained all the latest advances in mining. These were large indeed and comparable to those occurring in radar and guided missiles, Since then Soviet scientists have unquestionably continued improvements, including nuclear explosives, which have gone into the stockpile of mines assembled in various parts of the Soviet Union.

Most surface ships, submarines, and airplanes, with minor adaptations and some training, can lay mines. A few years ago the navy began building a class of fast modern surface minelayers with a capacity of 400 mines below deck and four launching tracks. The mine forces contain some 200 small ocean going craft and a similar number of coastal minecraft for sweeping or laying mines. Many of the larger ships have mine racks. These can be installed on any ship in a couple of days. Most of the Soviet Navy's huge fleet of submarines can lay mines, as can most of their aircraft. (Some of the navy's planes have made transatlantic flights to Cuba.)

The largest mine fleet of surface ships in the world could be easily augmented by Soviet fishing trawlers and merchant ships. Indeed, if the Kremlin planned another Pearl Harbor, merchant ships on normal commercial visits could carry one or two nuclear mines into ports of choice. Secreted in the hold the mine could be lowered quietly during the midwatch. The self-detonating mechanism would have a timer set for a precise hour weeks ahead. So laid in selected major ports of the world, the mines might in one moment end much of Western maritime power.

In mining, as in other fundamentals of maritime power, the U.S.S.R. manifests by deeds—not just words—its intention to develop the means to win the world to communism. Mine warfare capabilities seem adequate for this purpose.

In most of the fundamentals of maritime power Russia has already equaled or surpassed the United States. Amphibious capability is one of the few basic areas in which there is still some distance to go for overseas operations. But the Soviets rapidly acquire webs and are on the way.

The Soviets continue to learn from the United States and other navies and quickly adopt new, effective methods, such as vertical envelopment. Their helicopter carriers incorporate the latest concepts of amphibious warfare as developed by the U. S. Navy and Marine Corps. The Soviet fleets conduct assault landings as routine exercises during maneuvers, including those with European satellites.

Communist writers frequently point out that in limited or even nuclear war, amphibious operations inevitably become the final arbiter in many situations. And in no other way can Soviet power project itself overseas to a certain victorious conclusion against maritime nations.

Soviet leaders have experienced the benefits of their own amphious operations in war, and they have felt too often the impact of the United States' succcesses in cold war not to have gotten the point. From recent developments one cannot question that they intend to be ready to use this power whenever it suits their purposes.

In June, 1969, with clear foresight, the Center for Strategic and International Studies observed that the growth of Soviet amphibious capability "may provide an active deterrent to U.S. intervention in defense of allies and other interests."

The sources listed in Chapter IX served this chapter also. In addition, the following were valuable: *NAVSHIP Technical News; Dictionary of American Naval Fighting Ships* along with ship histories not yet in printed volumes; *Military Review* (U.S. Army Command and General Staff College); Naval *War College Review;* and amphibious studies.

12

Ocean Transport—
Lifeline of Nations

For her growth to world leadership Providence blessed the United States in many ways. One is a combination of broad territory filled with natural resources and a temperate climate that stimulates energy in its citizens. High on the list stands the type of government founded on the Declaration of Independence and Bill of Rights, which allows each man to work out his destiny in an environment of freedom under law.

Another blessing is the sea, which the U.S. is relinquishing to the U.S.S.R. The long open coastline on most of three frontiers, the bays, spreading harbors, and rivers reaching into the heartland of America are all manifestations of a maritime nation. On the oceans she was destined to find bounty and power.

This has proved to be true from the earliest days. In the colonial period the economy rested upon exports from farms, forests, and the sea. These paid for imports of manufactured items of every sort—salt (the deep freeze of the time), sugar, molasses, and rum. The economy prospered from the overseas traffic as many men turned to the sea as a way of life. The resulting large company of experienced seamen benefited the nation in several ways, not the least of which was the mine of experience to draw upon in time of war.

When the United States became independent, she was a seagoing nation, though a broad continent lay west of the blue mountains, awaiting the expansion a few generations would bring. During its first years the new republic's income stemmed almost entirely from excise taxes on overseas commerce, which has continued to grow like a rising tide.

Increasing Dependence on Commerce

The United States' surging growth into the world's number one industrial nation has not changed the trend or the categories of imports and exports. Products of her farms go not only to industrial nations but, via a steady flow of ships, to many countries with agricultural economies. Even rich Russia has tapped the cornucopia of American farms. So have most of the nations that support her.

American industry matches the farms in productive expertise. Factories can turn out nearly anything in excess of our domestic needs. Yet even as in colonial times, the United States continues to import manufactured goods of every sort from many lands.

Besides her rise to leadership in industry other changes have occurred that affect the use of the sea, some of which are of such grave import that every citizen should ponder them. One significant development is the fact that the United States increasingly has to import many raw materials by ship. Shortages in many critical areas increase with frightening speed. Right now we *must* import seventy to eighty different strategic materials that are crucial to our economy, military strength, and security. Others go to the very keel of industry and society.

While the industrial revolution continues to accelerate, so do America's overseas needs. As the leading steel manufacturing nation of the world, the United States at one time was thought to possess almost inexhaustible resources of iron ore. Yet today we are compelled to import in massive amounts. The iron ore comes not only from Canada but also from South America, Africa, and Australia.

The hunt for iron ore proceeds all over the world with an urgency almost matched by the quest for oil. Lakes have been drained in Canada to obtain rich ore. Railroads have been carved through the bleak vastness of Labrador; mountains have been stripped in Venezuela; and the jungle has been leveled in Brazil and Liberia.

The American steel industry grew up inland close to coal and iron deposits. Now giant complexes lie on waterways with deep channels opening to the sea. Bethlehem's largest plant has long been situated not in Bethlehem but in South Baltimore on the Chesapeake. In the 1950s U.S. Steel built one of the world's largest plants on the Delaware for seaborne imports.

As the demand for steel increases, giant ocean going ore ships have been built to help meet it. In 1970 the United States imported fifty million tons of iron ore—about four times the weight of every man, woman, and child in the nation.

From bauxite comes the alumina that refines into aluminum. This material goes into the nation's airplanes, which, in turn, comprise much of its economic and military strength. The United States must rely on imports to fill its needs for this basic ore. Streams of ships thread the Caribbean, transporting the output of mines in Jamaica, the Guianas, and elsewhere. The Soviet submarine base developing at Cienfuegos, Cuba, will gravely menace the United States. This fine harbor lies not far west of Guantanamo Bay, an important U.S. Navy training base developed after the United States helped Cuba to independence half a century before the present Communist enslavement.

Operating out of Cienfuegos, Soviet submarines will measurably increase the threat to the United States of ballistic missiles; these missiles launched from offshore are readily capable of reaching cities such as New Orleans, Kansas City, St. Louis, Chicago, and industrial centers situated along the East Coast. Submarines based there are also ideally stationed almost athwart the bauxite sea highways in order to choke off the flow of this crucial material. Should this happen, disaster would strike the air industry and the air strength of the army, navy, and air forceas well as the nation's domestic and overseas air transport.

Other ore ships ply the ocean, bringing such minerals as copper, nickel, and chrome in ever-increasing volume. Copper and other minerals help make possible the electronic miracles that enter into nearly every facet of civilian economy or military strength. Since the 1930s the field of electronics has grown with phenomenal speed. This science and its offshoots shape the future and weave through the whole economy. Furthermore, the bulk of our modern military hardware is dependent on electronic components or circuitry.

Nickel has a wide range of use in metal manufacture and the resulting products. Likewise, practically every major industry in the country needs chrome in its machinery, its tools, its stainless steel equipment. Yet through an unwise boycott of Rhodesia, the United States has made herself dependent upon the U.S.S.R. for much of her chrome—and pays through the nose for it.

World Hunger for Oil—and Dependence on Middle East

Nevertheless, petroleum outstrips all other commodities insofar as dependence on ocean transport is concerned. World consumption seems insatiable. The petroleum industry grew to global stature in the United States. For years she has produced more oil than any other nation—and until recently more than most regions. At the same time, she consumes the most. In fact, until the mid-1950s she consumed more than the rest of the world combined. Since 1950 demand for oil in the United States has more than doubled; for the rest of the world it has shot up five times.

The pinch of maintaining reserves in the United States becomes critical. Even as long ago as 1956 she proved only slightly more new oil than she took from the ground. With increasing consumption the situation has not improved. To maintain reserves wells go farther into the sea and deeper into the earth (about 5 miles down). The United States keeps up reserves at about twelve years of consumption by controlling production and importing foreign oil. Steadily increasing consumption has now reached more than 14 million barrels a day. The United States produces under 11 million barrels of crude and natural gas liquids.

To replace a single day's supply the United States must find or import* 600 million gallons of petroleum every twenty-four hours. She has to run as fast as she can just to stand still. Thus every American depends more and more upon ships.

With the rise in oil consumption, tankers have multiplied in number and have grown incredibly in size. Only as short a time ago as World War II the 17,000-ton tanker was the workhorse that met most of the navy's, the army's, and the nation's needs. In 1956 a tanker was completed at 56,000 tons, then the largest afloat. In the years since, tankers of 100,000 to 200,000 tons have become almost commonplace. As of this writing some 100 tankers of 200,000 to 300,000 tons are under construction or on order. Six 300,000-ton tankers sail the ocean highways already, and drawing boards contain plans for monsters of a million tons.

Some large tankers have already succumbed to the hazards of the sea. In December, 1969, while returning empty to the Persian Gulf, the Dutch tanker *Marpessa,* 207,000 tons, sank northwest of Dakar, Africa, after an explosion and fire.

Change sweeps the world, and most of all in the scientific/technological revolution. The curve of growth turns up sharply. In fact, it almost outstrips man's capacity to grasp it or control it, especially when the Kremlin ignites fuses to powder kegs in troubled lands everywhere. The revolution inexorably calls for more and more fuel. Discovery of new oil fields and development of existing ones do little more than match the increase in demand that rises faster than taxes. In the past decade alone world demand has almost doubled.

A similar ravenous appetite devours the world's reserves of natural gas and coal. Atomic energy plants are able to handle only part of

*About one-fifth of our imports now come from the Middle East, but this amount will increase.

the increased need. The situation began to become acute for the West in 1970 when a tractor "accidentally" broke the Transarabian Pipeline in Syria, with the government subsequently blocking repairs, and the Lybian government slowed production to force Western oil companies to come to terms on prices. Who would have thought a few years ago that in the autumn of 1970 the U.S. government would call upon industry and individual citizens to cut fuel usage by 10 percent in the winter ahead?

Although the United States produces and uses more petroleum than any other nation, most of the world's reserves lie in the Middle East and Africa. In the lands bounding the Persian Gulf the desert floats on seas of oil. No one knows how much lies beneath the sands. Current estimates of reserves run to over 270 billion barrels. The sheikdom of Kuwait alone, about 2 percent of the size of Texas, has estimated reserves larger than all of the United States. Saudi Arabia, Iran, Iraq, some of the Trucial Coast sheikdoms, and the bottom of the Persian Gulf itself have fabulous amounts of oil.

In 1958 knowledgeable men estimated that before 1980 the Middle East would have to supply about 18 million barrels of oil a day to nations outside the iron curtain. Halfway to that date, despite important new finds elsewhere, the Middle East already ships over 11 million barrels a day.

Oil in that troubled area yields itself not in reluctant trickles but in gushing fountains of black gold. Across the United States each of tens of thousands of wells patiently pumps a few barrels of oil a day. A well that produces a few hundred barrels almost seems like a gusher. The average for all wells in recent years has been under twenty barrels a day.

In the Middle East the average well produces several thousand barrels a day. Some years ago the saying there among oil men was that if a driller did not strike a 10,000-barrel-a-day producer by his third trial they would "exile him back to Texas."

Some of this oil fuels American ships, planes, and vehicles in the far Pacific. All services depended heavily upon it in the Korean and Vietnam struggles. Japan gets 90 percent of her petroleum from the Persian Gulf. Until a few years ago U. S. allies in Europe imported about 95 percent of their rising needs from the same area. The oil and gas discoveries in Moslem North Africa and in the North Sea and adjoining coast have, to some degree, reduced requirements from the Middle East. But the steep upward rise in consumption calls for more and more energy everywhere. In a few years the oil discoveries on Alaska's north slope and in Canadian territory to the east will help the United States, but the amount is a fraction of her future needs and of the Middle East reserves.*

Apart from the need for petroleum imports to feed the economy of the United States and its allies ashore, both the merchant marine and navy require oil to operate at all. The merchant marine has one ship propelled by atomic power—SS *Savannah*.

The U. S. Navy, pioneer in nuclear power, soon will have a hundred submarines with reactors but today has commissioned only four surface warships so equipped. It cannot have many more for several years to come even in the unlikely event of a crash construction program. Restrictions in the national budget, especially by the Department of Defense, have slowed to a snail's pace the progress in what seems a vital need for the United States. Consequently U. S. ships and forces overseas depend, in part, upon petroleum from the Persian Gulf.

Phenomenal Rise in Shipping as Nations Become One World

Besides the Middle East's ancient strategical values, this crossroads of civilization has thus become part of the West's life's blood, flowing through the arteries of the oceans. American aid and enterprise reach across the seas to any nation that will open its doors. These take many forms. Besides direct U.S. government aid, including food and machines, the State and Defense Departments, the Peace Corps, other government activities, many church groups, and other private organizations have programs helping especially underdeveloped nations. U.S. industry rapidly expands overseas, and U. S. citizens collectively —and, for the most part, individually—are committed to building a better world for all people. History has never before witnessed such an outpouring of men, money, and machines by a leading power.

As nations develop, they trade more. For those who believe that the United States' largest commerce is with nations shipping her the quantities of raw materials she requires, it may come as a surprise to learn that, in most cases, the opposite applies. The richest commerce flows between highly industrialized nations. In the Far East the United States' principal trade is with Japan; in Europe, with Britain and Germany; in the Western Hemisphere, with Canada.

International commerce rides on the keels of ships, and the demand for them continually increases. Even the spectacular increase

---

*SS *Manhattan's* historic voyage through the thick ice of the Northwest Passage indicates the value placed on water transport to move this petroleum from Arctic Alaska. A major shipbuilder has also submitted proposals to oil companies to construct giant nuclear powered submarine tankers for this purpose.

in air transport has the same result. Ships must bring in the aluminum ore to build the planes. In order for the planes to fly tankers must speed from shore to shore with fuel for their ravenous jets.

In 1939 the total world merchant marine plying the oceans numbered 12,798 ships of 80 million deadweight tons. War losses ran to about 7,000 ships of over 45 million tons. The miracle of U.S. production made up the loss in time. Then more and more ships came off the ways, mostly in other countries, to meet the mushrooming requirements of expanding global commerce. By the end of the Korean War merchant fleets exceeded in tonnage those of 1939 by two-thirds. Only fifteen years later world fleets have increased to some 20,000 ships of about 300 million deadweight tons—approaching four times the capacity of 1939's ocean going merchant ships.

Traffic between the North Sea and the Baltic—the sea frontier of much of the Soviet bloc—gives some indication of how the world depends upon shipping. In 1969 the Kiel Canal averaged 10 ships an hour, 24 hours a day, every day of the year, for a total of 87,000 ships. These came from 50 different nations bearing 60 million tons of cargo.

The more the industrial revolution races into tomorrow, the more nations need each other. As a corollary, the more they become one world and the more they need the sea. In 1970 U.S. foreign trade reached a value of $82 billion. For the world as a whole export trade just about doubled in the 1960s. What cosmic tragedy would befall free nations if the oceans did not stay free!

Calamitous Decline in U.S. Merchant Marine

Ships now transport two billion tons of cargo annually. The United States generates about a quarter of this vast commerce, yet her role in transporting it strikes a sad, even ominous note. In 1945 about a fifth of the world's shipping was registered in the United States. Thus U.S. flag ships could and did transport most of the overseas commerce.

After enjoying such preeminence, the United States then seems to have abandoned interest in the merchant marine, as she did in sea power in general after winning World War II. The bright merchant marine picture turned progressively more dismal, as will be detailed later. In 1970 her active merchant fleet has dwindled to about one-fifteenth of the world total, transporting scarcely 5 percent of the U.S.'s half billion tons of seaborne commerce.

At this writing world shipyards are building or have on order new ships for foreign nations with a tonnage in excess of four times that of the present U.S. merchant fleet. What a Herculean task confronts the United States if she wishes to recover her abandoned life-lines.

History has made clear that a leading nation with extensive overseas interests must possess a strong merchant marine as well as a powerful, well-equipped navy. It must control enough ships in peacetime to insure that its purposes and policies are enforced. In war the ships become a matter of life and death—not only active ones but a reserve of ships and seamen to meet the critical demands that won't wait for ships to be constructed or for seamen to be trained.

America has a reserve of sorts, but it is confined largely to aging World War II ships. Most of these uneconomical rustbuckets will soon be reduced to scrap. With them will go most of the country's reserve, and there certainly is no reserve of seamen.

Captain Stephen Roskill of the British Navy points up the importance of a merchant marine in his admirable *The War at Sea*. In World War II, he says, "throughout the whole of the first four years every strategic purpose conceived by the Allies, and every operation which they planned and executed was conditioned and controlled—and too often restricted—by the difficulty of providing the necessary shipping. . . . No other lesson is as clear as the importance to a maritime power of a large and modern merchant navy . . . with trained men to build and man ships."

The Vietnam War demonstrated how dangerously low the United States has sunk in ocean transport. Even though the government slowly marshaled force in Southeast Asia over several years, with ample time to activate aged ships remaining in the reserve fleet, many foreign flag ships had to be chartered.* How many of these would be available in a real crisis?

Large American companies own a number of ships that operate under "flags of convenience" such as Liberia and Panama. Primarily tankers and bulk carriers, they constitute a *possible* ready reserve of ships. During an international crisis, however, the flag governments might deny the use of the ships, or crews might refuse to serve or to bring the ships to U.S. ports. Furthermore, most of these are large and not useful for a wide range of military duties.

Reviewing the Vietnam War, the commander of the then Military Sea Transport Service (now Military Sea Lift Command) stated in 1969 that there is no "basis for optimism" with respect to effective U.S. control of this foreign flag fleet. It is not "the answer to the problem of where to obtain the augmentation of the American Merchant Marine in the event of serious need."

---

*In 1969 about 60 percent of the large petroleum needs of the forces there came in foreign flag tankers.

In order to maintain a modern merchant marine and navy a great nation such as ours must have numerous modern, efficient shipyards. Here too we have not made progress comparable to other nations. Secretary Robert McNamara even closed Brooklyn Navy Yard,* one of the nation's oldest, largest, and most important building and repair centers, located in the heart of one of the world's great port complexes.

Hope for the Future?

For years men in government and out have expounded on the danger to the United States represented by her precipitous maritime decline. The warnings continually fell on deaf ears, and no one did much to correct the problem. Today, with little time left, the tide may be turning, but can it turn fast enough?

Shipowners and shipbuilders, calling upon the ingenuity and energy that have been displayed in other American enterprise, have forged ahead in technology. They have taken the lead in development of the "container" ship. Loaded vans or other containers are lifted from the wheels that bring them from shipper to dockside. They are quickly stowed on board, taken across the waters, put on wheels again at port of destination, and carried to the consignee.

This door-to-door delivery has many advantages, but none is greater than the saving of time in loading and discharging cargo. The old ratio of "one day in port to one day at sea" for ships carrying general cargo now changes to a productive ratio of four days at sea to one day in port.

Container ship short turnaround time and greater size and higher speed begin to make the U.S. Merchant Marine competitive in ocean transport. It now boasts the world's largest container ship fleet, about eighty vessels, with others partially "containerized." It has led the way in the revolution in transporting general cargo from seller to buyer, just as tankers and bulk carriers have in oil, ore, and grain.

According to Maritime Administrator A. E. Gibson, some of the new American "container ships have proved to be so productive that they have captured more than 50 percent of the container trade in the principal North Atlantic and Pacific routes." U.S. corporations are also in the van in developing other advanced types of ships. One now building in numbers is LASH (lighter aboard ship). This offshoot of the container principle takes fullest advantage of cheap water transport with preloaded barges joining or unloading from the ocean going ship in deep water ports.

---

*He also scheduled closing the yard at Portsmouth, New Hampshire, but President Nixon reversed that decision.

This revolution in world shipping that has gradually generated speed for more than a decade, starting with the tankers, still has far to go. It offers new opportunity and new promise to the U.S. Merchant Marine. Relative innovations may become important factors in ocean transport tomorrow. Some experts believe that one of these will be the "Flying Shop."

Hydrofoils and ACVs (air cushion vehicles) have operated in several countries with success. One can now cross the English Channel at a speed of a mile a minute in an ACV, which carries up to 250 passengers and 30 vehicles. Larger craft are building for similar purposes. The U.S. Navy has had a large ACV under test for years and has used small ones effectively in combat in Vietnam. It may well be that in a reasonable time "flying boats" will skim across the oceans.

The foregoing record only some of the innovations underway to speed up and reduce the cost of shipping by water, historically the cheapest and easiest means of mass transport. The monumental 1970 report of Lord Rochdale's British Committee of Inquiry into Shipping looks into the future with this apt observation:

> . . . there is every prospect of a continuing rapid growth in the tonnage of ships. . . . The technological changes now so evident in the world shipping industry are probably no less significant than the replacement in the nine-teenth century of the wooden ship with that of iron, and of sail by steam. These changes are leading to a very big increase in productivity and thus reduction in the real cost of the transport.

Recently the U.S. government has also begun to act more vigorously but with something less than the speed of light. As he reiterated in 1970, President Nixon has often recognized that "the economic prosperity and well-being of our people rest heavily on the future use we make of the world's oceans."

It took some time for this concept to manifest itself in the budget. For fiscal 1970 (1969 budget) a mere $15.9 million was allocated to stimulate and aid merchant ship construction. However, the fiscal 1971 budget raised the ante to nearly $190 million, the largest since World War II.

In October, 1969, the president sent a message to Congress pointing up the crisis in shipping and the national need to reverse the course. He called for government support to construct 300 ships in U.S. ship-yards in the coming decade. In October, 1970, a bill to this effect passed Congress. Thus ten years after a similar program in 1960, which bogged down, the nation again slowly is getting underway. However, even if there are no hitches, the first ships will not sail before mid-1973. Americans should hope that this program will reach port. If so, it will help greatly, but at the best it can provide only part of the merchant men the United States must have to regain maritime viability.

The U.S.S.R. Passes the U.S.

The U.S.S.R. set a goal to transport 75 percent of its foreign trade under its own flag, and some time ago passed the 50 percent mark. In order for the U.S. Merchant Marine to carry even a third of this nation's overseas commerce (instead of the present frightening 5 percent) many more than these 300 ships will be needed. The United States has not constructed enough ships to replace the aging ones scrapped, much less to handle even a small portion of the increase in her ocean commerce.

American flag companies added about 200 ships during the decade just passed. In the same period the U.S.S.R. added nearly 700. In 1970 U.S. yards had 49 ships under construction or on order, whereas Soviet and other Communist yards had more than 500—one fifth of the ocean going vessels in the world and 10 percent of the tonnage.

Improvement in shipyards will, of course, help the United States to speed up the essential recovery of her maritime stature. As in yards elsewhere in the world, great changes have taken place, as will be noted in the summary of the Soviet yards. Use of computers and late developments such as lasers, along with automation, mechanization, and streamlining have speeded up shipbuilding. Two large new private yards have been built from scratch to take advantage of the advances. However, the total of all trained shipyard workers in U.S. Navy and civilian yards has not reached a quarter million men for many years. Currently it stands closer to 200,000.

Even the most modern yard takes time to build ships and to train new men during periods of expansion. In 1941, with two years of war in Europe providing preparation time, U.S. shipyards built less than 1.2 million deadweight tons of ships, twice 1940's output but only a start toward filling the desperate need. Not until 1942 did they hit their stride. In 1970 world shipyards had under construction or on order merchantmen *amounting to about four times the present active U.S. merchant fleet.* Of this total, U.S. shipyards had only 2 percent on their books. In the maritime administrator's words, the Soviets are "outbuilding us now at a rate of ten ships to one."

Massive Soviet National Effort in Shipyards

Catching up will not be rapid or easy. The United States has been in decline as a maritime power for a quarter of a century; the Soviets have been in full-throttle rise. They properly started with shipyards, first for the navy, and then for the merchant marine. After quickly rehabilitating those wrecked in the war, they began to build new yards. A 1970 study by the U.S. Naval Ship Systems Command covers seventeen major Soviet shipyards, which with several hundred lesser construction and repair yards scattered across the U.S.S.R. probably employ a million men or more, *at the highest average wage in Soviet industry.*

The excellent navy study reveals that five of the major yards, including four new ones, build merchant ships only, and eight of the other twelve build merchant as well as warships. In the first years of their surge to maritime power the major Soviet yards built only for the navy. Satellite countries and the West built auxiliaries and merchant vessels. The increased and improving shipbuilding facilities now make it possible to meet all of Russia's giant naval needs while at the same time building probably 40 percent of the merchant ships and a higher percent of auxiliaries and fishing craft.

For most of the rest of their maritime requirements the Soviets now draw upon satellites, especially the fine shipyards of East Germany and Poland, which extend iron curtain shipbuilding from Leningrad along the eastern Baltic to West Germany. While supplying fewer as a group than in the past, non-Communist nations from Finland and Denmark to Japan continue to construct merchant ships for the Soviet flag.

Of the major shipyards seven lie in the Baltic area, five on the Black Sea, one on the White Sea, two on inland waters, and two in the Far East. For each standardized type of ship the Soviets have a separate design bureau. Separate research institutes exist for different fundamentals of design and construction such as hydrodynamics, engines, electronics, welding, and metallurgy. The yards, especially the newest ones, take full advantage of automation, computer-controlled tools, sectional assembly off the building ways, assembly line production flow, enclosed building stations, covered ways for winter construction, and many other progressive techniques. According to Rear Admiral Nathan Sonenshein, who heads the Ship Systems Command, "The U.S.S.R. has modernized its shipyards, adopted advanced production and management methods, and has just about caught up with us in ship technology."

These modern and numerous shipyards have gone a long way toward reversing the maritime balance among nations. In 1945 the United States stood unchallenged as the first shipbuilder of the world, as she was first also in naval and total maritime power. The U.S.S.R. then ranked near the bottom in overall maritime strength and especially in the shipbuilding foundation. Yet by concentration of national energy, budget, and purpose she has forged ahead incredibly.

In the early stages the Politbureau set five-year goals for expansion of shipyards, navy and fishing fleets—and later the merchant marine. These have been consistently approximated or exceeded. When the Soviets got around to shaping a modern, strong merchant fleet, they found little on which to build. In 1950 the U.S.S.R. stood low on the totem pole with 432 deep sea merchantmen of 1,000 tons up—many of them old and slow, totaling 1.8 million deadweight tons. This placed her twenty-first among world merchant fleets.

At this time the Soviet Navy likewise ranked low, though it was making progress since Soviet and satellite shipyards were expanding, modernizing, and increasing their output. By the end of 1971, in fact, they will have launched nearly a thousand important combat warships, including powerful ballistic missiles, nuclear-powered submarines, and helicopter carriers. Aided by satellite yards, they will have completed about twice this many other warships (from small missile craft to large auxiliaries) and merchantmen, which are, in effect, naval auxiliaries. Simultaneously, the yards have had enough capacity to build thousands of modern deep sea fishing craft, which are also capable of serving naval purposes in peace or war.

The Soviets Will Leave the U.S. Far in the Wake Unless . . .

In 1971 the Soviet merchant fleet has grown to more than 1,800 ships, mostly modern and efficient, adding up to about 14 million deadweight tons. At the present pace it seems certain to expand to the goal of 20 million or more deadweight tons in 1980. This will put the U.S.S.R. far ahead of the United States unless many more ships join the U.S. fleet than are provided in the president's 300-ship program.

The current strong Soviet maritime posture has been accomplished from a position of weakness. What happened to the United States, the world's leading shipbuilder of less than a generation ago?

The record should alarm any American. In the past twenty years of massive shipbuilding, the United States has lagged dangerously. She has turned out only half the number of important surface warships, launched by Soviet yards and a fraction of other warships, merchant, and fishing vessels. Constant warnings from the navy, from some far-seeing political leaders, and from discerning journalists and other concerned citizens have not sufficed to keep the U.S. from its slide toward second place.

While the U.S.S.R. added over 12 million tons by mid-1971, the United States has allowed her merchant fleet to decline by about three times this amount. On VJ Day, 1945, the United States had about 5,000 merchantmen totaling better than 50 million tons. In 1971 this armada of commerce has shrunk to under 700 active ships (the majority of which are over 25 years old) plus 400 other ready reserves, totalling under 10 million deadweight tons.

The U.S.S.R.'s merchant fleet carries over 50 percent of her foreign commerce and from a negligible factor in 1950 has become an important influence in certain aspects of world trade. The United States, with far greater need for ocean transport, must depend upon foreign flags for nearly all her overseas commerce.

It will take the utmost vision, cooperation, and energy of government, industry, and labor to regain for the United States the merchant marine stature she must have to be certain of survival.

Soviet leaders do not want the merchant fleet just to compete in world commerce or to be an indispensable component of naval power. They see in it a strategic tool, far reaching and irreplaceable, to further world power ambitions. A look at the globe suffices to show that sea transport does and will play a ruling role in war, cold war, and economic and political influence. A recent Soviet publication states, "The Russian maritime fleet is to be considered as a weapon in the competition with the capitalist countries, and it must contribute toward breaking the expansion of certain capitalist countries . . . in order to support the developing countries."

Special attention should be given to the last clause. The swiftly expanding Soviet merchant fleet is composed primarily of small and medium size ships suitable especially for entry into the smaller harbors of developing nations.

For the Soviet leaders, merchantmen along with the fleet have become powerful means to expand Communist ideology and influence, which, in turn, can promote unrest and subversion. We already have ample indication of the purposes to which this growing strength at sea is being put. Day after day ships under the Soviet flag have unloaded in Haiphong the deadly AA missiles, radars, fire control equipment, armament, and munitions that have killed Americans and their allies and have kept North Vietnam in the war.

These same ships have disgorged tanks, artillery, airplanes, and weapons of many types in Latakia, Syria. They have twice brought in the vast quantities of armament, from guided missile boats to aircraft and from tanks to SAM launchers (types II and III) with their accurate missiles, to make Egypt a bristling servant of Mars. A steady stream of ships and heavy Soviet aid sustain Castro in Cuba. In 1962 Soviet ships brought to Cuba nuclear warhead missiles that could devastate much of the United States. When the chips were down, the Soviet fleet, being much weaker then, supposedly took them away again. They probably brought materials for a submarine base at Cienfuegos, Cuba, in 1970.

Wherever there is chance to topple an existing government by parties favorable to the U.S.S.R. or to support an existing leftist regime, the Soviets have ships that can aid.

The Kremlin has found the new instruments at sea most valuable for entry to almost any nation, thus opening new opportunities for intrigue and manipulation. Soviet merchant ships now visit more than ninety different countries. Whenever in the cycle of economies a surplus of world shipping exists, the U.S.S.R. can affect shipping rates in general. With the state controlling prices and commerce, the Politbureau can start a sales war in selected commodities, thus accelerating its economic penetration. In fact, this has occurred frequently.

As long ago as the mid-1950s the Soviet Union had enough tankers and petroleum to begin to undercut world prices. The Soviet oil trust sold its exports at a discount of as much as 40 percent in order to get a trade foothold in various nations. By 1965 the U.S.S.R. oil trust had emerged as the world's third largest exporter (after Standard Oil of New Jersey and Royal Dutch Shell) and was furnishing Western European nations 8 percent of their petroleum imports.

Wherever the Soviet ships trade Soviet commercial organizations spring up and become centers of propaganda, intrigue, and conduct of Soviet national policy. This is an important reason for the Politbureau's continuing to give the maritime industry a large share of the budget and to favor sailors as well as shipbuilders with special treatment. During 1959–1965 the state raised the pay of Soviet sailors 33 percent, against 22 percent for the total labor force.

The Soviet leaders have gauged maritime capability as a whole. They fully comprehend the potential for influence and power that lies in a strong merchant marine. It serves in peace to advance state policy, whether economic, political, or military. In war every ship becomes a naval auxiliary if needed—and we can be sure that the Kremlin builds and controls its merchant fleet with this purpose ever in mind.

Storm Warnings

The U.S.S.R.'s phenomenal surge toward maritime predominance has no precedent in our era. Largely self-contained, the Soviet Union, with its adjoining satellites, has only modest need for foreign trade to balance the economy. This vast nation spanning two continents has no long, open seacoasts inviting ocean commerce, as does the United

States. She has no fundamental need for shipping services to balance foreign expenditures. She has no forces of consequence overseas requiring a flow of ships. Yet she is rapidly building one of the world's largest merchant fleets.

On the other hand, the United States, a nation enveloped in the sea, desperately requires it for her economy, her overseas forces and commitments, and for her allies. The largest trading nation in the world *must* have a merchant fleet to survive. Yet through apathy and neglect she has let it decline even more than her navy.

Why the blind piloting by the United States? Why the all-out turn to the sea of the Soviet Union?

For the United States there seems only one answer: lack of understanding by her citizens. The average American can judge international problems only through accurate information that comes to him from the media and through forthright leadership from his elected representatives in Washington. So the responsibility falls on that portion of media reporters and Washington political leaders who have failed to point up the dangerous developments at sea.

Years ago Admiral Arleigh Burke evaluated Soviet leaders with his customary perception as "hard, cold, and ruthless strategists. They have keenly and accurately appraised the geographical nature of the Free World . . . a vast oceanic confederation."

There is sound theory behind the rising threat of Soviet buildup on the oceans, in which the merchant fleet has a special role. When the Soviets become first at sea, as they have long been ashore, the storms of the past two decades will seem like summer calms.

13

Oceanography and Allied Uses of the Sea

OCEANOGRAPHY and its related sciences are fundamental to maritime power. Research in the oceans, by which the harmonies of nature are preserved, will immeasurably influence man's future—in naval success, commerce, food supply, weather information, navigation, mining, and petroleum extraction.

The term "oceanography" can have a restricted or a broad meaning. To this writer any science or art that has marine application would seem in some way to fit into the scope of the term. Hence, this chapter will touch not only on the ocean itself, from its restless surface to its darkest depths, but also on various interrelated scientific, engineering, and development uses.

Soviet leaders seem to have comprehended fully the vast potential in the oceans for projection of national power, for commerce, and for other notable benefits. In recent years, therefore, they have set full sail to surpass the United States in oceanography and in other types of maritime strength.

They set themselves a large task, for just as the United States played a memorable role in seagoing commerce for generations, so she had an outstanding record in oceanography. Notable contributions began in the 1700s as Americans followed in the wake of their seafaring ancestors of the British Isles. Benjamin Franklin's observations and experiments in the Gulf Stream, the most famous of that period, led to publication of a chart of the stream that speeded transatlantic crossings. After Franklin, Commodore Thomas Truxtun stands out next. He carried on Franklin's ocean studies and prepared a book about navigation solidly founded upon expert practice and theory.

Nathaniel Bowditch, who credited Truxtun with "the knowledge we possess of the Gulf Stream," is the third great American student of the sea in this early period. Mathematician and merchant mariner, he also became a famous navigator. As master of the ship *Putnam,* he climaxed a voyage of thousands of miles from the East Indies when he made Salem, Massachusetts, "on the nose" on Christmas Eve, 1803, in a blinding snowstorm that cut visibility to zero. His *Practical Navigator,* first published in 1802 and revised and enlarged over the generations and translated into many languages, still is used widely. Since 1867 the navy has published it through its Hydrographic (now Oceanographic) Office.

Pathfinder of the Seas

Among those after Bowditch, one scientist stands out like a meteor. Lieutenant Matthew Fontaine Maury, "Pathfinder of the Seas," was the leading oceanographer of all times. He placed his magic touch also upon other fields of activity, thus benefiting mankind. Indefatigable student, talented writer, profound thinker, man of dedication and deep faith, Maury studied and contributed to his profession from the day he entered the navy as a midshipman. In the 1830s, after years of experience and study at sea, he published *A New Theoretical Treatise on Navigation,* which became a U.S. Navy textbook. A few years later he brought the U.S. Navy's observatory world distinction as a result of its accomplishments in astronomy.

In the 1840s he began analyzing wind, current, and meteorological entries in old ship logs to determine the normal paths of storms, the winds, and currents met on shipping lanes. By prodigious labors with the mass of data he determined and published information on favorable sea tracks that measurably shortened passage days on key routes. He said his charts and sailing directions would *"blaze a way* through the winds of the sea by which the navigator may find the best paths."

Knowledge of their value spread like wildfire when ships following his directions sharply cut passage times. In 1848 a barque out of Baltimore that sailed Maury's recommended track made Rio de Janeiro in 35 days, versus the normal 55 days. Soon the average passage from New York to San Francisco dropped from 180 to 133 days, and the clipper ship *Flying Cloud* raced over the 15,000 miles in a record 89 days and 21 hours.

As a next step Maury promoted an international conference in 1853. This resulted in a system of cooperative reporting of weather, meteorological, and sea data by men of war and merchant marines of all nations. Each ship, as he said, was "a temple of science." This successful pattern for productive international cooperation still continues.

Overseas Maury became the nation's most famous citizen. Many countries decorated him for his "eminent services to science and mankind." At the outbreak of the Civil War he resigned to serve his native state of Virginia. When the news of his resignation reached Russia, he was invited to establish himself there under the patronage of the government with full financing and "no conditions of engagement." Thus he could continue his indefatigable research. Maury declined because of a sense of duty to his state.

To this day Maury's work remains a foundation for modern oceanography, astronomy, and meteorology. Widely used pilot charts prepared by the navy's Oceanographic Office appropriately bear the inscription "founded upon the researches made in the early part of the 19th Century by Matthew Fontaine Maury while serving as a Lieutenant in the United States Navy." *

In time the navy separated oceanographic and astronomical work into parallel but separate activities. Were Maury to review them today, he would see dreams come true in each. The Naval Observatory, a world leader in the study and use of the heavens, greatly advances man's safe and swift passage of the seas, of the air, and into the reaches of infinity. The observatory's aid ranges from the Nautical Almanac and other studies and publications to the atomic time clock using a cesium beam atomic oscillator that divides a second into a thousand million parts.

The station's achievements have not only contributed significantly to the navy's operating efficiency at sea but they also figure into every American's life and into a wide range of scientific and technological advances, such as the precise navigation essential for space operation.

The Oceanographic Office concentrates upon research and measurement of all levels of the ocean, from the frigid to the torrid zones in both hemispheres by ship, buoy, submersible, airplane, and satellite. The office's charts, other publications, and separate data have worldwide application far beyond their invaluable contributions to naval operations for the security of the nation.

Intensive research in meteorology has increasingly broadened knowledge of the "atmospheric ocean" that envelops sea and land and inter-

---

*Contemporaries of Maury also made important contributions to understanding the oceans. These included Lieutenant Charles Wilkes, USN (Commodore by courtesy) in his famous four-year expedition to Antarctica and the South Seas; Commodore Matthew Calbraith Perry and Lieutenant Silas Bent, during the historic mission that opened Japan, whose oceanographic work included the first definitive study of the Japan Current; and Commodore John Rodgers and others in Arctic exploration and survey. Many other naval officers, including Commander George Dewey, conducted extensive hydrographic surveys during this century.

mingles with them to affect all life. The U.S. Weather Bureau represents Maury's concept of a center to receive weather reports from thousands of stations and volunteer observers. Naval officers have headed it, and many have served in it. Reports from navy ships and planes flow in routinely. Navy and air force "Hurricane Hunters" now fly regularly through the violent winds and turbulence of hurricanes into the strange, calm "eye" in order to chart the character of these awesome cyclonic disturbances and to give early warning to communities in their paths.

Expansion of U.S. Oceanography

The navy has habitually cooperated with and supported work in oceanography of other government agencies and private organizations. During most of the nineteenth century naval officers commanded and staffed coastal survey ships and those of the Fish Commission.

Civilian scientists participate in the countless facets of naval research and development both in the naval-civilian teams of its own excellent laboratories and in the outside laboratories receiving naval support.

In World War I Secretary of the Navy Josephus Daniels established the Naval Consulting Board of noted scientists, headed by Thomas Edison. This group made salient contributions in gunnery, ASW, and numerous other fields, including oceanography.

Out of Edison's service came also the Naval Research Laboratory (NRL), which, along with other naval laboratories, has figured prominently in the navy's effectiveness. Formally established in 1923, NRL incorporated as its Sound Division the men and equipment responsible for charting new courses in this field at the Naval Engineering Experimental Station, across the Severn from the Naval Academy. Here in 1921 Dr. Harvey C. Hayes developed the sonic depth finder—a breakthrough of great import to underwater operations of every type.

The interval between world wars brought increasing interest in oceanography outside the government. Celebrated private oceanographic laboratories, such as Woods Hole in Massachusetts and Scripps Institute in California, matured. They worked closely with and, in fact, almost as a part of the Naval Hydrographic Office. Receiving funding and material support from the navy, including the loan of ships, these laboratories (and subsequently others) have demonstrated the benefits of coordinated but independent research.

In World War II the Secretary of the Navy appointed a coordinator of research within the department. He worked with President Roosevelt's National Defense Research Council, which sought to achieve maximum use of scientists in the national effort.

Following in the coordinator's wake, in 1946 the Office of Naval Research (ONR) was formed to "plan, foster, and encourage scientific research." ONR was given cognizance over NRL and certain other naval activities while working in coordination with the navy's great specialized laboratories.

Cold Latitude Research

Expansion of research in the oceans proceeded apace after World War II, among the most impressive of which took place in the polar regions. These operations continued the nation's long history of achievement in icy seas that began with American whalers and Commodore Wilkes during the last century. A generation before World War II, in 1909, Admiral Peary reached the North Pole, and some years later Commander Richard E. Byrd began his notable series of explorations that included the world's first flights over each pole. In 1946 the navy launched "Operation Highjump" with Byrd, then a rear admiral, having overall direction. Rear Admiral Richard Cruzen commanded the task force of thirteen ships and over four thousand men that carried out the largest assault on Antarctica in history.

Operating airplanes and the first helicopters in the Antarctic, the expedition discovered more territory than all previous ones combined. Its research across the board in cold weather operations, including studies relating to oceanography, achieved monumental results. The next notable operation was the first "deep freeze" expedition to Antarctica in 1955–1956, under Rear Admiral George J. Dufek. A similar one the following year dedicated the U.S. Navy's South Pole Station on 23 January 1957.

These prepared for the International Geophysical Year 1957–1958. The latter was so successful that the country organized a long-range Antarctic research program within the National Science Foundation. The navy has continued to participate and has provided each year the transportation and logistic support for all American scientists on the frozen continent.

Scarcely had the geophysical year ended when at the other end of the globe USS *Nautilus* set another historic first. In late summer, 1958, she cruised under the ice over the top of the world from the Bering to the Norwegian Sea, traveling "right through the North Pole." Other submarines have since researched under the polar cap on this short underwater route between the two great oceans.

A decade after *Nautilus*, U.S. oil companies enlarged and strengthened SS *Manhattan*. Then they sent this large tanker on her dramatic conquest of the thick ice of the Northwest Passage to the oil discoveries on Alaska's Arctic slope.

The army, air force, other federal departments, and industry and university laboratories have conducted much low temperature research in the labs and in the field. Navy experimental work ashore has complemented the practical work of ships and planes at both ends of the earth and in the cold depths of the oceans. This includes the Naval Arctic Research Laboratory on the Arctic Ocean, with its outlying ice island stations. Through research, development, and continuing practical experience the coast guard is a master of the art of opening a way through frozen waters.

The sum total of new knowledge is impressive in the fields of gravity, magnetism, physical and chemical oceanography, underwater acoustics, ice physics, and other fields. From the studies have come a rich flow of benefits such as improved survival techniques, better ice transit, bathymetric charts of the Arctic, and the navy's ability to forecast ice conditions anywhere.

Despite the U.S.S.R.'s unrivaled experience of living and working in and using the Arctic regions, it would seem that the United States has comparable capabilities insofar as they pertain to oceanography and other activities in the colder regions of earth.

Ocean Research between the Poles

Work in the sea has been so extensive in the past two decades that in this brief space we can do justice to only a minute cross section of it. In the 1950s the navy initiated "Project Magnet," a continuing airborne magnetic survey of the world. This project expanded the research of World War II spurred by Germany's use of magnetic mines and torpedoes and by the progress in employment of airborne magnetic detection in antisubmarine warfare. Other work valuable in measuring and predicting the environmental conditions in which submarines would operate also moved ahead.

On the ocean's surface the navy established its Optimum-Track Ship Routing program, which advises ships on the best routes to follow for favorable wind, current, and weather conditions. Descended from Maury's revolutionary track charts, this program has saved many millions of dollars, has speeded passage, and has lessened storm hazard and damage.

The National Science Foundation, with its comprehensive book *Oceanography 1960–1970,* and the navy, with its forward-looking document *Ten-Year Program in Oceanography,* set the course for achievement in the past decade. The federal Council for Science and Technology, with its Interagency Committee on Oceanography, increased coordination between government agencies working in the sea, including the navy, coast guard, Coast and Geodetic Survey, bureau of fisheries, Atomic Energy Commission, and a score of others. The cooperative National Oceanographic Data Center, under navy administration, developed early from the committee's proceedings.

The Secretary of the Navy, in 1966, gave the Oceanographer of the Navy centralized control over naval marine science programs in the various bureaus, commands, and laboratories. This directive coincided with important legislation. In 1966, Congress established the National Council on Marine Resources, chaired by the vice-president, and the Commission on Marine Science, Engineering, and Resources.

The Council has acted on scores of major policy decisions and issued annual reports entitled *Marine Science Affairs.* The commission's multivolume study of national activity in oceanography, published in January, 1969, as *Our Nation and the Sea,* is a milestone in the nation's progress at sea. Among the many recommendations to strengthen the United States' marine programs was the formation of the National Oceanic and Atmospheric Administration (NOAA).

NOAA was established under the Department of Commerce in late 1970 to incorporate and concentrate the federal government's nondefense activities in all phases of marine science, technology, and resources. It should vitalize the nation's progress in the science and use of the sea.

As a seagoing science oceanography needs every type of platform available to study this salty environment that covers most of the globe. In the last decade, though not with the emphasis in surface ships of the Soviet Union, the United States has progressed rapidly in constructing vessels and vehicles for operations from the depths of the sea to the upper atmosphere. Satellites, airplanes, fixed platforms at sea, buoys,* test ranges, and submersibles all have their parts to play, but the burden of work in ocean sciences and engineering will long be borne by surface ships. They provide the speed, mobility, endurance, helicopter platform, and ample laboratory and working spaces to accommodate large amounts of equipment and numerous scientists. Thus a single ship can acquire and process vast amounts of data.

---

*The navy has about twenty oceanographic buoys positioned in the oceans supporting its research work and environmental prediction services. These include two forty-foot diameter Monster Buoys for the North Pacific. The Monster measures 100 meteorological and oceanographic factors simultaneously and transmits the information automatically to distant shore stations.

As part of its essential continuing test and evaluation of "hardware" and techniques, the navy also has several test ranges serving oceanographic functions. One of these is AUTEC (Atlantic Undersea Test and Evaluation Center), with principal facilities in the Bahamas and Virgin Islands. AUTEC has a wide scope of capabilities to test U.S. vessels, weapons, weapons systems, sonobuoys, oceanographic instruments, etc.

The last decade has been a fruitful one for the navy. Until a few years ago all of its ships performing oceanographic functions were on temporary assignment from other duties or conversions. A ten-year program initiated in 1960 provided for ships built from the keel up to accommodate a rush of new, more rapid, and precise types of oceanographic instruments, along with digital and analog computers. The Oceanographic Office established an Instrumentation Center (now transferred to NOAA along with Data Center) in 1962, which in coordination with industry has speeded up advances in instrumentation and automation.

Some sixty ships were requested for oceanographic surveying, hydrographic surveying, or oceanographic research duties. Like other naval shipbuilding programs, this one has also lagged severely behind the nation's needs. About one-third of the ships have so far been built. The construction of many more in the near future is dubious. In fact, scarcely had some of the new ships been commissioned when the 1969–1971 budget cuts forced the navy to lay them up. Important programs on the world oceans had to be sharply curtailed.

The new ships are among the finest afloat for ocean study. The research type, designated AGOR,* conducts fundamental research in studies of physical, chemical, biological, and geological characteristics and their manifestation in wave motion, sea-ice features and properties, oceanographic acoustic properties, marine organisms, sea floor and bottom strata, geomagnetism, and gravity. Nearly all of this basic and applied research enters directly into the navy's submarine and anti-submarine operations for the nation's security.

About ten oceanographic surveying ships and hydrographic surveying types operate in direct support of the fleet. The latter provide the basic data for the ever-improving charts that daily serve the navy, merchant marine, and indeed all who sail the sea. The Oceanographic Surveying ships, with an array of splendid instrumentation, have advanced shipboard survey systems for automatic collection of geophysical, hydrographic, and oceanographic information. The new ships can anchor in depths up to four sea miles. They can maintain position exactly through control of cycloidal propellers fore and aft (or trainable bow thrusters) and can conduct several studies at once.

A single "fish" (set of instruments) lowered from one of the sixteen separate winch systems may measure ambient light, depth, salinity, sound velocity, and temperature. The fish also transmits the measurements for digital or analog use. Other measurements include such areas as gravity, magnetism, and seismic profiles.

---

*One of the new AGORs revives the catamaran hull for large ships.

Instead of sixty ships, the Oceanographer of the Navy now has only about twenty under his control or overall supervision. Some of the AGOR serve as pool ships for navy laboratories. Others are operated by private institutions such as Scripps or Woods Hole or universities working under navy contracts. The ships are manned, operated, and controlled by the institutions concerned, with the navy retaining only broad supervisory control. This latitude of freedom has paid off handsomely in research results.

The navy also owns some small craft with oceanographic functions. Other government agencies such as the coast guard, the Bureau of Mines, and NOAA have valuable ocean research vessels. A number of universities and private research institutions have furnished craft for research or instruction. Frequently one of these may be employed in a project of national interest with funding support from the navy or the National Science Foundation. This would customarily be basic research, which the navy and the National Science Foundation have long stimulated. Over a hundred academic institutions offer courses in marine sciences or engineering and related fields, and the majority of them award graduate or undergraduate degrees in these disciplines.*

Some Economic and Other Uses of the Sea

With this broadening foundation, we may hope that the United States will make even more rapid progress in the 1970s. She needs to pay special attention to some areas such as fisheries. In a relatively short span of time the nation has seen this fundamental element of maritime strength give way disastrously to superior ships, techniques, and energy of the Soviets and of the far-ranging fishermen of other countries such as Peru and Japan. In 1945 U.S. fishing craft supplied most of the nation's requirements. In 1971 foreign fisheries are the principal source.

On the other hand, the nation can be proud of achievements such as those uncovering the mysteries of the polar regions; the navy's broad programs from aerial survey to deep submergence; the state, university, industry, and private laboratory achievements from the ocean depths to the atmosphere; and the remarkable accomplishments of

---

*Since its inception over 125 years ago, the U.S. Naval Academy has given all midshipmen some instruction in oceanography in the courses on navigation, seamanship, and the basic sciences. During the past few years the addition of splendid new laboratories and computers has led to more specific courses in ocean sciences. In 1970 the Academy accelerated emphasis on oceanography by establishing a separate discipline (Department of Environmental Sciences) and offering majors as part of the Academy's progressive curriculum. At this writing more than 500 midshipmen are carrying specific courses in ocean sciences, besides the instruction all receive in naval science and other fields associated with oceanography.

private industry in mining the sea (as in petroleum), stimulated by the government's depreciation allowance.

In its 1969 report *Our Nation and the Sea,* the Commission on Marine Science, Engineering, and Resources makes this prophetic comment:

> How fully and wisely the United States uses the sea in the decade ahead will affect profoundly its security, its economy, its ability to meet increasing demands for food and raw materials, its position and influence in the world community.

The uses of the sea are legion. In addition to national security and oceanography they include most basic sciences such as biology, geochemistry, geophysics, and geology. A few applied fields in which the U.S. and her economy (and that of all nations) will benefit as the vast ocean storehouses are unlocked should be noted here.

Weather

Man's most common topic of conversation, weather makes a good starting point. The meeting point of sea and air is a giant world-circling factory that manufactures weather twenty-four hours a day. Growth in understanding of this global machine has already been of great significance to many nations. For instance, more knowledge of hurricanes gained through the valiant flights of navy and air force hurricane hunters, the use of radar (first developed by the navy) to guide planes around storms, and many Weather Bureau advances in forecasting have already saved thousands of lives and hundreds of millions of dollars. Ocean buoys, satellites, submersibles, planes, and surface ships will improve forecasting further. Those who know, like Rear Admiral O. D. Waters, past Oceanographer of the Navy, say that more knowledge of what goes on in the sea-air factory "would be worth billions of dollars to the country every year."

Transportation

Advances in knowledge of the sea and weather have long benefited shipping, the life's blood of the world economy. Progress today is almost as spectacular as that fathered by Maury in the 1840s. For generations the navy has furnished time checks, charts, and daily bulletins to merchant seamen as well as warships that help insure safe passage across the oceans. Now it has added recommended routing determined from predicted sea states. This information, obtained from the Naval Weather Service Command, can save a ship many thousands of dollars on a single trip. This increased knowledge of the sea will help to stimulate revival of the U.S. Merchant Marine. America has exposed herself to grave peril by dependence on foreign flag ships to transport the swelling flood of critical imports that sustain the economy.

Fishing

As noted before, the United States has fallen far behind in this ancient skill of farming the sea except in certain endeavors such as tuna, shrimp, and salmon fisheries. The science and knowledge are available. As a byproduct of its oceanographic research in connection with ASW operations, for example, the navy, in coordination with the Bureau of Fisheries, demonstrated that use of the information on temperature gradients can conceivably triple the catch. The incentive should exist, for the United States provides the most lucrative market in the world. American enterprise and government stimulus should find a solution at least comparable to that accomplished by the Soviets.*

Aquaculture

Scientific farming of the sea, employing a controlled environment, is in its infancy as a major supplier of world food requirements. Trout and oyster farming hint at the possibilities that promise much larger yields per acre of high-grade proteins than the most fertile land (provided we take major steps to stop polluting the oceans as well as inland waterways).

Medicine

Healing drugs will come from the sea in addition to those already extracted, such as iodine. Scientists are turning to the sea, where a higher percentage of organisms than those found ashore contain an active biological agent. For instance, what agent in a sea cucumber inhibits tumor growth, as demonstrated in mice? How can a starfish regenerate lost arms? In these and other sea creatures scientists hope to find agents that may lead to cures for cancer, heart ailments, and other ills.

Mining the Sea Bed

Tremendous progress has been made in petroleum and sulphur recovery, especially by American private industry. Diamonds are scooped up off the coast of Africa, and gold is obtained from Alaska. Tin and coal come from mines under the sea. A start has been made in developing commercial dredging methods to recover the mineral nodules that form in the oceans and that in some parts of the Pacific almost pave the bottom. They contain greatly needed manganese, which the

---

*Besides fish, other foods or supplements, such as agar, come from the sea; the future will bring much more.

United States must import, and also other minerals including cobalt, copper, and nickel. After a pilot test with something resembling a deep ocean vacuum cleaner near the close of 1970, Tenneco announced plans to form an international consortium to recover and process the almost limitless quantity of nodules.

Mining Sea Water

Only as resources began to dwindle ashore did man begin to mine the ocean bed. For thousands of years he has mined sea water for salt. In recent years the unresting waves have also become an important source for magnesium and bromine. The waters are filled with other minerals and chemicals that will be recovered in growing amounts as scientific technology uncovers them and economical means develop them. To be sure of this one has only to realize that more gold and silver are suspended in the ocean than have ever been mined ashore; estimates go as high as 10 million tons of gold and 500 million tons of silver.

Power

A mariner has only to ride out a typhoon at sea or witness the assault on the shore of a hurricane's waves to appreciate the awesome force pent up in the massive oceans. Hungering for energy, men will accelerate past efforts to harness the tides and ocean temperature gradients to do the work of the world.

Fresh Water

Next to air, water is probably man's most precious environmental legacy. Water in the universe is rare in liquid form except on earth. For decades ships have converted salt water into potable water. Now desalinization plants begin to multiply ashore from the arid Middle East (employing flare gas from the oil fields) to areas of the United States short of water, such as Southern California. Recent advances by the U.S. Government and by industry hasten the day when it may be possible to desalinate sea water on a large scale economically. Atomic power will contribute to a marked degree in this boon to man as it does increasingly in filling his wants for energy.

Because of immediate returns the largest effort in all the applied fields has gone into recovery of petroleum and natural gas offshore. Already the ocean depths furnish one-sixth of the world's petroleum and much natural gas. The huge discoveries in the North Sea and on the Arctic slope will add to the percentage, which will rise steadily. Oil men estimate that 40 percent of future recoverable oil will come from the ocean floor. They predict that before 1980 systems will be available to explore and produce in ocean depths up to 6,000 feet.

Numerous ocean science and engineering developments enter into the exploration and recovery of these hidden riches. All the hydrographic programs of the navy, its weather service, and its sonar and other advances well serve in this effort on behalf of the nation, as do programs of other government activities. Industry has gone to sea with vigor, especially in ocean engineering and technology in exploration and construction.

Tugs tow monstrous mobile drilling platforms to distant parts of the world. More than two hundred of these now serve in the insatiable search for oil in many waters. In 1969 a giant underwater oil storage tank, as tall as a twenty-story building, proceeded under tow to the Persian Gulf. Submerged there it forecasts extensive use of underwater storage. Huge fixed development and production platforms now stand in depths up to 340 feet; in a few years structures will rise out of water double this depth, successfully meeting the awesome force of the waves. Flow from wells at greater depths can be piped to the fixed platforms, one of which may handle the production of a score of wells.*

In the 1950s geologists explored with scuba gear. This exploration led to stratographic drill tests at shallow depths. Today ships frequently drill for bottom cores at depths up to a mile, and the specially built *Glomar Challenger* (functioning in the national ocean sediment scientific drilling program) has obtained cores at remarkable depths of as much as three sea miles below the surface and penetrating far into the bottom. Equipped with satellite navigation, automatic dynamic positioning equipment, and the latest technical developments in automated drilling devices, the ship's achievements set the course for deep sea petroleum drilling in the future.

Since fixed surface production platforms probably cannot be built for depths beyond 1,000 feet, alternate methods are now being developed to place the operating equipment on the bottom or on a platform submerged below the reach of the waves. In fact, the navy and industry have already developed techniques in diving and working in the sea that make these concepts feasible.

Submersibles and Man in the Sea

The oceans are earth's last frontier, abounding in resources for man's survival. Just as its horizons have drawn him on throughout history to great wealth, now its depths make possible the same promise.

In the last two decades notable progress has been made in developing the capability to descend into the depths and to live and work

---

*In the latter half of 1970 Humble Oil began drilling a wildcat well off California in 1,500 feet of water, the greatest sea depth for oil well drilling recorded to date.

there. Today the United States leads the world in saturated diving experience, undersea habitats, and submersibles for scientific investigation, exploration, and underwater work.

Trieste, built by the Picards, father and son, represented a significant forward step in depth exploration. Purchased by the U.S. Navy and manned by Lieutenant Don Walsh, USN, and Dr. Jacques Picard, *Trieste,* on 23 January 1960, set a historic record when the two men descended to 35,800 feet in the Pacific, the oceans' greatest known depth.

From these and other efforts there evolved the navy's Deep Submergence Systems Project, with the ultimate goal of operating submersibles, manned and unmanned, at any depth anywhere in the oceans. For the first phase the navy established five major programs.

Sunken Submarine Location, Escape, and Rescue
This involved the development of a small submersible capable of descending to at least the collapse depth of present deep-running submarines. There it would mate with the sunken boat through an escape hatch and rescue the crew. DSRV-1* (Deep Search and Rescue Vehicle) has been constructed around three special steel spheres, with an operating depth below 3,500 feet. It can be flown to the area of need. There a nuclear submarine with special equipment added can leave its regular duties and become a mother submarine of the DSRV for rescue operations.

With the DSRV attached piggyback, the mother submarine proceeds to a point as close to the stricken submarine as feasible, employing sonar and homing on the sunken boat's radio buoys. The DSRV then detaches and with television cameras, powerful lights, sonar, and viewing ports locates one of the sunken submarine's escape hatches, clearing away debris with its mechanical arm. Linking with the hatch is a delicate operation made possible by the DSRV's stern propeller, four duct thrusters that control heave, pitch, surge, sway, and yaw, with liquid mercury shifting between tanks helping to minimize roll.

Deep Search Object Location and Small Object Recovery at Depths Far Beyond Past Capabilities
This program's objective is a submersible capable of searching to 20,000 feet. It will not be as cumbersome, slow, or inflexible as *Trieste.* Marked progress has already been made in this area of activity, as evi-

*DSRV-2, launched August, 1970, should complete trials in 1971–1972. Requiring the development of new technologies, the DSRV has large strategic and economic implications.

denced by the navy's recovery from 2,850 feet of water of the nuclear bomb dropped from a plane off Palomares, Spain, in 1966, and of the small submersible *Alvin* (lost underway while operating for Woods Hole), from 5,105 feet. In 1970 budget cuts forced discontinuation of the submersible, but certain studies continued, and the project will probably be renewed later.

Large Object Salvage

Methods utilizing saturation diving techniques and pontoons are being developed to raise objects weighing as much as 1,000 tons from depths ranging to 1,000 feet.

Man in the Sea

This program is designed to enable men to perform useful and prolonged work in and out of habitats at depths to 1,000 feet. Using normal equipment, a diver can work at 250 to 300 feet for only a short period of time. Then he must spend about six times as long in slow ascent and decompression.

Captain George F. Bond of the U.S. Navy Medical Corps achieved a critical breakthrough in the advancement of saturation diving. By breathing a balanced mixture of gases* equal to the pressure of the sea depth around him, the diver can work for long periods before coming up and decompressing. If an underwater habitat is provided to maintain the outside sea pressure, the aquanaut stays saturated at this pressure both when working in the sea and when returning to his sunken home. He can remain in this pressure environment for weeks at a time and undergo decompression only upon his return to the surface.

The progressive Man in the Sea program has made tremendous progress. Beginning in 1964 a series of Sealab experiments at depths to 600 feet have demonstrated that man can live and work for prolonged periods under high pressure without harm. The experiments have contributed greatly to scientific knowledge concerning new items of equipment and modes of living in the sea.** They have particularly expanded the range of uses for saturated diving. In 1968 two members of

---

*Oxygen and helium below one hundred feet.

**The aquanauts had some unexpected experience with food under pressure. Aquanauts cannot use fresh eggs because they give off a sulphide gas in the pressurized oxygen-helium atmosphere. Dehydrated foods, when opened under the high pressure, dissolved into powder. Unexpected medical findings of great value have also come from Sealab, a major laboratory for the navy's research in biomedicine. As one example, patients suffering with gangrene have been successfully treated when subjected to oxygen at high pressure.

an aquanaut team preparing for a Sealab experiment set a world record in a 1,025-foot dive simulated in a pressure tank.

With Sealab as a pathfinder, the United States commenced a series of tests called *Tektite,* with NASA, the navy, the Department of the Interior, General Electric Company, and scientists of a number of private institutions. The tests began in 1969 off St. Johns in the Virgin Islands, where four aquanauts lived and worked in the sea and in wet and dry laboratories of their habitat submerged at 50 feet for 60 days. Other tests followed in 1970.

Construction of a Nuclear-Powered Deep Submergence Research and Ocean Engineering Vehicle
This submersible, abbreviated NR-1, joined the fleet in 1969. The small submarine carries seven men. She has viewing ports, underwater lights, television and movie cameras, and a remote control manipulator arm. Bow and stern thrusters make it possible to adjust position over a submerged object with great precision. Capable of reaching extreme depths and of cruising at maximum speeds for long periods, NR-1 is proving very useful in a broad spectrum of scientific and engineering missions as well as in other naval assignments.

As part of its deep ocean technology accomplishments, the navy is working in many fields such as fuel cells to provide quiet, prolonged endurance at less weight and expense than nuclear power; hydraulic systems employing sea water instead of oil; and structural materials of high strength to weight ratio, such as glass.

NEMO (Naval Experimental Manned Observatory), a two-man submersible sphere of clear acrylic plastic allowing 360 degree vision, has been tested in a pressure vessel in depths surpassing 4,000 feet. While not designed for great depths, NEMO demonstrated its usefulness in dives to 600 feet in 1970. Developed by the navy's civil engineers, this "crystal ball" with virtually unobstructed vision could serve as a model for research vehicles, cabs on seafloor trucks, bulldozers, excavators, and other heavy equipment.

As the navy's efforts expand, providing more reliable systems for operations on the ocean depths, NOAA, other government agencies, and industry continue to contribute their own innovations to most phases of ocean science and engineering.*

American industry, often with navy or other government support, has built a number of small submersibles for civilian use. Most of

---

*This also includes unmanned underwater research vehicles such as *Curve.* Equipped with sonar and television and designed for torpedo recovery, *Curve* surpassed its test capability in attaching a line to the Palomares bomb. Its capabilities have been increased, and one that will operate at 20,000 feet is in design stage.

these provide space for two or three men. They bear names such as *Deep River, Deep Quest, Roughneck,* and *Deep Star.* Usually they are equipped with arms to aid in underwater tasks.

Academic institutions and laboratories such as Scripps and Woods Hole have conducted some work with submersibles chartered from industry or on loan from the navy. Scientists from numerous institutions participated in the *Tektite* experiments. Most laboratories and universities with oceanographic capabilities participate in the government's overall efforts. The institutions in turn receive many research grants and contracts from the government. From these are derived some of the nation's finest accomplishments.

For instance, MIT built the intricate integrated control and display system for the navy's DSRV. It is comparable to the control navigation system of Apollo spacecraft, and it needs to be at least as effective. In some respects the DSRV's task in the hostile depths, amidst enormous pressures and dense darkness where there are no stars or other navigational aids, is more complex than a lunar landing.

The United States currently leads the world in submersibles for working beneath the sea. However, it may or may not hold the lead. Budget restrictions have markedly slowed naval programs under the sea as well as elsewhere. When man leaves the surface of Earth, whether plunging into outer or inner space, he pays for it. The deeper he penetrates into the strange, dark, crushing pressure of the oceans, the more difficult and expensive it becomes. Because of cost differential, habitability, and working space, surface ships will probably always play the primary role in most aspects of oceanography, ocean science, and engineering. But the ventures into the depths must continue because they hold great rewards for all mankind.

Soviet Oceanography Surges Ahead

With attention centered on the U.S.S.R.'s successes in space flights too many people in the United States have failed to appreciate the Soviet's spectacular and more significant advances in all areas of maritime power, including knowledge of the sea.

When Russia made the military decision to break out of Eurasia, she greatly expanded oceanographic work and other maritime activities. The Soviets then lagged far behind, but in recent years they have significantly altered their position in the oceanographic race. As early as the International Geophysical Year 1957–1958 the U.S.S.R. conducted the largest oceanographic program of any country. In 1971 she carries out widespread activities ashore and in all oceans.

From the time Peter the Great forged a powerful navy and brought

Russia's frontiers to waters opening into the world's oceans, the Russian people have explored and studied the seas. A century after Peter's school for training naval officers got underway, Ivan Kruzenstern, noted world navigator and oceanographer, headed it for sixteen years.

Kruzenstern, an able naval officer who received oceanographic training in England, was the first Russian to circumnavigate the globe—in 1803–1806. For the rest of the century Russian navigators averaged about three circumnavigations a decade, and these voyages were complemented by studies of the oceans. As already noted, Russians greatly admired Matthew Fontaine Maury and tried to induce him to settle in their country.

Now the Soviets have moved to the forefront in the study and uses of the sea except in such areas as petroleum exploration and deep submergence research. By reason of a crash building program the Soviets today operate the world's largest fleet devoted to ocean research, approximately 200 ships. Numerous academic institutions and laboratories ashore support the fleet, but the principal training, along with much of the most important laboratory work, is conducted afloat.

Soviet areas in ocean research are roughly parallel to those in the United States. The principal activity falls under: (a) the navy, (b) the Hydrometeorological Service, (c) the State Committee for Fish Economy, (d) the Ministry of Geology and Mineral Resources, and (e) the Academy of Sciences.

The academic system is linked with these, and the total operation comes under the broad control of the State Committee for Coordination of Scientific Research. All groups, including the academic institutions, work directly for and are controlled by the state without the stimulating influence of free enterprise and research. But the Soviets overcome these weaknesses by massive effort.

Like the United States, the U.S.S.R. has established an overall coordinating group, entitled the National Council for the Utilization of the Resources of the Sea. Cooperating with other nations, including the United States, the Soviet Union has incorporated the knowledge of each into its own progress. The extensive ship and laboratory building programs have especially benefited from advanced Western instrumentation.

Ocean Science Ashore

The U.S.S.R. has some one hundred specialized laboratories or academic institutions that concentrate much or all of their work in oceanography and related research. Examples include such important ones in Moscow as the Academy of Sciences Institute for Oceanology, the Institute for Microbiology, the Acoustic Institute, and the Chief Directorate of the increasingly powerful Hydrometeorological Service.

In Leningrad we find the Hydrometeorological Institute and the Arctic and Antarctic Research Institute. The Polar Research Institute of Fisheries and Oceanography is located at Murmansk in the north; the Pacific Hydrometeorological Scientific Institution at Vladivostok is in the Far East; and the Ukrainian Academy of Science at Sevastopol is in the south.

The U.S.S.R. Academy of Science and other academic organizations such as the Marine Hydrophysical Institute emphasize basic research. Most applied research falls under the Hydrometeorological Service and the various ministries, with the navy's Hydrographic Service and the State Industrial Fisheries Commission playing important roles.

Types of Research

The range of Soviet research covers physical oceanography from the atmosphere and the surface of the sea to the lower depths. This includes wave action and energy exchange at the surface, interaction of sea and air, currents, dynamics of circulation, turbulence, mixing of waters, and depth of the mixed layers. In ocean chemistry Soviet scientists advance in such fields as salinity, composition of marine sediments, radio nuclids in the bottom layers, and hydrochemistry.

In biology they have opened all the stops in applied research for the support of fishing. As will be summarized later in this book, this has been quite successful.

Most research is directed with practical goals of direct benefit to naval operations, particularly submarine and ASW, ocean transport, fishing, petroleum, and mineral recovery. For example, the U.S.S.R. has long excelled in Arctic oceanography.

Following the historic pattern of Czarist times, the Soviets pressed scientific investigation and use of the northern polar regions at an early stage. The 6,000-mile frigid frontier from Lapland to the Aleutians becomes increasingly active. Icebreakers extend the open season of the northern sea route for passage of warships and merchantmen, spurring the development of this formerly empty region.

The Arctic Institute, probably the equal in its field of any group in the world, has had a distinguished role in this advance. For years it functioned under the Northern Sea Route Administration, but as the Soviet surge to the sea gathered headway in the early 1960s, the Hydrometeorological Institute took over.

Research Afloat

One can learn the sea only by living with it. It is in ships and their employment—more than in shore laboratories and institutes—that we witness the most striking evidence of the Soviet's dynamic turn to ocean research. Since 1963 the Soviets have added an unbroken flow of commodious, splendidly outfitted research ships to cover all types of ocean research. They not only build in numbers and employ sup- plementary ships such as fishing trawlers, but many of the ships con- tain laboratories for all disciplines and large scientific staffs. The Kremlin has pulled out all stops. Cost is not important when com- pared to the goal.

The ships are assigned to the several activities working in the oceans, but priority goes to the navy, the Hydrometeorological Serv- ice, and organizations working with fisheries.

The navy's Hydrographic Service has achieved unprecedented oceanwide survey capability as the recipient of many large new oceanographic vessels. These include eleven or more of the *Subov* class built in Poland. The expanding Hydrographic Service has some twenty-five new ships replacing old conversions. With a combina- tion of naval and academic scientists on board these ships travel all seas and visit ports in many lands.

The Hydrometeorological Service, which is controlled directly by the Council of Ministers, has likewise made tremendous strides in adding new research ships. Its numerous craft include most of the seven splendid *Akademik Kurchatovs,* the largest class of purely oceanographic research ships in the world.

Over eighty scientists work in twenty or more laboratories on each of these ships to make them truly mobile research centers. Even as late as 1964 American scientists visiting fifteen leading marine insti- tutes and laboratories in the Soviet Unon saw only one computer operating, which indicated backwardness in the use of this important tool. Yet each of the *Kurchatovs* has computer facilities. The ships also have bow thrusters, stabilizing fins, helicopter pads, meteorologi- cal rocket launchers, and other equipment that demonstrates that the Russians are among the world's best.

Several ships of a newer and smaller class, the *Passats,* built in Poland, have joined the Hydrometeorological Service in the last few years, probably for upper air, general meteorological, and oceanogra- phic research, and useful, as well, for all types of naval operations including submarine ballistic missile firing.

The numerous laboratories of these ships contain the most modern instrumentation. In this field the Soviets lagged well behind the

U.S. until recently. Neither facilities nor experience to produce the required instruments existed in the U.S.S.R., or it did not exist in sufficient amounts to implement oceanographic as well as other programs. So the Soviets borrowed heavily from the West. Now more and more of the required instrumentation comes from Soviet plants, often excellent reproductions of instruments produced elsewhere.

Current estimates credit the Soviets with more trained and practicing oceanographers and other ocean scientists than the United States. In the ocean sciences, as in all other fields of science and engineering, Russia has a massive training program underway. The number of trained men with seagoing experience mounts yearly. The Soviets' 200 ocean research ships provide an extraordinary amount of practical experience; they don't sit in mothballs for lack of funds. Some vessels of the large fishing fleet also carry scientists. Adding to all these seagoing billets, in the 7,000-ton *Bataisk* the U.S.S.R. has the only full-time oceanographic training ship afloat. She carries some 250 teachers, trainees, and technicians on working cruises.

Oceanographic authors within the U.S.S.R. show intimate knowledge of Western work and of reports in foreign scientific and technical journals to which they have long subscribed. Published Soviet articles reveal special interest and skills in underwater acoustics and all the many variables and phenomena that affect sound transmission and reception in water. This knowledge, of course, carries immediate urgency for offensive and defensive submarine operations. It also has another immediate value, highly beneficial and lucrative.

Soviet Fisheries

One of the reasons that Moscow invests heavily in oceanography is fishing. In this industry, as in the merchant marine, the Russians perceive very important economic benefits. Not only do the merchant and fishing fleets directly stimulate economic health but, as adjuncts of the Soviet Navy, they play a significant role in Soviet strength at sea.

Soviet fishing and whaling expanded with startling speed after the early 1950s. At that time the U.S.S.R. was a heavy importer of sea foods; now her situation has reversed. In the decade beginning in 1955 Soviet fleets increased their fishing catch 140 percent, while the United States' annual catch remained unchanged. By the late 1960s the United States had dropped from second to sixth place in world ocean food production, and she continues to slide down the list. Once an exporter of food from the sea, she now depends heavily upon imports.

Some 100,000 craft fish the inland waters of the U.S.S.R. and greater seas. Small vessels account for most of these, but recent years have brought a swift increase in quality, tonnage, and numbers of those engaged on the oceans. Because of heavy state investment, the Soviet flag now flies over the largest and most modern deep sea fishing fleet in the world. It claims about 4,000 vessels, ranging from trawlers capable of cruising halfway around the world to huge floating factories and "mother" ships.

These include numerous refrigerated trawlers that operate as far as the Indian Ocean and the southern seas. The fine new trawlers mount the latest electronic devices to detect schools of fish vertically and horizontally. And they process the catch on board as they make it.

The tuna "factories" carry up to eight sloops, which are sent out in favorable waters to harvest the sea. The large ship then cleans and packs the fish to go directly to the customer upon return to port. Giant whaling factories of about 44,000 tons now cruise where in past generations American whalers predominated.

Each year the Soviet gains more sophisticated ships with the latest equipment, built mostly by East Germany and Poland. Much research goes into fishing to make it a major national industry. The Ministry of Fisheries conducts a good share of this, but it receives special support from the other ministries as well. The All-Union Research Institute of Marine Fisheries and Oceanography operates some sixty research ships. These may sail to far parts of the world, as did *Akademie Knepovich,* which visited Antarctica in 1968 to initiate large scale research there for commercial purposes.

The research fleet includes two converted submarines. They hunt fish, observe their behavior, and aid in improving fishing equipment and techniques. From a submarine cruising behind trawlers the Soviets have made still and motion pictures of trawler action to determine ways of improving the effectiveness of the craft.

Applied research that has made Russian fishing an efficient business includes, for example, reproduction of the sounds of predatory fish. When a trawler plays these into the water, the fish dart to the bottom, where the bottom trawl easily snares them.

As a collateral function, fishing vessels aid in oceanographic research. Certain of them carry special equipment for weather reporting, survey, study of winds, currents, and acoustic conditions. The scientific and military service of the vessels is second only to the economic benefits.

Numerous institutions such as the Sakhalin Maritime School train men for the fishing fleet as well as for the merchant marine. Some technical training may last as long as four years. In addition, retired men from the navy and naval reservists serve in the crews. Active navy files undoubtedly join those ships, which are equipped to spy electronically and occupy intelligence stations from the Chesapeake Capes to the Mediterranean and the Far East.

Year in and year out, large fishing fleets (including those with oceanographic and intelligence duties) swarm off the U.S. coasts. Among them appear stern trawlers, side trawlers, factory ships, and large fish freighters that shuttle processed fish to market. While with the fleet these large vessels serve as base ships. They have various comforts on board, including good medical and dental facilities and small hospitals.

The large fleets are supported for months at a time far from home. Tugs accompany them to handle breakdown and repairs. Tankers join for refueling. Passenger ships bring replacement crews. This is a truly sea-based operation, in which the Soviets have become highly skilled in sea logistic support and endurance under the most rigorous conditions. The skills acquired serve the Russians well in all other operations at sea. Thus the fishing fleets are not only economic aids and valuable naval auxiliaries, but they constitute a priceless training school that furnishes a large reservoir of experienced seamen. The U.S. lacks this reservoir.

The base pay is good. The Soviets draw upon the capitalist system of incentive and provide bonuses as high as 150 percent. Part of this bonus is guaranteed because of long absences from home; the remainder depends upon the trawler's meeting her annual quota. If the ship exceeds the quota, all hands share in the income from the extra catch.

One hundred or more trawlers may operate together as a fleet, with outlying scout trawlers. A controller receives reports twice daily and directs changes in position to reap the richest harvests. So many trawled down the East Coast in 1969 that Congressmen flew out to survey them. Some lawmakers, such as Representative Jack Edwards of Alabama, took the floor to warn fellow Congressmen of the "great fishing offensive" that sweeps the world.*

The number operating off the United States varies with the seasons. At times it may exceed 500, but it usually averages between 100 and 300 vessels. In March, 1970, for example, 338 fished off U.S. shores, mostly along the Atlantic and Alaskan coasts.

In 1966 the Soviets formed a western hemisphere overseas "fishing fleet command," based in Cuba. This now includes cold storage plants, canneries, warehouses, ship repair yards, and docking facilities capable

---

*Congressional Record, House, 17 April 1969, H2766.

of handling more than 100 vessels at a time. Cuba has a growing fishing fleet with accompanying large, modern refrigerated trawlers. The Kremlin has also assisted Fidel Castro in establishing an oceanographic service that can serve the U.S.S.R.'s purposes as well as Cuba's.

Vessels from Poland and East Germany have also fished off the U.S. coasts. Like those of the Soviets, many of these craft use small mesh nets, illegal in America, and dangerously deplete the fishing grounds. Insult is added to injury when some of the fish processed on board promptly enter the United States. Among the imports are blocks—compressed frozen slabs of filets, which the factory ship machinery produces. A fishing fleet off New England is not distant from the French islands of Miquelon and St. Pierre, south of Newfoundland. After processing, the blocks go in fish transports to these islands. There they transfer to U.S. ships for import—as into Gloucester, Massachusetts—at a price below cost for local fishermen. Thus as Americans eat the filets they are weakening the U.S. fishing industry and aiding the Soviets.

The efficiency of these large, new fishing fleets and their heavy, unregulated fishing have accelerated the decline of U.S. commercial fisheries except in areas such as shrimp and tuna fishing. Since 1955 U.S. consumption of fish products has more than doubled. Since her catch has remained static, she is now forced to import two-thirds of her needs.

Freedom of the seas is one of man's chief blessings, and it must be preserved. Yet like other freedoms, that of the sea has its responsibilities and must consider the interests and welfare of other nations With their maritime supremacy, Great Britain and the United States accepted these responsibilities afloat. Hence none benefited more from freedom of the sea than the smallest and weakest states.

The case may be different when the Communists gain control if we may judge from what has happened to her slave satellites behind the iron curtain ashore. Insofar as fishing is concerned, the results began to show up several years ago. They are well set forth by Senator Warren G. Magnuson in his 1964 Committee report *The Postwar Expansion of Russia's Fishing Industry:*

> As a result of the intrusion of the prowling and ravenous fishing fleet of the U.S.S.R. into the traditional fishing grounds of a number of nations around the globe, the orderly pattern of activity of many fishing communities has been painfully disrupted, contributing a new and dangerous source of conflict. . . .
> . . . If the drive is continued unabated, it can be expected to work further havoc with the hitherto orderly exploitation of the fishery resources of the world for the equal benefit of all nations.

The Soviets are making a full-scale assault on the sea and its inner space that far surpasses their operations in outer space. They have already experienced the immediate and lasting benefits the sea offers to all who seek them. They perceive greater potential rewards—rewards that place no frontiers on the extension of their power and influence.

Sea power is a blend of many things. Important among them are knowledge of and experience in this medium that exerts its vast influence throughout the earth. With their expanding navy, merchant marine, and oceanographic and fishing fleets the Soviet effort on the oceans is truly prodigious. Like a rising tide it sweeps across all seas with one goal—control of the world.

Some of the significant results already achieved appear in the following chapter.

Numerous sources have contributed to this necessarily brief view of U.S. activity in oceanography. The most valuable have been those mentioned in the first pages of the chapter and the admirable summary survey of Rear Admiral O. D. Waters, "The Ocean Sciences and the Navy" in the U.S. Naval Institute's *Naval Review, 1969*, with updating from current naval periodicals and reports and material in *Navy Times, Navy, The Magazine of Seapower, U.S. Naval Institute Proceedings*, professional notes, *Ordnance,* and *Oceans.*

Those wishing to explore the growth of oceanography under Maury will find fascinating his *Physical Geography of the Sea* and the biographies, *Matthew Fontaine Maury: Pathfinder of the Seas,* by Charles L. Lewis, and *Matthew Fontaine Maury: Scientist of the Sea,* by Frances Leigh Williams.

Information about Soviet progress was taken from some of the foregoing items but especially from the excellent series of articles entitled "Okeanologii," by Robert D. Plunkett, in *Oceans,* beginning with the July, 1969, issue; the comprehensive volume *Soviet Sea Power,* published by the Center for Strategic and International Studies, Washington, D.C.; and various articles in the *U.S. Naval Institute Proceedings.*

14

Soviet Outreach by Sea

T HE U.S.S.R. has turned to the oceans with purpose and frightening speed, and it forges ahead in the full spectrum of uses of the sea. Only the most naive could imagine that this drive into the waters of the world does not have a global goal. Directed by the cold and calculating men of the Kremlin, this long-range purpose bodes no good for all nations.

If anyone doubts how Russia intends to exercise this power afloat, he has only to examine how it has been used in the decade just ended. As their sea power has grown stronger, the Soviets have ventured near and far with increasing boldness. The past surely presages the future— and what it foretells for the United States is not pleasant.

Change always produces tension. The more rapid the change, the greater the tension and revolt. Witness the rising passions currently raised by the winds of unrest even in richly favored America. In the mounting tide of turbulence that is washing across the world, free nations will find it no easy matter to survive. And they will surely fail if they lose the sea.

Nuclear Missile Challenge from and over the Sea

A century and a half ago the Monroe Doctrine enunciated a cardinal principle of American foreign policy. It informed European nations that any attempt to extend a repressive political system to the western hemisphere is dangerous to our peace and safety.

257

Today, thrusting ever outward, the Soviet Union takes large and ominous steps that challenge the tenets of the Monroe Doctrine.

The challenge can come only from across, under, or above the oceans. North America has properly been called a continental island. Despite the shrinkage of time and space in the age of air, missile, and satellite, the comparison still applies. To reach America the enemy must make his approach over water, under it, or through the sky above it. Thus the safest place to meet him is as far overseas as possible.

The gravest threat stems from sea- or shore-based nuclear missiles. In shore-based missiles (as we have seen) the Soviets have forged ahead to surpass the United States, by about 1,400 launchers to 1,054. Not content with such a margin, the Kremlin continues to increase the number of launchers and the size and power of their missiles. Admiral Moorer reports that they have likewise placed priority on improving "the accuracy, survivability, and defense penetration capability" of the ICBMs.

Production has specialized, particularly on the huge SS-9, designed to knock out even hardened Minuteman sites. The Soviets have achieved superiority ashore, posing a security problem of considerable magnitude for our nation.

Today the Kremlin is restrained only by the United States' superiority afloat in the Polaris-Poseidon submarine force. But what of tomorrow when this superiority vanishes? As was noted earlier, this will certainly happen. While the United States stands still with forty-one of these undersea champions, the Soviets are rapidly and aggressively building ballistic missile submarines of their own.

The massive increase in Soviet shipbuilding facilities and the large number of submarines now on the ways indicate trouble for the United States. South Carolina's L. Mendel Rivers, who struggled hard in Congress to see that America maintains a strong offensive and defensive posture on the world scene, advised his colleagues in October, 1970, shortly before his death, that "The present Soviet drive to overtake us in all categories of submarines is irreversible—irreversible."

Today Soviet submarines cruise, hidden beneath the surface, off both American coasts. They maneuver unseen, with nuclear missiles targeted on American cities from Boston and New York to Jacksonville and Miami; from Chicago to Kansas City and New Orleans; from Seattle to Los Angeles and San Diego. Tomorrow there will be more of them and by 1975, if not before, more than in the U.S. Navy.

The United States has blindly ignored much evidence of the Communists' intention to take over the world. She has not heeded many of their plainly spoken purposes, such as the statement of the Minister of Defense, Marshall Andrei Grechko: "The Americans are fooling themselves. The only war to fight to win is an atomic one, and that is what we shall be prepared for."

The Ocean Moats

The first line of defense against nuclear missiles is as close to the launch point as possible. If the launcher can be destroyed before the missile can be launched on its course, this gives 100 percent defense— a fact that surely motivates Moscow in building for the purpose of superiority.

U.S. leaders manifestly cannot consider a first strike. They *can* take the next best defensive step and place the first line of defense as far forward as possible. This should constitute three complementary parts, each of which is of primary importance.

(1) *SABMIS (Shipborne Antiballistic Missile System)*. These missile destroyers would meet the ICBM in the early part of its flight and have a chance to destroy it on the far side of the ocean.

(2) *Effective ASW (Antisubmarine Warfare)*. If the launcher is a Russian submarine, it is imperative that the United States have dependable long-range detection, close surveillance, and strong ASW forces of ships and planes to destroy the underwater attacker at point of launch.

(3) *Ballistic Missile Submarines on Station*. These should be situated as close aboard the U.S.S.R. as feasible to provide a sure massive second strike and, therefore, virtually certain prevention of a Soviet preemptive first strike against Minuteman, strategic air bases ashore, and submarines at their bases. Mobile, dispersed under the sea, and very difficult for the Soviets to locate, the Polaris-Poseidon submarines still give the United States an enormous advantage. But that advantage is rapidly dwindling. The subs can and should be supplemented with ballistic missiles mounted in surface ships; these have the same advantages of mobility and dispersal, though they lack the element of concealment. They cost less than hardened Minuteman sites ashore or submarines and should be beneficial for the U.S. to employ in preserving security and peace.

Of these three essentials the United States does not possess the first at all. As far as the second is concerned, she has a good long-range detection, but she lacks the critical number of ASW forces—air, surface, and submarine. In the last two years, even while the Kremlin continues to build, Washington has severely cut back the U.S. Navy.

The reduction affected mostly older ships. Nevertheless, it has *placed the United States in its weakest position afloat since 1950—*

when the Communists capitalized on American unilateral disarmament by striking into Korea.

With respect to the third requirement, the United States has long possessed the necessary elements in the remarkable Polaris submarine fleet, which USS *George Washington* initiated with her commissioning in 1959. But after launching forty-one of these mighty deterrents the U.S. rested despite the mounting menace of Soviet power and has built no more.

Nor has the U.S. allotted funds to place ballistic missiles in surface ships. There is no possible means for an enemy surprise attack to destroy all missiles mounted in these forty-one submarines—and probably not all that might be mounted in surface ships. Hence, with enough of these seaborne missiles the U.S. Navy would have the assured capability of devastating the foe regardless of his first strike.

With the large number of nuclear attack submarines commissioned or under construction, the Soviets can hope to contain a counterattack unless the United States acts quickly to put more deterrent force at sea.

America's second line of defense rests in ABMs launched from within her frontiers to intercept the enemy missiles offshore or, as a last resort, to intercept them over the target. These are less desirable than ABMs on mobile platforms afloat, but this shore system protecting Minutemen sites helps to create a posture of sure deterrence. Washington has started to develop it.

Challenge Ashore in the Western Hemisphere

Thus in her first imperative of security and peace—protecting home base—the United States falls behind. This knowledge and the confidence engendered by growing maritime strength enter into the Kremlin's increasing boldness in the western hemisphere.

The Soviets' first notable success within the bounds of the Monroe Doctrine came before they achieved distant sea power. Fidel Castro had close Communist contacts in Mexico and received training in Soviet tactics of "wars of liberation." From the outset of his takeover, the Kremlin has poured in support. This has included naval and other military aid as well as vast economic aid, for which the Cubans pay dearly.

With the growth of its merchant marine the Kremlin found new opportunities for economic, political, and psychological probes overseas and for shoring up the military strength of Communist-inclined nations. But in 1962 Khrushchev ventured a step further when he introduced Soviet medium-range missiles into Cuba, thus making the island a forward launching site, a nuclear menace pointing at the heart of the United States.

Strong American counteraction forced him to back down and theoretically remove the missiles. Many Americans, however, believe that some of these missiles or others with simpler launching requirements are in Cuba today. Caves filled with military hardware are reported to exist.

Starting in 1962 the U.S.S.R. has transferred to Cuba missile boats, torpedo boats, and patrol vessels. A naval mission accompanied them and constitutes part of the large Soviet contingent now with Castro. Listening stations on the island undoubtedly monitor space and missile shots from Cape Kennedy, including the navy's latest Poseidon. It would not be surprising to learn that the Russians have installed underwater equipment in the area for long-range tracking of U.S. submarines. Shore stations probably keep tabs on the U.S. Navy's fleet operations in the area. Out of Cuba operate some of the Soviet spy ships that patrol the U.S. East Coast to monitor military radio and radar emissions.

By 1970 Soviet maritime power had reached such stature that the Kremlin played its next gambit. Following an earlier visit in 1969, Russian naval task forces boldly cruised the Caribbean. Warships mounting powerful missiles approached to within thirty-five miles of the Florida and Louisiana coasts. The Soviets began building what was probably an advanced submarine base at Cienfuegos, on the southern coast of the island across from Havana. This undoubtedly included missile upkeep and storage facilities ashore or in barges and submarine tender afloat.

Protests by the U.S. government *may* have brought results. But there was probably a quid pro quo; and whatever the Kremlin promise may be, we must always question whether it will be kept. Long ago Lenin cynically set the course for Communists. "Promises," he said, "are made to be broken."

A fundamental thesis of the Communist doctrine is that the end justifies the means. In the half century since the Bolshevists took over Russia their record of treaty violation is not one to inspire confidence.

Even if construction does not go ahead ashore, a submarine tender and barges provide a suitable advance base. The Russian Navy obviously intends to use Cuba for this purpose. Thereby time on station will be greatly increased for Soviet submarines operating in the Gulf of Mexico and off the southeastern United States.*

When America possessed overwhelming nuclear and naval superior-

---

*Work at Cienfuegos will undoubtedly continue under the cover of its development as a commercial port. This has already included an electricity generating plant and the shift there of Cuba's largest crane, both of which would serve naval installations well.

ity, the Soviets lit fuses to powder kegs from Korea to the Middle East. As the margin of superiority fades, it will become increasingly difficult to resolve problems arising from Moscow's intrigues across the sea.

In Cuba the Soviets have a prize of utmost importance: a large and populous island nation lying just off Florida and athwart the vital trade routes into the Gulf of Mexico, Panama Canal, and South America. Castro's policies and Moscow's presence multiply America's defense problems, especially for the navy. More of the fleet must be kept there than would normally be the case. Still more may be required in the future if Moscow maintains warships in the Caribbean on a continuing basis. As events have demonstrated in the Middle East, the Soviet naval buildup is not aimed at peace and stability but toward tumult, anarchy, and Communist takeover.

Cuba also gives Moscow a splendid takeoff point for projecting agents into other Latin American nations. These have taken some part in the unrest that has invaded numerous countries in recent years. On the surface the U.S.S.R. seems opposed to Castro's active spread of revolution and appears to be advocating the soft pedal. Yet Russians assist in terrorist training in Cuba; staffs increase in Soviet embassies in Latin America; and new embassies continue to open. This escalation obviously has political and subversive overtones, for Russian foreign trade with these nations remains small.

Each year some 1,500 selected youths from Latin America journey to the U.S.S.R. to study. When they return, the embassies keep in touch. At least some of these youths become Marxists.

In 1965 the U.S.S.R. reopened relations with Chile and established an embassy that soon developed close relations with Chilean leaders. Five years later Dr. Salvador Allende, head of a Marxist-dominated front, won election as Chile's president by a narrow plurality.

In Peru, Venezuela, and elsewhere Communists play an increasingly significant role. As Soviet maritime and diplomatic presence in the western hemisphere mushrooms, will the Monroe Doctrine be violated by nuclear maritime power from without and subversion from within?

The Soviet Sun Rises in the Pacific

In examining employment of Soviet maritime power during the past few years, we might steer from the western hemisphere into the Pacific. Here U.S. destiny has been shaped since her first merchant sailors ventured across the far longitudes to China and the East Indies in the eighteenth century.

The Russian merchant marine has had much impact in the Pacific during the past few years. Tens of thousands of dead and wounded

Americans attest to its use and influence. Week after week and year after year Russian ships have unloaded deadly SAM weapon systems, rockets of many types, artillery, tanks, munitions, vehicles, and supplies to bolster North Vietnam's aggression in the south. Soviet maritime power can claim credit for making it possible for North Vietnam to prolong the war (with resultant loss and cost to the U.S.).

The Soviet merchant ships have also contributed their share in the growth of U.S.S.R.-Japanese trade, which has quadrupled in the last few years. A joint project is being considered between the two nations to exploit the Siberian forest resources. Japan has launched many merchant ships for the U.S.S.R. and is helping the Soviets to build a new port on the Soviet Pacific coast.

Pressures within Japan and Okinawa force the United States to speed up its timetable for withdrawal from the extensive base on this island—bought with so much toil, blood, and resources in the bitterly fought drive across the Pacific. The conqueror submits to the conquered.

On the other hand, just north of Japan lies the strategic Kurile chain of islands, seized by the U.S.S.R. with scarcely a shot fired when she entered the Pacific war at the last minute. From these islands, owned for centuries by Japan, the Russians have taken into custody hundreds of Japanese fishing boats that ventured inside territorial waters. As for return of the islands, the Soviets will not even discuss the matter.

Control of the Kuriles makes the Sea of Okhotsk practically a Soviet inland sea. Far to the south, at the strategic Strait of Malacca, where vital sea highways converge, the U.S.S.R. achieves peaceful penetration of similar importance. As Britain withdraws from east of Suez, including the magnificent port and naval base of Singapore, the Kremlin fills the vacuum.* Soviet merchant ships are already using the superb docking and repair facilities, the finest in the Far East. Soviet influence grows in this world port, which dominates the Strait of Malacca and the South China Sea.

The U.S.S.R. Defense Minister Andrei Grechko has been credited with masterminding the seizure of *Pueblo*. Afterward, as U.S. warships converged off North Korea, so did massive contingents of the Soviet Navy.

Then and since Soviet warships have shadowed U.S. Navy ship move-

*Britain's present government has announced cancellation of full withdrawal of warships, but the diminished size of her navy makes it appear that the Soviets will still have dominant force in the area from Singapore to Suez unless the United States acts.

ments; they have harassed them, often forcing an eye to eye confrontation. Realizing their strength, the Reds are betraying by their deeds that they are beginning to feel ready to challenge the United States in any ocean, including the largest.

Anyone who questions the global extent of the Soviet naval expansion should have seen proof in Exercise "Okean." During late spring, 1970, the Russian Navy carried out the largest naval exercise in its history and, according to the chairman of U.S. Joint Chiefs of Staff, "the widest in scope ever attempted by any nation." Warships spanned the world in three oceans and nine seas, including extensive units in the Pacific.

From Petropavlosk and Vladivostok, Soviet Pacific Fleet headquarters, missile submarines regularly patrol off U.S. Pacific bases in Okinawa, the Philippines, Guam, Hawaii, and the West Coast. Soviet surface warships regularly conduct large exercises (including, at times, well over a hundred ships) and make visits throughout the vast area. These have included Chile and Peru, both of whose governments now lean far left.

Moscow does have its problems in Peking—but these are problems within the family, so to speak. Hairpulling may occur at home, but outside the iron-bamboo curtain a united front rises. Differences between the two giants of the Communist world did not prevent full support by each to Soviet forces in Korea and later in Vietnam. In future crises the two awesome powers can be counted on to close ranks again to injure the West. They will do so behind the Soviet Navy buildup that is part of the overall Communist design.

Russia and China, who divide most of Asia between them, cannot be checked in the Pacific without a powerful U.S. Navy. Acting as shield and spear, the navy must keep open the sea highway to the handful of non-Communist countries in Southeast Asia, South Korea, and the barrier of offshore nations from powerful Japan and Nationalist China to Indonesia, Australia, and New Zealand.

President Nixon's strategy relies on these nations to increase their defensive strength. As a means of insurance, the United States must continue military aid and some direct support, as she is doing in South Korea, South Vietnam, and Thailand. She will continue to need strong forward bases like those in Guam and enough ships and planes to dominate the ocean from its depths to the atmospheric sea above. Considering the growing Soviet Navy, how can the United States do this with her own navy diminished beyond the danger point?

Will the Indian Ocean Become a Soviet Sea?
The magnificent distances of the Indian Ocean extend from the Cape

of Good Hope north to the Horn of Africa and the Arabian peninsula, thence to the Indian subcontinent and far beyond to Indonesia
and Australia. Its wide empty spaces and adjoining lands east of Suez
become the latest stage in the modern drama of world geopolitics. As
England withdraws from this third of the world and the United States
treads water, the Russians move in.

This simply follows the pattern of Soviet foreign policy since World
War II—to probe for soft spots and to take advantage of the West's
weakness wherever uncovered. As the Soviet fleet becomes ever more
active in the Indian Ocean it will curb the West's ability to act along
the southern rim of Eurasia.

Soviet naval operations in the Indian Ocean doubled from 1969 to
1970. Late that year the Russians had some twenty warships in this
area: missile cruisers and destroyers, submarines, an amphibian, and
oiler and supply ships. How ironic that this region where Britain long
blocked the southward reach of the Czars through Persia and Afghanistan now goes by default to more dangerous Communist successors.
Here the Kremlin expands its empire unchecked at a time when the
area has achieved a new importance.

The northern gate of Afghanistan, which controls strategic Khyber
Pass, opening into the plains of Pakistan and northwest India, has become almost dependent on the U.S.S.R. Hundreds of millions of rubles
have gone into improving roads along which Russian trucks move
southward toward the sea. These roads tie in at the border with the
Soviet Union's road and river network. A tunnel pierces the Hindu
Kush, the massive and storied mountain range that for thousands of
years barred the way to conquerors from Asia into the rich plains of
the Indian subcontinent.

Pakistan, whose national religion causes her people to abhor atheis-
tic communism, long stood stalwart on the side of the West. When the
United States checked the flow of military equipment after the short
Pakistan-India war of 1965, this populous Moslem nation turned to the
two giants to the north. Trade with both Communist China and the
U.S.S.R. has increased. The Soviets have helped Pakistan improve
Guadar, near the Gulf of Oman approaches to the Persian Gulf, as a
"fishing port." Russian warships visit Pakistan's important port and
training center of Karachi. Merchant ships bring in cargo, including arms. Soviet agents import subversion and play on local problems
to create disorder and chaos from which Communist rule can evolve.

Relations between Pakistan and the United States have recently
improved. Americans can only hope that Washington will strive for
still greater improvement and will provide whatever arms Pakistan
requires.

The Pakistanis are straight thinking people. They have entered into arrangements with the Communist giants, realizing the possible consequences—probably better than the United States did in allying with Stalin during World War II. Undoubtedly they think they can escape Russia's influence and avoid becoming a near-satellite like Afghanistan. We can only hope that this will come to pass, for west Pakistan dominates the approaches to the Persian Gulf and the Arabian Sea.

Since becoming an independent nation, India has considered herself a third world. Presumably neutral in the West's struggle to preserve freedom from Russia, India has nevertheless leaned strongly toward Moscow. Early in her short career she often highlighted small Soviet aid but gave little notice of extensive assistance from America.

With the growth of Soviet maritime power there has been a steady rise in economic, political, and military influence of the U.S.S.R. in this nation of more than a half billion people. The Kremlin has invested about three times as much in India as in Pakistan, including steel mills and an aircraft factory to build MIG 21s. Soviet-supported newspapers flourish. Communist-dominated governments control two populous states. Merchant, fishing, and oceanographic vessels under the Soviet flag increasingly ply these distant waters.

As part of an extensive military aid program, Moscow has furnished warships from landing craft to submarines and submarine tenders. These now cruise in company with ex-Royal Navy ships—shades of the glory of the British empire. The Russian-built warships base at Vishakhapatnam on the Bay of Bengal, which the Soviets are helping to develop into an important submarine and naval repair base. It can be useful also to the Soviet Navy in its active operations on both sides of the subcontinent.

Ceylon's leftist government, elected with Communist backing, has brought this nation into a morass that may end in Communist dictatorship. Then two of the fine harbors of the world—Colombo and Trincomalee, which the Allies developed during World War II into one of the most extensive naval and air bases in the eastern hemisphere—could wind up as Soviet bases. Roughly midway between Malaysia and Africa, these ports lie athwart the great sea highways bearing traffic east and west—such as the huge oil flow from the Persian Gulf to Japan and Vietnam.

Yemen, South Yemen, and the nations along Africa's east coast tell a similar story of Soviet penetration that accompanies its rising maritime power. In late 1970, the leftist government of Sudan, washed by the Red Sea, agreed to work with Egypt and Libya in forming a federation (Syria later joined the compact). South of Sudan, using Arab clients, the Kremlin masterminds Eritrean guerrilla action to establish a separate state out of this province of Ethiopia.

Across the Red Sea, Yeman and Aden of southern Yemen control the Strait of Bab el Mandeb, which joins this steaming sea to the Gulf of Aden and the vast waters beyond. In each of these countries the Soviets have predominant influence. Aden, so long a strong point on Britain's lifeline to India and a naval base of tremendous strategic import, now welcomes Soviet merchantmen and warships. Soviet-supplied aircraft, arms, and advisors abound. Revealing her clear understanding of Aden's key maritime importance, Moscow maintains a fifty-man embassy there.

Late in 1970 the Russians landed a survey team on the island of Socotra,* where the British once had an air base at the mouth of the Gulf of Aden. Nearby to the west, occupying the Horn of Africa, lies Somalia, independent since 1960. In the same Communist boat as Sudan and Egypt to the north, Somalia obtains most of her arms from the U.S.S.R. In this new nation that controls the southern shore of the Gulf of Aden the Kremlin has conducted a vigorous economic and military aid program and has recently augmented the number of advisors. The Soviets are helping to modernize the port of Mogadishu in the southern half of this crescent-shaped nation and are rebuilding facilities in the good natural harbor of Berbera, almost due south across the water from Aden.

Thus the U.S.S.R. fully dominates the southern gateway to the Red Sea, just as she does the northern entrance at Suez.

Countries astride strategic choke valves on the ocean lifelines particularly appeal to the Kremlin. Control of these pivotal points from Suez to Singapore can bring immeasurable benefits to the U.S.S.R. The Soviet rulers understand that much of the history of civilization is the history of domination of convergence points of vital maritime routes.

The Kremlin leaders have learned that a modest naval force can have large and lasting effect in their penetration of many nations of the eastern hemisphere. The Indian Ocean fleet engages in classic naval diplomacy, conducting exercises and showing the flag in ports from Singapore and Ceylon to Africa and the Middle East. The *Soviet Military Review* typically boasts:

> The population of maritime cities in India, Ethiopia, Somali, Tanzania, and other countries warmly welcomed Soviet sailors as envoys of peace and friendship. . . . The Soviet Union does not threaten anyone.

---

*The Russians are reportedly building a naval communications station and other facilities, which could include an air base and an ammunition depot.

Far down in the Indian Ocean east of Madagascar lies the diminutive island nation of Mauritius, an independent member of the British Commonwealth. In 1970, only its third year of independence, this island outpost that the free world sorely needs completed a maritime aviation agreement with the U.S.S.R. This establishes a joint fishing enterprise, gives the Soviets refueling and docking rights for trawlers (fishing and intelligence) and landing rights for Aeroflot, the Soviets' civil airline. There tankers can load fuel for warships ranging the Indian Ocean.

The Russians have laid mooring buoys in Mozambique Channel and elsewhere; among other purposes they may serve for submarine refueling. They use this ocean to monitor space operations and have recovered one space capsule there.

The closure of the Suez Canal heightened the already significant strategic value of South Africa. Sea highways converge at the Cape of Good Hope so that more than 10 million tons of ships steer past every week. In the Republic of South Africa the United States could have a strong, stable, and sturdy ally in a focal point of world maritime struggle. Yet Washington's policies toward the republic, like those of London, have tended to establish a gulf between nations that need each other very much.

In late 1970 Prime Minister Edward Heath of Great Britain wisely reversed the policy of his predecessor government. He stated that England will again sell warships and other weapons to South Africa because it is in the interest of Great Britain "to defend the Indian Ocean and Cape of Good Hope sea routes." However, Black African Commonwealth nations have opposed the decision and could possibly abort it.

This change and the slowing of British withdrawal from Singapore are favorable moves, but they may not be sufficient to check the Soviet onrush in this area. Certainly the United States does not contribute much. Except for its small Middle East Force and occasional other ship visits, she has let the area go almost by default. This is in marked contrast to Moscow's policy as enunciated by Admiral Gorshkov: "We must be present in all waters."

Recently the United States has demonstrated some indication of stronger action in this strategic ocean. Near the equator north of Madagascar and Mauritius lies a group of small, widely scattered islands comprising the British Indian Ocean Territory. On one of these, Diego Garcia, the United States will construct a joint British-American communications center, air base, and naval refueling station. The communications facility could replace in an emergency the U.S. communications and satellite tracking station in Eritrea (now troubled by leftist guerrilla activity), which has served the U.S. Navy and NASA well for many years.

This action in Diego Garcia will modestly buttress the West's weakening posture in the third world ocean, but it scarcely begins to counter the Russians' growing presence there.

Moscow has set an undeviating course to build up its "Strategic Indian Ocean Fleet," which will surely shape the destiny of all the lands bordering these great waters. Following England's announcement of plans to reduce commitments east of Suez, Soviet warships entered the Indian Ocean and have cruised there continuously for the past three years in increasing numbers of warships and oceanographic, fishing, and intelligence vessels.

The more one ponders what has happened in this strategic region, the more one believes that what was wrong with the British Empire was not that it existed but that it ceased to exist too soon. It brought enduring benefits to the lands around the Indian Ocean with fair, just, honest, and capable administration. The record of history reveals that empires don't just fade away to be replaced with good government, peace, and liberty for all citizens. This may happen in some instances, but too often the opposite occurs. Ambitious leaders, lustful for power, frequently take over and are accompanied by corruption, lawlessness, and anarchy.

This sets up precisely the conditions desired by an ambitious new empire. We witness such a course of events today. With her great land strength bearing down from the north, her economic and military penetration of the nations of Africa and the Indian subcontinent, and her growing maritime preponderance in the Indian Ocean, the Soviet Union already dominates this part of the world. The dreams of the Czars seem to be coming true for the kings of the Kremlin.

The Persian Gulf and the Lengthening Shadow of the Bear

From antiquity the Persian Gulf has been a pearl-diving center. But all the pearls of history cannot begin to compare with the value of Middle East oil, nearly all of which lies in the countries bordering the Gulf. These fabulous and almost incredible riches bring in several billion dollars a year of direct and indirect income to the Gulf states.

More important from a geopolitical standpoint, this oil fuels ships, planes, factories, and vehicles of a formidable part of the world. A ceaseless stream of about four hundred tankers a week transits the Straits of Hormuz at the entrance to the Gulf. Outward bound tankers steer for Africa, Europe, the United States, India, and nations of the

Pacific. This arm of the sea leading to the plains of Mesopotamia has taken on a global maritime meaning of utmost importance to the future.

If the flow of tankers steering out of the Gulf should suddenly cease, catastrophe would strike from West Europe to Japan. One can thus understand why Moscow eyes the Middle East even more hungrily than did the Czars of the past.

The area retains its ancient strategic values as the crossroads of continents and highway to India, Africa, and control of the Indian Ocean. But in a sense it has become a highway to the entire world, through its immense energy resources in a civilization in which transportation and national economies insatiably demand more mechanical energy. If the Persian Gulf should come under Moscow's control, what tremendous political and psychological power this would give the Kremlin over the economies of other nations.

Stalin did not realize the incredible oil resources of the Middle East or their meaning to leading world nations when he made the infamous pact with Hitler in 1939. The area's enduring geographical values were great enough for him to write in the treaty with the Nazis, as a condition of Communist cooperation, agreement that Germany would recognize "the area south of Batum and Baku in the general direction of the Persian Gulf . . . as the center of aspirations of the Soviet Union."

This pact is dead, but the desire still lives. During the late 1960s, for the first time in over a century, Russian warships began showing their flag in the Persian Gulf. As the hammer and sickle appears, Britain's proud ensign that for so long stood for stability in this region grows dim over the horizon.

Iraq and Iran, both oil rich, lie between the U.S.S.R. and the Persian Gulf—while Iran and Afghanistan constitute the land bridge from the Soviet Union to southern Asia. For years Iraq, like Afghanistan, has been almost a Soviet satellite. Economic aid, arms, equipment, and military advisors flow steadily from the north. In southern Iraq, where the Tigris and Euphrates Rivers join as the Shatt al Arab to flow into the Persian Gulf, the U.S.S.R. has gained access to an oil concession. Thus, in a sense, she at last stands ashore on the Persian Gulf even as her warships enter it by sea from the south. Engineers and rubles aid Iraq in developing a proved oil field, building a textile mill, and expanding other enterprises. Trade and economic assistance are the opening wedge for Communist agents. Intrigue follows among the leftists, who at this time seem particularly to flourish in most countries of the Middle East.

Aeroflot wings Communists back and forth between Moscow and Baghdad and other parts of the Middle East. Moscow sends in ample funds to support the radical newspapers and broadcasting stations. Arab Communists, trained in the Soviet Union and elsewhere, operate in most of the countries, following standard Soviet policy wherever there is air or maritime access.

The control of Iran, strategically situated between Iraq and Afghanistan, has long been a goal of Moscow's imperialistic ambitions. The wise Shah Mohammed Reza Pahlevi in Tehran is thinking clearly. He and the citizens of his great and proud land have not forgotten the long record of conquests by the Czars, which snatched the Caspian Sea and bordering lands from Persia or Persian vassals. Nor have they forgotten Russia's aggrandizements of this century, including Moscow's effort in 1945 to liberate into the iron curtain Iran's northwest province as the Republic of Azerbaijan. Likewise, Iran's leaders cannot be unmindful of the U.S.S.R's chief export of subversion, "people's war," and Communist tyranny.

Yet the Soviets' enormous power presses down on Iran's northern frontier. Their presence in Iraq and Afghanistan outflanks her on the east and west. This encirclement, added to the rise of Soviet global sea power and decline of Anglo-American influence in the Middle East, has led Iran to make what has been called a "spectacular rapprochement" with her giant neighbor.

Excluding oil, more than a quarter of Iran's exports now enter the iron curtain countries. Major Soviet aid in hand or underway includes military vehicles, guns, a steel mill, and other industrial developments. It also includes the necessary engineers, administrators, advisors, and, camouflaged among them, agents with the unchanging mission to conquer from within.

To pay for the aid it has been arranged that a pipeline leading north through the massive Elburz Mountains will deliver gas over a fifteen-year period. This is an arrangement in which Moscow has undoubtedly driven the usual hard bargain, selling at inflated retail prices and buying wholesale. The U.S.S.R. has an added advantage in that Iran's gas replaces a similar amount now flowing from Soviet wells to West Europe and brings Moscow prized hard money.

Petroleum will add increasingly to the northward flow of trade. With the depletion of the U.S.S.R.'s European oil fields, by Moscow's edict Soviet satellites turn to the Middle East for their needs. Iran already has oil export arrangements with Bulgaria, Czechoslovakia, and Rumania. Thus Iran is drawn more and more into the economic orbit of the Soviets.

Moscow's growing influence in Iran and throughout the Indian Ocean area will profoundly affect the future. As Russian trade, shipping, and warships multiply east of Suez, the Soviet Union will find the cheap Persian Gulf oil of special benefit to her ambitions. And the Kremlin rulers unquestionably plan for the day when this petroleum, so conveniently situated for their plans, will be even cheaper. Manipulated change of government can lead to expropriation, which has already occurred in Iraq.

British and U.S. companies have been the principal developers of this vast oil wealth, with some input from other nations. Most of the relative calm that has prevailed in the Persian Gulf area of the Arab world in turmoil has resulted from British influence and the strong governments of Iran and Saudi Arabia.

England's influence has been especially beneficial in the sheikdoms of the Trucial (Pirate) Coast, at the south end of the Gulf (to which Britain brought order and peace last century). During recent years major oil strikes in some of these small, barren domains have made them suddenly very desirable. Because of their sparse populations it would take very little "volunteer" aid for any coup to succeed.

Britain's empire, on which the sun once never set, has been important also to the Sheik of Bahrein at the center of the Gulf and to oil-rich Kuwait at the north end. What happened in Iraq could happen much more easily in any of these sheikdoms along this water highway. It could also happen with engineered revolt and Soviet-backed puppet governments in Saudi Arabia (home of the world's largest oil reserves) and Iran, the vast petroleum deposits of which the Kremlin surely covets. If all of the Gulf should fall under Communist domination and most of the world's petroleum become Communist-controlled by nationalization, what a tremendous difference it would make in the world's economic and military balance.

Storm Clouds over the Sea of History

Events in nations of the Levant and North Africa forecast what may be the future of other lands of the Mediterranean as well as those east of Suez; and the barometer predicts storm.

The gathering hurricane has many causes. Prominent among them are: (a) the disruption caused by the Israel question, which sets up a chronic crisis situation; (b) the shattering tensions as many of these countries leave the age of Abraham and move into that of the jet and nuclear missile; (c) Moscow's liberal and relentless export of subversion, guerrilla instructors, and training in terrorism and revolt; (d) Soviet economic, political, and military expansion throughout the area; and (e) the U.S.S.R.'s powerful maritime presence in the Mediterranean not only in her warships—visible evidence of power and purpose—but also in her merchant ships, which disgorge economic and military aid and advisors.

The Soviet Union's visible and active sea power is extremely influential in the slide of the area toward communism. As late as 1966 scarcely half a dozen Russian warships cruised the Mediterranean. After the 1967 six-day war between Israel and Egypt the U.S.S.R. began to project power into this strategic sea on a grand scale. Her Mediterranean fleet has become comparable in size to the United States' 6th Fleet except for carriers. Citizens of the Arab world might nevertheless find it easy to agree with Soviet propaganda that the Soviet fleet equals the 6th Fleet in power because of overwhelming superiority in ship-to-ship missiles and because of ship visits to ports denied to the U.S. Navy. In fact, it might appear that the United States has abandoned the southern and eastern Mediterranean to the Russians.

This appearance of weakness is heightened by the fact that the 6th Fleet too often lies in port to the west when it should be showing our flag to the east. According to the Stratton Subcommittee of the House Armed Services Committee (after a visit to the Mediterranean) budgetary restrictions on the navy seriously affected the fleet's state of readiness in the autumn of 1970.

The committee's report states, "This problem is related not only to spare parts but to recent drastic cutbacks, ordered for budget reasons, in allowed steaming and flying time . . . [leaving] the carrier sitting at anchor much of the time, a very dangerous situation in the present circumstances." Growing barnacles in port is fatal in the long run at any time, for only by continuing exercise and operation can a fleet act with maximum efficiency.

Ordinarily thirty to forty warships flying the Russian flag now sail the Sea of History. But at the height of crisis the number may rise to over sixty. Submarines are especially significant in the Soviet threat. As the Stratton Subcommittee report highlights, "The 6th Fleet desperately needs additional help for its antisubmarine warfare capability." Thus besides attack carriers the United States ought to station an antisubmarine warfare carrier regularly in the area.

The Soviets still preserve the myth of their having no bases in the Mediterranean. Yet they make beneficial use of Port Said and Alexandria in Egypt, and visit Latakia in Syria and the splended ex-French naval base at Merz-el-Kebir, Algiers.

Early in the game Moscow pitted Israel against the Arabs. Then realizing the bigger spoils on the other sides of the deserts, she cynically shifted her allegiance. Against her economic, political, and strategic interests, the United States has been drawn into the Middle East vortex as a whipping boy. This has brought tremendous emotional and irrational gains for the Russians. The United States has become the devil of the Moslem world, and the U.S.S.R., the angel in the southern and eastern littoral of the Mediterranean.

In part as a consequence of this topsy-turvy state, Syria has become, through military and economic aid, almost a Soviet dependency. In this only Arab nation that does not outlaw the Communist party, Russia wears the disguise of protector and guide. The good port of Latakia just below the Turkish bulge would make a splendid Communist naval base. But the Kremlin has larger goals than this. Added to Iraq, Syria completes the virtual encirclement of Turkey with her straits leading from the Black Sea, coveted for centuries by Russia.

This is only one of several factors that have caused even Turkey to soften toward the Soviets. Foe for centuries of Russia (since the 1600s the two have fought each other, averaging more than one war a generation) and eastern anchor of NATO, Turkey's relations with the United States have nevertheless weakened deplorably. The maritime balance the Soviets have achieved must inevitably have played a part in this dramatic change of attitude.

Growing economic ties to the north are an additional factor. Trade with the U.S.S.R. has multiplied several times. Soviet aid helps to build an oil refinery near Izmir, an aluminum plant, and what will be Turkey's largest steel mill. In late 1970 the two nations reached agreement that Turkish produce trucks could travel behind the iron curtain to northern markets. In return Russian trucks may cross Turkey bound for the Middle East with "commercial" cargo.

Turkey's changing stand has also been influenced by greater activity of Communists and leftist journalists whose newspapers are subsidized by Moscow. Stimulated violence has made it difficult even for the 6th Fleet warships to visit Turkish ports.

Thus the Kremlin brings closer its goal of control of the vital water exit from the Black Sea to the Mediterranean. To the south the Russians have long since clutched Egypt, which sits astride another of the world's great connecting maritime arteries. It is no accident that Moscow early grasped opportunity in this ancient land that contains the world's most important canal. Via Suez, Soviet ships can save thousands of miles between the Black Sea and the Indian Ocean. The canal and the Red Sea beyond form the connecting link between the Mediterranean and the wealth east of Suez.

Egypt is firmly in the Soviet camp. Its military forces are under Soviet control; its economy has been shifted in orientation from the West to the U.S.S.R. Its territory is a Soviet economic-military enclave. The death of President Nasser in the autumn of 1970 apparently has not disturbed the Kremlin's control. Although Middle East turmoil has closed the Suez Canal temporarily, the Russians can look to the day when it will open again—not as a lifeline for Britain but as a Soviet highway of economic, political, and military expansion.

In 1969 Libya, with her newly discovered oil wealth, and Algiers have likewise swung into the leftist fold. Tripoli, where Commodore Edward Preble and Captain Stephen Decatur won imperishable fame, may now serve Soviet buccaneer rather than Barbary corsair. Nearby lies the huge Wheelus Air Force Base complex, developed by the U.S. at great expenditure of money and effort. It once supported nearly 3,000 landings and takeoffs each week for NATO. The Soviets may gain without effort or expenditure one of the strategic sites of the Mediterranean, which overlooks the east central area of the sea from Crete and Greece to Malta and Sicily just across the waters.

In fact, along all the North African coast and much of that of Asia Minor the United States has no air base rights. On the other hand, through her presence in the area the U.S.S.R. has rights in several countries and probably could take them in most.

Libya's leftist regime has meanwhile drawn close to Egypt. As a step in the compact for unity the two nations have established joint air training at Wheelus with Soviet participation. At Port Susah in Libya the two African nations are organizing a joint naval academy, in which Communist skills and instructors will undoubtedly direct the course.

Algiers adds markedly to potential Soviet air and naval capabilities on Africa's long northern coast. Looking at the map, one can see the significance of this large country to the security of the western Mediterranean and Gibraltar. Moscow has looked and studied carefully. Airfields in Algiers have been extended to accommodate jets and equipped to meet other Soviet requirements. Russian planes come and go from them. Marshall Grechko and other high Soviet officials have landed on the fields. Hundreds of pilots fly to the U.S.S.R. each year for training.

The maritime picture is similar. As part of a manifold increase in trade between the two nations Soviet ships bring in tanks, artillery, and other military equipment. Russian guided missile and patrol boats make up most of the little Algerian Navy. Moscow looks with keen interest at the fine naval base of Merz-el-Kebir, with its extensive underground facilities. This splendid deep water base could serve the Russian fleet well and play a large role in control of the western Mediterranean highways that govern the destiny of most of the nations bordering that historic sea.

Not content with the advantages this base offers on the approaches to Gibraltar—strategically and economically the most important strait in the world—Russia's leaders see to it that Soviet warships frequent open sea anchorages where the sea bed rises off the Spanish Isla de Alboran halfway from Merz-el-Kebir to the Rock. Similar anchorages extend across the Mediterranean, especially at such focal maritime points as just off Malta and in the Aegean Sea.

For more than two decades peoples of the Mediterranean have looked upon the 6th Fleet as keeper of the peace. Twenty years ago ships flying the stars and stripes could visit almost any port in this long sea. In 1971 nearly all ports on the south and east coasts are closed to the U. S. With them have gone valuable training grounds and missile firing areas. Now Soviet warships enter instead, disguised as friend and protector.

Steadily the Russians build a broad base on these shores for extension of power. Almost two centuries ago the first Russian fleet entered the Mediterranean and soon was trying to win strategic points such as Malta. The Soviet fleet repeats the maneuver today but under far more favorable circumstances. NATO has blocked the U.S.S.R.'s ambitions to expand the central front in Europe. Now on this fluid southern frontier the Russians execute an end run against the "soft underbelly." With their penetration ashore and their strong fleet they have come a long way toward completely outflanking NATO.

In its report the Stratton Committee points up the profound change:

> The greatly increased Soviet naval activities in the Mediterranean together with the Soviet ability to use the northern shores of Africa on short notice require that there be a reorientation of NATO defense strategy . . . toward the new Soviet threats coming from the south.

Soviet success has already markedly altered the strategic balance in this sea that for thousands of years decided the course of history—and shapes it fatefully again today.

The momentous strategic gains that would be brought by control of the Arab world—and the Persian Gulf oil is a rich prize—to be sought with all the vigor the Kremlin displays. Yet the larger prize of western Europe still remains the principal objective. Russia strides toward capability in the Mediterranean and Middle East to menace and choke off the tankers and much of the merchant shipping that sustain Europe's economic life.

This arm of the ocean, under the protection of the 6th Fleet, has been the strength and joy of NATO nations in the south. It has been a safe highway and secure frontier especially for Turkey, Greece, and Italy. Yet today it becomes a perilous one, as does any highway that is not strongly held. The West's bastions in the Mediterranean and Middle East are weakening. If America and its NATO allies permit a complete collapse of their defenses, the dangers to the West will be incalculable.

NATO's Waning Power

To the west, past the Gates of Hercules, is NATO's broader main—the North Atlantic Ocean. This maritime alliance has had and must always have three essentials:

(a) An economically and militarily powerful United States, steadfast in purpose.

(b) A strong Western Europe, united in purpose to stand ashore and to aid at sea. Greece and Turkey are the natural eastern extensions of this oceanic alliance.

(c) The cement of sea power. NATO must maintain maritime superiority in the North Atlantic and its Mediterranean arm reaching far eastward to the seats of empire of the Middle East. Without this superiority nothing can bind North America and Western Europe together and sustain them in the grave hazards they face.

The need for the first two of these foundations is obvious, so attention will be directed principally to the third. However, it should be noted that if any one of the three should fail, all would fail. The sea alliance would collapse, and Moscow's goal of world conquest would be attained. Western Europe, which the Kremlin considers the balcony to the great Russian house, would go first. Then America would stand alone.

As pointed out in the preceding pages, not only has Turkey mended her fences with the U.S.S.R., but the West's naval superiority in the Mediterranean has been seriously weakened. Considering Soviet inroads through the Middle East and North Africa, one might even say that the superiority has vanished. Thus in a very few years NATO's posture on the southern flank has greatly deteriorated.

The Iberian peninsula forms the western shore of this sea. This extension of the larger peninsula of Western Europe juttting seaward from Eurasia likewise forms part of the eastern boundary of the Atlantic. Without the Iberian peninsula the West would have no hope of holding the Strait of Gibraltar and therefore the Mediterranean.

Without the peninsula and its oceanic dependencies, such as the Azores, the Atlantic shipping and defense problems would also sharply expand.

Thus Spain and Portugal have notable roles to play in the alliance of freedom. Naval and air bases in both nations augment the control of the western Mediterranean and the crucial sea lanes to South America, Africa, the Indian Ocean, and the Persian Gulf. More and larger ships crowd these sea lanes, swelled in recent years by Europe's ravenous need for petroleum.

Despite the foregoing, the unfathomable vagaries of diplomacy have kept Spain out of NATO. Fortunately for the West Spain has held to her anti-Communist stance. Also, in considerable part because of the efforts of Admiral Sherman, Chief of Naval Operations in the early 1950s, Spain has granted valuable base rights. U.S. installations there, which serve as NATO defense elements, include two large air bases (with a third one in reserve) and the valuable facilities at Rota, west of Gibraltar, for Polaris submarines.

Portugal is a member of NATO. The United States and other member nations have nevertheless treated this maritime nation with less than wisdom over her firm handling of incited terrorism in Africa.

Regardless of the political cold shoulder of her allies Portugal has continued to support the aims of NATO. She makes a number of valuable contributions to the alliance, the most important of which is the grant to the United States of base rights in the Azores, essential in any struggle to keep open the Atlantic lifelines. The passing of Antonio de Oliveira Salazar from the political scene has so far not diminished Portugal's pivotal role in NATO and U.S. security. Whether the same will apply to Spain when age carries General Francisco Franco beyond the horizon one cannot know.

France has withdrawn from the integrated action of NATO; hence the alliance has lost strength. When the chips are down, however, she will be on the right side, for the combined power of NATO is fundamental to her security—just as she is necessary for the effectiveness of NATO because of her central position, military force, and sea coasts on both the Atlantic and Mediterranean.

With her extensive sea frontiers and ever rising requirements to use the ocean highways, France critically needs the U.S. Navy. So do her smaller neighbors to the north—the Benelux group: Belgium, the Netherlands (for centuries a sturdy people of the sea), and Luxembourg. Indeed, every nation of the alliance depends upon the United States to contribute the major share of the power that must be afloat to permit these people to maintain their independence.

West Germany must, first of all, possess solid land and air defense capability, for she is the bulwark the U.S.S.R. would have to breech to conquer western Europe by conventional force. Yet West Germany's function at sea is almost as important since the Baltic and the North Sea wash her coasts. In NATO's combined sea power her chief responsibility is defending the Baltic. This could be very important because of Soviet amphibious capabilities.

Along with Denmark and Norway in NATO, West Germany has significant responsibility to defend against the Russian Navy's breakout through the Cattegat and Skagerrack. The performance of these responsibilities may or may not suffer from the Willy Brandt government's detente with the U.S.S.R. and Poland in 1970. The negotiated treaties will certainly not cause the duties to NATO to be performed better.

The United Kingdom furnishes a sizable segment of NATO's power. All non-Communists should be heartened by the present government's reversal of the fatal decline of the British Navy.

The main British Isles, with their northern extension of the Orkneys and Shetlands, and Denmark's Faroe Islands are of tremendous strategic value for allied air and naval operations. They have similar value for surveillance of Russian naval, air, and missile operations from the Norwegian Sea into the North Atlantic toward America.

Norway to the northeast and Iceland to the northwest have special duties to carry out for the alliance. Norway contributes early and greatly to the vital need to know what Soviet operations are on, under, and above the waters. With its long and extensive coastline, Norway occupies a tender strategic position for the U.S.S.R. The Soviet Navy conducts frequent exercises in the Norwegian Sea. Aircraft patrol it, and submarines pass submerged through it. During Operation Okean in 1970, large air, surface, and submarine operations embraced this region. As part of the exercise planes conducted round-the-clock flights into the North Atlantic for five days.

The Kremlin yearns to extend the iron curtain to encompass this strategic sea. Secrecy is at the core of the Communist conspiracy. Hence Moscow has tried in the past to persuade Norway to quit NATO and will surely continue to do so.

Norway's potential sphere of influence extends from the U.S.S.R. northern routes into the open sea to those from the Baltic through the Skagerrack. With Britain and Denmark Norway forms the long northern reach of NATO, a narrow sea barrier against Soviet expansion in the area.

A giant stepping stone toward America, Iceland rises from the ocean bed hundreds of miles to the west. Her capital city of Reyk-

javik thrives roughly midway in longitude between New York and
Soviet naval and missile bases on the Barents and White Seas east
of Norway. From these bases a large percent of the Russian submarine fleet operates. This ocean outpost has served NATO well. In
turn NATO, via U.S. sea power, has provided Iceland with the defense
and security she needs.

Iceland's strategic location between Great Britain and Greenland
provides an irreplaceable base for surveillance of submarines sailing
out of the U.S.S R.'s northern bases into the Atlantic. As with Norway
and other members of NATO, Moscow has continually urged Iceland
to withdraw from the ocean alliance. Iceland's indigenous Communist
party, which religiously follows Moscow's party line, exerts similar
pressure on public opinion. Under the guise of the Labor Alliance
party, the Communists regularly win about one-sixth of the seats in
Iceland's parliament, the Althing. To encourage neutrality in support of the local Communists, Soviet warships visit the island.

Greenland and Canada bridge the final gap in the sprawling seaborne pact that spells security for every nation involved. The alliance involves peoples ashore, their commitment to the principles of
freedom, their economy, and their military strength. Most of NATO's
area of influence comprises vast stretches of salt water, as with other
American pacts overseas. In this alliance alone the amorphous arteries
stretch from Washington some 6,000 miles to Turkey's farthest Black
Sea port. They flow up the western coast of Europe into the frozen
Arctic. From these they continue in a huge bulging arc to Greenland's
northern tip, down Canada and North America's long east coast—tens
of thousands of miles of sea highways, millions of square miles of ocean.

Each nation has the charge to perform its mission for the good
of all. Yet if every other duty is perfectly performed and sea power
cannot maintain mastery of the ocean arteries, NATO as a working
alliance will fail. So I end this chapter, as it began, with the warning
that this foundation of strength and security is waning. Moscow fully
understands that the nation that controls the sea controls the world.
Too many Americans, while living in a land based on and strengthened by the sea, have forgotten this immutable truth to their peril.

In July, 1971, Iceland's new coalition government, which includes communists,
asked the U.S. to remove its military forces. These consisted principally of those
stationed at Keflavik Air Base in connection with watchdog flights over the northern
sea approaches.

15

Hurricane Warnings

AMERICA heads into the most dangerous period of this century for her future as a great nation and for the future of freedom. Although the twentieth century has brought a series of crises—World War I in the second decade, the Depression in the thirties, massive World War II in the forties, the Korean conflict in the fifties, and the Vietnam War—the years to come could prove to be the most perilous yet.

Strong, dedicated leadership in the highest echelons of government and faith and integrity among citizens in all walks of life will be necessary to survive the storms that lie ahead. The Soviets, playing their familiar role on the international stage, continue to widen their influence and power over nations around the globe, sowing subversion, activating trouble spots, and employing every economic, political, and military means to extend their control.

In the 1950s Kremlin leaders made their decision to wrest the sea from the United States. Their progress has been phenomenal, as the foregoing pages have demonstrated. Mass apathy in the United States (especially in many of her political leaders and journalists) toward the decline of the navy and merchant marine has greatly aided the Soviets in making progress toward their goal. In the future, with a shrunken U. S. Navy and the Soviet fleet deployed on the seven seas, the task of checking Soviet imperialism will be far more difficult.

As the preceding chapter outlined, in a very short span of time the Soviets have markedly altered the world balance of power through their gains overseas. Politically, commercially, and militarily they have penetrated most of the countries encompassed by the Indian Ocean and those of the Middle East and North Africa, and they have stretched their sphere of influence into the western hemisphere, including Cuba, on the virtual doorstep of the United States.

Russia—A Global Military Power

We have not seen the end. Senator Henry M. Jackson correctly said in the summer of 1970: "The Soviet Union is now, for the first time in Russian history, a global military power. Looking ahead, the somber prospect is a Soviet Union increasingly bolder in its policies . . . to extend Soviet influence in new areas of the world."

Whenever a vacuum develops, the Kremlin, with a strong navy and merchant marine, waits ready to move in. The overly hasty withdrawal of colonial powers from southern Asia and Africa, leaving many nations unprepared for self-government, increased Moscow's opportunities. They were like ripe plums ready for the picking by any ruthless adventurer. A number of such ruthless characters came equipped with subversion and guerrilla training received in the U.S.S.R. or in Communist schools of revolution established in numerous nations, including the United States.

The Russians have developed subversion as a science, and they skillfully employ this effective tool in the expansion drive—both in the nation up for takeover, such as South Vietnam, and in the United States, boring from within to create dissension and to weaken and destroy the national will.

The Communists seem to be pursuing a policy of encirclement of the United States and the free nations of the West. This policy, combined with subversion, efforts to demoralize American youth, and the vanishing American lead at sea, gives the Kremlin leaders the strongest playing cards in their history.

Once the Communists assert their apparatus of control of a country, they insure that the reverse process of regaining freedom is not easy. Events have borne this out from Cuba to Czechoslovakia. The Communist path becomes a one-way street.

Thus the Soviets have leaped over strong, free nations to form a checkerboard of leftist governments, giving the Kremlin power to put the squeeze play upon nations in between. Employing their maritime strength, they gradually gobble up the world through a series of limited gains. This route could mean the end of freedom as surely as nuclear war.

So far, while still lacking superiority at sea, Moscow has refrained from using the U.S.S.R.'s armed forces directly in takeover of countries not adjacent to Russia's frontiers. But planes, tanks, guns, and volunteers have played a significant part in power coups and changes. Open military action by Soviet armed forces has been reserved for use against peoples nearby already regulated by established Communist governments, Red China, and the satellites chained behind the iron curtain. Nearly every satellite, and some more than once, has felt the brutal lash that considers neither tolerance nor mercy.

With maritime capability playing such a key role in Communist world takeover, we can rightly ask why has the United States not awakened. Why has she reduced strength instead of increasing it against the darkening future? Late in 1970 Secretary of the Navy John H. Chaffee remarked in a speech that, when he took the helm, "our fleet consisted of 934 ships. By July of next year we will have just under 700* . . . a net loss of some 235 ships. In the same time we'll have cut our manpower by 150,000. But there is a limit below which we can not safely go, and we will be at that limit next July."

The U.S. Security Gap
In 1968 Presidential aspirant Richard M. Nixon forthrightly stated the need for more rather than less strength:

> The hard truth is this: the present state of our defenses is too close to peril point, and our future prospects are, in some respects, downright alarming. We have a gravely serious security gap. . . . If we allow our superior strength to become second best, if we let those who threaten world peace outpace us— in time we will generate tensions which could lead to war: first, by our display of physical weakness and flabby will; and second, by tempting an aggressor to take risks that would compel us to respond.

Thus in 1968 the United States was already near or below the safe limit in her defenses. The progressive cuts in the navy since then and the buildup of the Russian Navy have taken it past the safe limit to a critical point well below the danger line unless two unlikely events occur: (a) the Kremlin ceases to increase and modernize the Soviet Navy and (b) Moscow calls a halt to its campaign of international subversion and power grab. Unless assured of such action by the U.S.S.R., the United States ought to be increasing rather than decreasing her strength at sea.

One can sympathize with the president and the leaders in the defense establishment as they face difficult political and internal problems. One can understand the philosophy of cutting defense in order to try to balance the inflated budget. Nor is it difficult to understand the hope that a one-fourth smaller navy, fortified by new construction,

---

*Later revised slightly upward.

can accomplish more in the 1970s than could the larger navy of 1968. One can understand, but he can also question whether the hope has validity. The Soviet Union does not stand still at sea. It has a dynamic expansionist policy. Each year better submarines, better surface ships, and better planes and missiles strengthen the Soviet's fleet. In part, the new units represent replacements for older and less efficient ones, but the trend has been toward not only better ships, planes, and missiles, but a greater number of them.

Is not the United States, therefore, courting the peril of shipwreck with a national strategy that tolerates unacceptable international risks to appease the antimilitary and to divert funds needed afloat into domestic programs?

At intervals throughout history there are periods during which the struggle between despotism and freedom loving peoples rises to a climax that determines the whole stream of civilization thereafter. We are living now in such an era.

Behind their global maritime power structure the Russians have forced the West into retreats and partial surrenders that hasten the approach of their goal of world communism. They have often stated that the future belongs to them. Decades ago Communist leaders said that the struggle with the West was the "axis" of life and "the second half of the twentieth century will bring the complete victory of communism throughout the world."

Russian accomplishments to date must increase Moscow's confidence in that prophecy. Though we cannot pierce the veil of the future, we can predict with certainty that the U.S.S.R. will succeed unless the citizens of the West, and especially the United States, resolve firmly otherwise.

The issue may not be decided by Armageddon but rather in the spirit of men, which will be shaped in part by strength at sea. The United States has lost most cold war struggles in negotiating with the Russians. One principal reason has been Communist refusal to back down. Trickery, deceit, intransigence, and propaganda have also contributed their share to Soviet success. But the most compelling reason can be found in Russia's tough power base and its *undeviating resolution not to compromise.* Followers of Marx and Lenin, Soviet leaders are also students of Clausewitz. They cling to his principle that "He who engages in battle with the fixed determination not to be the first to yield is already half victor."

When the United States set a firm course with equal resolution and had the power to back it, she prevailed—as in saving Greece, establishing NATO, and forcing the removal of the missile threat from Cuba. Past experience with the Communists has demonstrated that they respect strength and determination and have only contempt for equivocation and appeasement.

The course of the twentieth century is still in contest, as it has been for most of its stormy track—and the oceans will figure significantly in its ultimate outcome. From the golden age of Greece to the soaring space age men of foresight have perceived that he who commands the sea commands the world. With all that sea power has meant to America, how incredible it seems that in the 1970s those who steam full speed ahead to win the seas are the men of the Kremlin, not America's Congress and executive branch.

We cannot overemphasize that the Kremlin is not stopping with present strength. Looking to the future, Soviet leaders build not only more ships but progressively improved ones. They emphasize research and development, which determine whether tomorrow's ships and weapons will excel technically. In 1960 the United States spent 50 percent more than the U.S.S.R. on military and related research and development. Yet a decade later, according to Dr. John S. Foster, Director of Research and Engineering, Department of Defense, the Soviets have shot ahead and now spend 15 to 35 percent more than the United States in this vital field. If the trend continues, he believes that by 1973 the Soviet Union will become technically superior.

Though the U.S.S.R. has a gross national product half that of the United States, the Soviets spend more on defense and related projects than does this country. Thus, percentagewise Moscow devotes twice as much as Washington to military endeavors. Considering the lower pay and depressed scale of living in the U.S.S.R., the ratio becomes even higher.

One does not meet this type of competition and hope to survive by retrenchment. In late November, 1970, from his position of responsibility and knowledge, Dr. Foster gave Americans this clear warning:

"In many kinds of important weapons, both nuclear and non-nuclear, the Soviets are drawing ahead on quantity. On quality, I believe it's a horse race, with the U.S. now ahead by a neck but falling back."

The Urgent Need to Hold the Sea

Problems facing the weakened U.S. Navy begin with nuclear missiles. The nation ought to have more nuclear warfare deterrent forces afloat—offensive, ABM defensive, and ASW—against the mounting menace of the Soviet ballistic missile submarines. With its present resources the navy would have problems beyond its capabilities to prevent nuclear holocaust in America. It would consequently be hard put to prevent even nuclear blackmail.

Before the 25 percent reduction in number of ships, the navy was strained to carry out the nation's commitments in the cold war while sustaining limited war in Vietnam. With the reduction of U.S. forces and bases ashore overseas, demand for sea-based strength to fill the gap climbs steadily. Where will the ships come from?

Certainly the requirements for naval strength off troubled shores near and far will not decline. Scarcely had the administration announced another in a series of cutbacks in late summer, 1970, when crisis reared its head in the Middle East far away and the Caribbean close at hand. On North America's doorstep was the problem of a possible Soviet submarine base in Cuba. A third of the way around the world yet pregnant with possibilities of shattering America's future was civil war in Jordan, in which Soviet tanks under Syria's flag joined against King Hussein. Egypt, heavily strengthened by the U.S.S.R., and Israel seemed on the point of striking. Moscow despatched more ships to its Mediterranean fleet. For a time it appeared that the feared Middle East explosion was at hand.

Before the height of the crisis, with much strain on depleted resources, Washington despatched two task forces to bolster the 6th Fleet. One centered on the helicopter carrier *Guam* with a Marine Battalion Landing Team. The other was built around the powerful attack carrier *John F. Kennedy*.

Already the nation's economy moves at sea had struck the reef of reality. The navy had to scratch and scramble to produce the second task force, which seriously reduced the reserves in the western hemisphere. In fact, the total ready reserve in attack carriers was USS *John F. Kennedy*, the only one that could be hurriedly sent to the trouble area. As the *Christian Science Monitor* later reported, "In a defense establishment that thinks always of available options, to be reduced to the simple one of sending the *Kennedy* or not, with nothing else available, was disquieting."

The addition of the two task forces boosted U.S. and NATO naval power in the Mediterranean so that it outmatched the Soviet Fleet on the scene. Again by the narrowest of margins, power at sea may have averted larger war or collapse of the Middle East to Soviet domination.

By all rights, this quick lesson in preparedness, occurring so soon after fleet reductions, should have awakened Americans to the necessity for more ships. Yet we have little indication of this in the nation's actions, nor of realization that the future holds other, perhaps graver crises from the Middle East to the western hemisphere. The sea and freedom are indivisible. The international development of Soviet sea power insures that points of Soviet intrigue and friction with the United States will multiply.

Crises eventually reach a solution for better or worse. Even wars such as Korea and Vietnam come to some sort of an uneasy ending. But the Soviet challenge at sea will loom like a rising storm long through world history. The U.S.S.R.'s maritime growth, the appearance of her warships around the globe, and her growing capabilities in all quarters carry the import of an alarming turn in the tide of history.

Despite this obvious fact of life the United States is passing through a political mood marked by retrenchment in defense. Is it not possible for leaders in both political parties and the press to see the danger and to devote their energies to awakening the American people?

If the United States lets the Russians surpass her at sea through their aggressive building or her inaction, disaster is assured. Despite the warnings and efforts of numerous men in government and out, America is on the brink of losing the sea. Too many leaders refuse to heed the tolling of the bell and the lesson of history that war occurs when aggressor nations grow strong while peace-seeking nations weaken.

The United States has many problems besides holding the sea. Success there alone will not assure survival. Yet if she fails at sea, nothing else will matter. The internal problems now disturbing citizens will dwindle compared to the Communist plight that could end the long American dream.

Before our eyes the Soviet Union is wresting from the United States the oceanic strategy by which the land grew great. If America, the most capable nation of history, cannot find the will to reverse the course of events, she will deserve the fate reserved for the soft and the weak. If she cannot be persuaded to accept the sacrifices and trials necessary to supply the maritime strength the country must have, then the Communist tide will surely engulf the world.

Before the desperate risks of his first and most momentous victory, the Battle of New Orleans, Admiral Farragut put into words the answer to America's danger: "God alone decides the contest, but we must put our shoulders to the wheel."

Ever since the American Revolution the United States has grown

Bibliography

BOOKS

Anderson, R.C. *Naval Wars in the Baltic during the Sailing-Ship Epoch, 1522–1850.* London: G. Gilbert-Wood, 1910.
———. *Naval Wars in the Levant, 1559–1853.* Princeton: Princeton University Press, 1952.
Baldwin, Hanson. *Strategy for Tomorrow.* New York: Harper & Row, 1970.
Baxter, James P. *The Introduction of the Ironclad Warship.* Cambridge: Harvard University Press, 1933.
Bemis, Samuel F. *A Diplomatic History of the United States.* New York: Holt, Rinehart, and Winston, 1965.
Bird, Harrison. *Navies in the Mountains.* New York: Oxford University Press, 1962.
Brassey's Annual: The Armed Forces Yearbook. London & New York: Various publishers, 1886 to present.
Cagle, Malcolm, and Manson, Frank. *The Sea War in Korea.* Annapolis: U.S. Naval Institute, 1957.
Field, James A. *History of United States Naval Operations: Korea.* Washington: GPO, 1962.
Forrestel, Emmet. *Admiral Raymond A. Spruance, USN: A Study in Command.* Washington: GPO, 1966.
Furer, J. A. *Administration of the Navy Department in World War II.* Washington: GPO, 1959.
Georgetown University, Washington, D.C. Center for Strategic and International Studies. *Soviet Sea Power.* Washington, 1969.

Gullion, Edmund A., ed. *Uses of the Seas*. Englewood Cliffs, N.J.: Prentice-Hall, 1968.

Heinl, Robert Debs, Jr. *Victory at High Tide*. Philadelphia: J.B. Lippincott, 1968.

Holmes, W.J. *Underseas Victory*. New York: Doubleday, 1966.

Howeth, L.S. *History of Communications-Electronics in the United States Navy*. Washington: GPO, 1963.

Jane's All the World's Aircraft. London & New York: Various publishers, 1909—.

Jane's Fighting Ships. London & New York: Various publishers, 1898—.

King, Ernest J. *The United States Navy at War, 1941–1945: Official Reports to the Secretary of the Navy*. Washington: GPO, 1946.

Klyuchevski, Vasili. *A History of Russia*. 5 vols. London: J.M. Dent & Sons, 1911–1931.

Knox, Dudley W. *A History of the United States Navy*. New York: Putnam, 1948.

Larrabee, Harold. *Decision at the Chesapeake*. New York: Clarkson N. Potter, 1964.

Lewis, Charles Lee. *Matthew Fontaine Maury: the Pathfinder of the Seas*. Annapolis: U.S. Naval Institute, 1927.

Lord, Walter. *Incredible Victory*. New York: Harper & Row, 1967.

Maury, Matthew Fontaine. *Physical Geography of the Sea and Its Meteorology*. ed. by John Leighly. Cambridge: Harvard University Press, 1963. Prepared from the 8th ed. Published in 1861.

Mitchell, Mairin. *The Maritime History of Russia, 1848–1948*. London: Sidgwick & Jackson, 1949.

Morison, Samuel E. *History of United States Naval Operations in World War II*. 15 vols. Boston: Little, Brown, 1947–1962.

——. *Old Bruin: Commodore Matthew C. Perry, 1794–1858*. Boston: Little, Brown, 1967.

——. *The Oxford History of the American People*. New York: Oxford University Press, 1965.

National Council on Marine Resources and Engineering Development. *Marine Science Affairs*. Washington: GPO, 1970 (and reports for earlier years).

Oceanographer of the Navy. *The Ocean Science Program of the U.S. Navy*. Alexandria: Office of the Oceanographer, 1970 (and reports for earlier years).

Polmar, Norman. *Aircraft Carriers*. New York: Doubleday, 1969.

Potter, Elmer, ed. *Sea Power: A Naval History*. Chester W. Nimitz, assoc. ed. Englewood Cliffs, N.J.: Prentice-Hall, 1960.

Reynolds, Clark. *The Fast Carrier*. New York: McGraw Hill, 1968.

Roskill, Stephen. *The War at Sea, 1939–1945*. London: HMSO, 1954–1961.

Saunders, Malcolm, ed. *The Soviet Navy*. New York: Praeger, 1958.

Sharp, Admiral U. S. G., and Westmoreland, General W. C. *Report on the War in Vietnam*. Washington: GPO, 1969.

Smith, William W. *Midway*. New York: Thomas Y. Crowell, 1966.

Troebst, Cord. *Conquest of the Sea*. Trans. by Brian and Elsbeth Price. New York: Harper & Row, 1962.

Tuleja, Thaddeus. *Climax at Midway*. New York: W.W. Norton, 1960.

U. S. Commission on Marine Science, Engineering, and Resources. *Our Nation and the Sea*. Washington: GPO, 1969.

U. S. Department of Defense. *Report of the Secretary of Defense, and the Reports of the Secretary of the Army, Secretary of the Navy, Secretary of the Air Force*. Washington: GPO, 1947–.

U. S. Government. *Civil War Naval Chronology, 1861–1865*. Washington: GPO, 1971.

U. S. Government. *Destroyers in the United States Navy*. Washington: GPO, 1962.

U. S. Government. *Dictionary of American Naval Fighting Ships*. Washington: GPO, 1959.

U. S. Government. *Riverine Warfare: The U. S. Navy's Operations on Inland Waters*. Washington: GPO, 1968.

U. S. Government. *The Submarine in the United States Navy*. Washington: GPO, 1969.

U. S. Government. *The United States Navy: Keeping the Peace*. Washington: GPO, 1968.

U. S. Marine Corps. Historical Branch, G-3. *Marines in Lebanon, 1958*. Washington: GPO, 1966.

U. S. Naval History Division. *Aviation in the United States Navy*. Washington: GPO, 1968.

U. S. Office of Naval Operations. *United States Naval Aviation, 1910–1960*. Washington, 1960.

U. S. President's Science Advisory Committee. Panel on Oceanography. *Effective Use of the Sea*. Washington: GPO, 1966.

Wallin, Homer. *Pearl Harbor: Why, How, Fleet Salvage and Final Appraisal*. Washington: GPO, 1968.

Westcott, Allan F., ed. *American Sea Power since 1775*. Philadelphia: J.B. Lippincott, 1952.

Weyer's Warships of the World. Annapolis: U.S. Naval Institute, 1967.

Williams, Frances. *Matthew Fontaine Maury, Scientist of the Sea*. New Brunswick, N.J.: Rutgers University Press, 1963.

Wilson, E.E. *Slipstream*. New York: McGraw-Hill, 1950.

——. *Kitty Hawk to Sputnik to Polaris*. Barre, Mass.: *Barre Gazette*, 1960.

PERIODICALS

Aerospace Technology. Washington: Volume 1, 1956.

All Hands. U.S. Bureau of Naval Personnel. Washington: Volume 1, 1942.

Antarctic Journal of the United States. Washington: Volume 1, 1966.

Armed Forces Journal. Washington: Volume 1, 1968.

Aviation Week and Space Technology. New York: Volume 47, 1947.

Data. Washington: Volume 1, 1956.

International Defense Review. Geneva: Volume 1, 1968.

Marine Corps Gazette. Quantico: Vol. 1, 1916–.

Military Affairs. American Military Institute. Washington: Volume 1, 1937.

Military Review. Fort Leavenworth: Volume 1, 1922.

Naval Aviation News. U.S. Office of Naval Operations and U.S. Naval Air Systems Command. Washington: Volume 1, 1919.

Naval Engineers Journal. Washington: Volume 1, 1889.

Naval Research Logistics Quarterly. Office of Naval Research. Washington: Volume 1, March 1953.

Naval Review. Annapolis: Volume 1, 1962.

Naval Ship Systems Command Technical News. Washington: Volume 1, 1952.

Naval War College Review. Newport, R.I.: Volume 1, 1948.

The Navy Civil Engineer. U.S. Navy Civil Engineering Corps and U.S. Naval Facilities Engineering Command. Washington: Volume 1, 1960.

Navy:The Magazine of Sea Power. Navy League of the United States. Washington: Volume 1, 1958.

Navy Times. Washington: Volume 1, 1951.

NATO's Fifteen Nations. Amsterdam: Volume 1, 1956.

Ordnance: Land-Sea-Air-Space. Washington: Volume 1, 1920.

Revue Maritime. Paris: Volume 1, 1861.

Under Sea Technology. Arlington, Va.: Volume 1, 1960.

United States Naval Institute. Annapolis: Volume 1, 1874.

United States News and World Report. Washington: Volume 1, 1933.

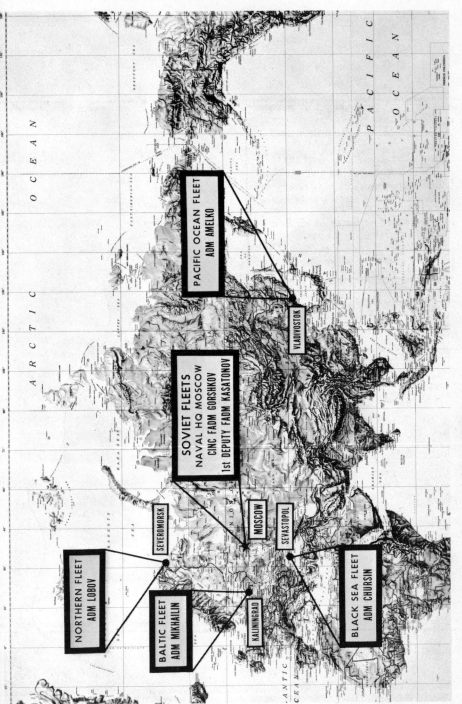

SOVIET FLEETS
NAVAL HQ MOSCOW
CINC FADM GORSHKOV
1st DEPUTY FADM KASATONOV

PACIFIC OCEAN FLEET
ADM AMELKO

VLADIVOSTOK

SEVEROMORSK

MOSCOW

SEVASTOPOL

NORTHERN FLEET
ADM LOBOV

BALTIC FLEET
ADM MIKHAILIN

KALININGRAD

BLACK SEA FLEET
ADM CHURSIN

Headquarters for Soviet fleet activities, 1968.

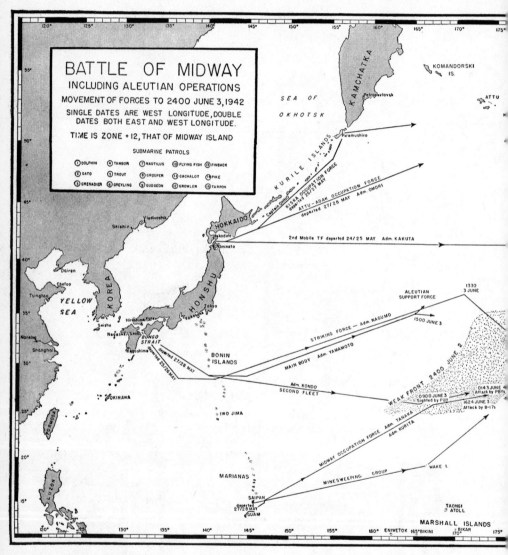

The Battle of Midway.

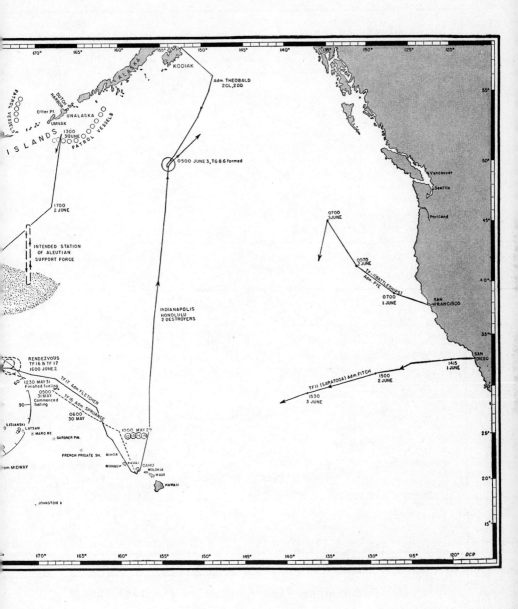

KODIAK

Adm. THEOBALD
2 CL, 2 DD

PATROL VESSELS

ALASKA

DUTCH
HARBOR

Otter Pt.

UMNAK

UNALASKA

ISLANDS

1300
3 JUNE

PATROL VESSELS

0500 JUNE 3, TG 8.6 formed

1700
2 JUNE

Vancouver

Seattle

Portland

0700
3 JUNE

INTENDED STATION
OF ALEUTIAN
SUPPORT FORCE

0070
2 JUNE

TF-I (BATTLESHIPS)
Adm. PYE

0700
1 JUNE

INDIANAPOLIS
HONOLULU
2 DESTROYERS

SAN
FRANCISCO

RENDEZVOUS
TF 16 & TF 17
1600 JUNE 2

60°

1230 MAY 31
Finished fueling

0500
31 MAY
Commenced
fueling

TF 17 Adm. FLETCHER

TF 16 Adm. SPRUANCE

0600
30 MAY

90

LISIANSKI

LAYSAN

120°

MARO RF.

GARDNER PIN.

FRENCH FRIGATE SH.

NIHOA

1000 MAY 29

from MIDWAY

NIIHAU

KAUAI

OAHU

MOLOKAI

MAUI

HAWAII

JOHNSTON I.

SAN
DIEGO

1415
1 JUNE

1500
2 JUNE

TF II (SARATOGA) Adm. FITCH

1530
3 JUNE

DCR

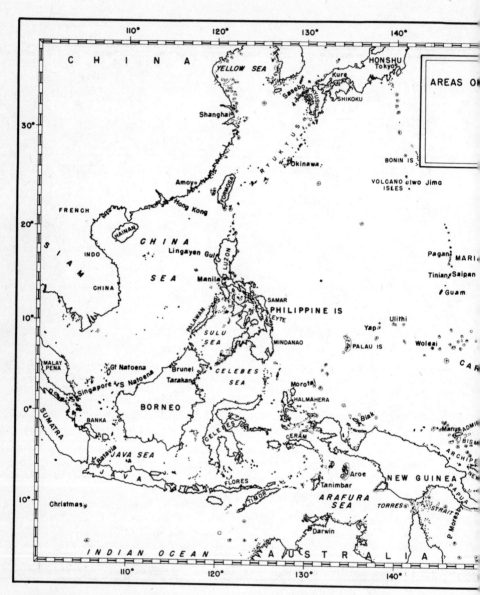

The Pacific Ocean areas of U.S. naval operations, 1944–1945.

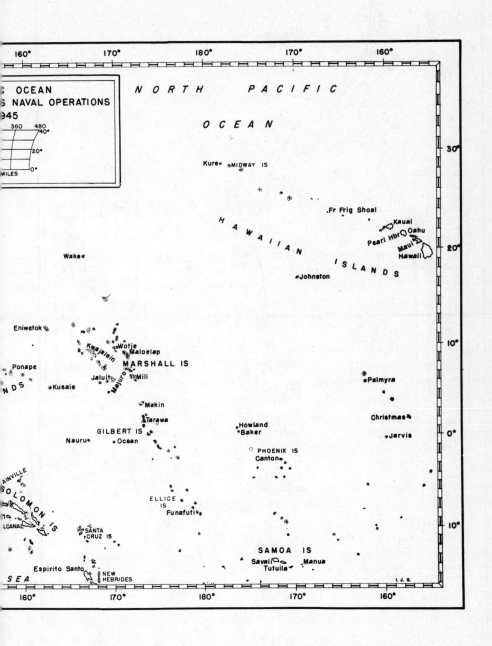

C OCEAN
S NAVAL OPERATIONS
945

N O R T H   P A C I F I C
O C E A N

30°

Kure• •MIDWAY IS

•Fr Frig Shoal
Kauai
Pearl Hbr• Oahu
Maui
Hawaii

20°

H A W A I I A N   I S L A N D S

•Johnston

Wake•

Eniwetok•

10°

Kwajalein •Wotje
•Maloelap
MARSHALL IS
•Ponape
Jaluit• •Mili
•Kusaie

•Palmyra

NDS

•Makin
•Tarawa
Christmas•

GILBERT IS
Nauru• •Ocean
•Howland
•Baker
•Jarvis

0°

PHOENIX IS
Canton•

AINVILLE
SOLOMON IS

ELLICE
IS
Funafuti•

10°

LCANAL

•SANTA
CRUZ IS

SAMOA IS
Savaii•• •Manua
Tutuila•

Espirito Santo
NEW
HEBRIDES
S E A

I. J. G.

160°   170°   180°   170°   160°

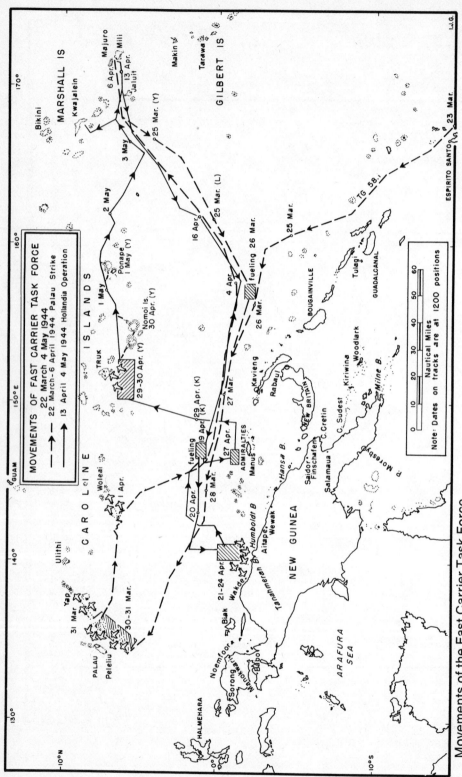

Movements of the Fast Carrier Task Force.

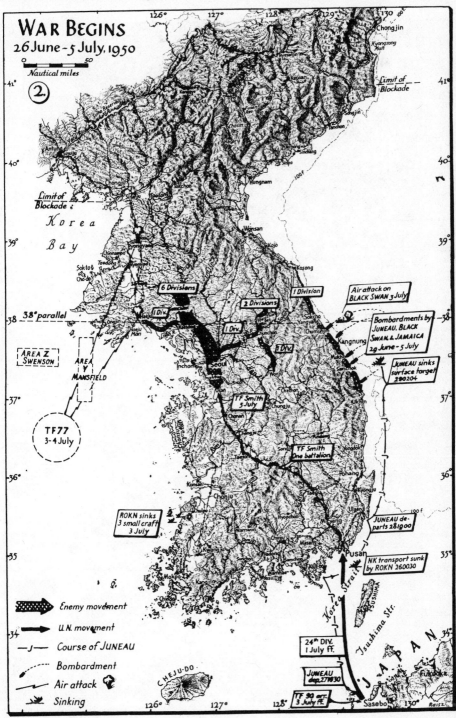

WAR BEGINS
26 June - 5 July, 1950

0   50
Nautical miles

②

41°

Chongjin

Kyongsong Man

Limit of Blockade

Antung

Limit of Blockade

Korea Bay

40°

Hungnam

Wonsan

Kojo

39°

38° parallel

6 Divisions

2 Divisions

1 Division

Air attack on BLACK SWAN 3 July

Bombardments by JUNEAU, BLACK SWAN & JAMAICA 29 June - 5 July

1 Div.

1 Div.

1 Div.

Kangnung

JUNEAU sinks surface target 290204

AREA Z SWENSON

AREA Y MANSFIELD

Seoul

Inchon

Wonju

38°

TF 77 3-4 July

TF Smith 5 July

TF Smith one battalion

37°

ROKN sinks 3 small craft 3 July

Taegu

Pohang

36°

JUNEAU departs 281900

Mokpo

Pusan

NK transport sunk by ROKN 260030

35°

Korea Strait

TSUSHIMA

Tsushima Str.

Enemy movement

U.N. movement

Course of JUNEAU

Bombardment

Air attack

Sinking

24th DIV. 1 July ff.

JUNEAU dep. 271930

TF 90 arr. 3 July ff.

CHEJU-DO

J A P A N

Fukuoka

Sasebo

War begins in Korea.

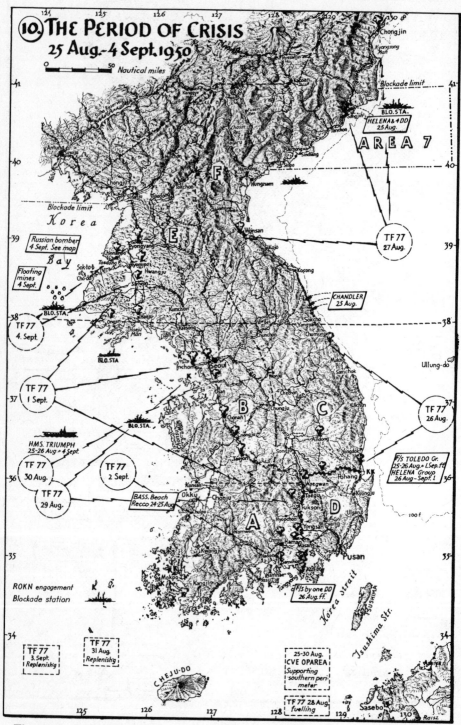

The period of crisis 25 August–4 September 1950.

South Vietnam.

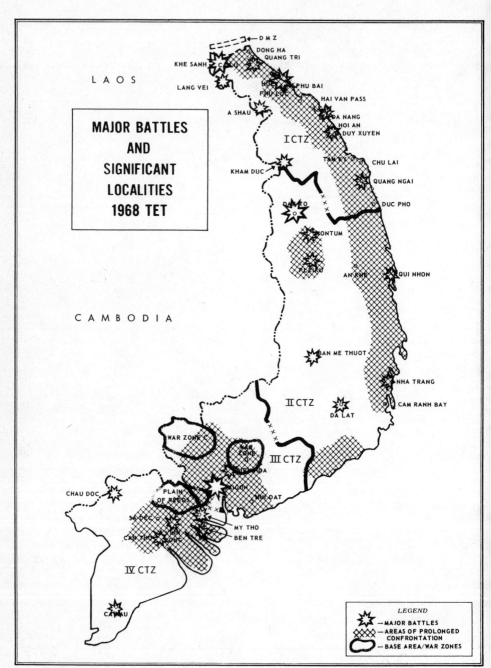

MAJOR BATTLES
AND
SIGNIFICANT
LOCALITIES
1968 TET

LAOS

CAMBODIA

DMZ

KHE SANH
LANG VEI

DONG HA
QUANG TRI
HUE
PHU BAI
PHU LOC
HAI VAN PASS
A SHAU
DA NANG
HOI AN
DUY XUYEN
I CTZ
TAM KY
CHU LAI
KHAM DUC
QUANG NGAI
DUC PHO
DAK TO
KONTUM
PLEIKU
AN KHE
QUI NHON

BAN ME THUOT
NHA TRANG
CAM RANH BAY
II CTZ
DA LAT

WAR ZONE C
WAR
ZONE D
BIEN HOA
III CTZ
SAIGON
PLAIN
OF REEDS
VUNG TAU
CHAU DOC
SA DEC
MY THO
BEN TRE
CAN THO
VINH LONG

IV CTZ

CA MAU

LEGEND

✦ —MAJOR BATTLES
▨ —AREAS OF PROLONGED
    CONFRONTATION
⬭ —BASE AREA/WAR ZONES

1968 Tet. Major battles and significant localities.

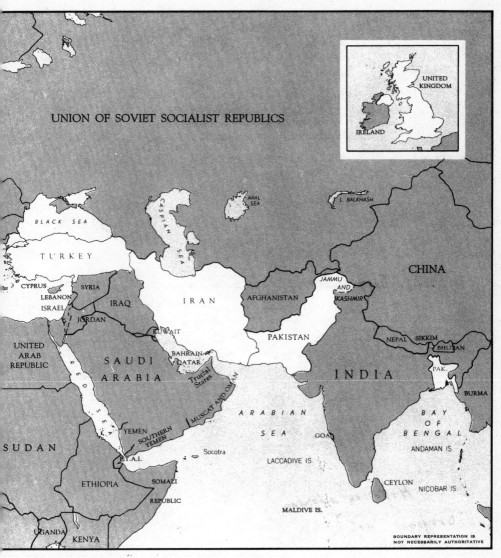

Union of Soviet Socialist Republics.

UNITED STATES COLLECTIVE DEFENSE ARRANGEMEN

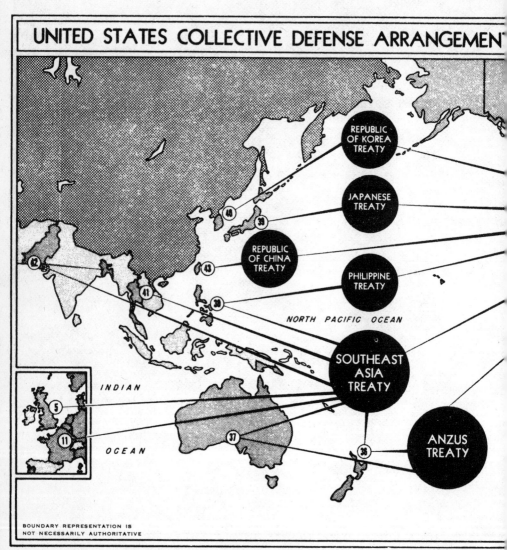

United States collective defense arrangements.

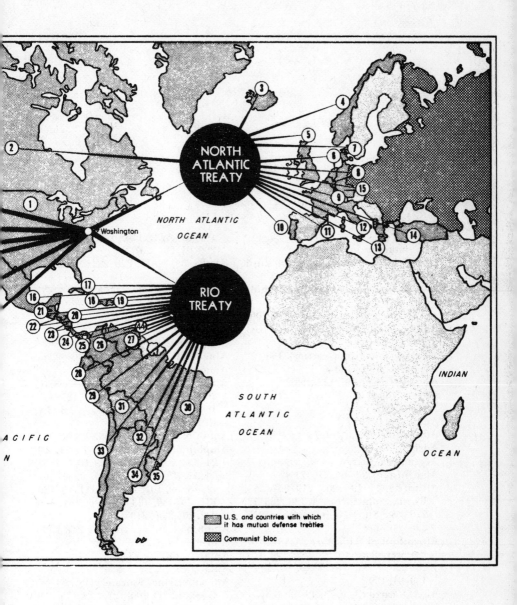

Index

306